Associative Democracy

Associative Democracy

New Forms of Economic and Social Governance

Paul Hirst

The University of Massachusetts Press
Amherst

Copyright © Paul Hirst 1994
First published in 1994 by Polity Press
in association with Blackwell Publishers
Printed in Great Britain
All rights reserved
First published in the United States of America in 1994
by the University of Massachusetts Press
ISBN 0–87023–896–5 (cloth)
ISBN 0–87023–897–3 (paper)
A CIP catalogue record for this book is available from the
Library of Congress

For Jamie

Contents

Acknowledgements

A great many people have helped me to formulate the argument in this book both through their writings and discussion. I would like to thank Anthony Barnett, Joshua Cohen, David Held, Barry Hindess, John Matthews, Rev. David Nicholls, Joel Rogers, Charles Sabel, Philippe Schmitter, Grahame Thompson, Garry Wickham, Erik Olin-Wright and Jonathan Zeitlin. I am especially grateful to Joanne Robertson and Joanne Winning for their help in preparing the manuscript and to the School of Architecture, University of Western Australia, for providing a congenial environment in which to write a substantial portion of it.

1
A Changed Conjuncture

At the end of the twentieth century we are witnessing the exhaustion of the great competing intellectual systems of social organization, liberal democratic capitalism and collectivistic state socialism, that came to fruition in the nineteenth century. These ideas set the terms of political debate and struggle for the next one hundred and fifty years. The recognition of the waning of these heretofore ruling ideas is no mere *fin de siècle* mood, rather the collapse of state socialism as a political project, and the fundamental stagnation of liberal democratic ideas, reflect important changes in both social relations and the expectations of individuals that have accelerated rapidly in the West since the 1960s.

The great conflict between liberal democracy and state socialism was at least in form a struggle over what was to be the predominant type of property relations, private property or collective ownership. This issue was the *differentia specifica* of a conflict that at times took the form of a bitter social war. In other respects, the two systems claimed (or had) actual common features. Liberal and socialist states both claimed to be democracies, and each claimed to represent a superior kind of democracy to the other. In both the socialist East and the liberal West the common social fact of greatest significance has been the growth of large-scale hierarchical administration, the growth of large-scale mass production, and the growth in the powers and functions of the state. Centralization and bureaucracy were common features of social systems that were radically divergent in their outcomes. However, in both types of society they were perceived as stemming from social and economic necessities that equated the large-scale with efficiency. It is that equation which is in question today.

Changing social relations are challenging the notion that bureaucracy and mass society are inevitable. In the West people have become increasingly sophisticated and individuated, they wish to control their own affairs by their own choices and refuse to be treated as part of a 'unit of administration' by officials. It is for these reasons that another set of ideas about social organization that was developed in the nineteenth and early twentieth centuries, associationalism, has once again become relevant after a long period of eclipse by state socialist and liberal democratic ideas. The late twentieth century offers new conditions in which ideas marginalized for many decades can be redefined and developed to serve as an alternative, radical means of reforming and reorganizing economic and social governance in Western societies.

These ideas lost all credence by the end of the 1920s because they seemed ill-adapted to a world dominated by the imperatives of hierarchical organization and bitter social conflict, which indeed they were. Collectivist socialism captured and continued to hold the imagination of an important section of the Western intelligentsia, as they sought to criticize their own society and to find an alternative to it. Social democracy was always a pragmatic halfway house that lacked ideological appeal, despite its vast practical achievements in social reform and economic management when in government. Social democracy accepted representative democratic institutions on the one hand, and liberal collectivist concepts of social provision on the other. It was thus defined by these compromises with liberalism. Vast quantities of intellectual energy were consumed in trying to find a model of socialism that would not share the brutal and authoritarian features of the Soviet system. This obsession with 'true' socialism drained away much of the energy and talent from other forms of radicalism. That diversion is now virtually at an end. Collectivist state socialism is finished as a viable alternative to liberal representative democracy and market-based economies. Actually existing socialism consistently failed to deliver either greater political freedom or greater economic equality, let alone prosperity, than Western democratic states. That has long been obvious to the mass of workers, since communist and radical socialist parties have been consistently rejected by mass electorates in Western democracies.

The intelligentsia's search for socialism has ended, but it has taken the implosion and collapse of Soviet socialism (and that of its satellites) to finally destroy that illusion.

Yet liberal individualism and free-market capitalism have gained no decisive victory from this failure of socialism. This is not just because the collapse of the latter has occurred at the same time as the onset of a major slump and myriad social problems in the West. Western liberalism has atrophied as a radical body of ideas committed to freedom, in part because the contest with the Soviet system was too easy, and in part because liberals retreated before the apparently inescapable demands of state bureaucracy and corporate power. Representative democracy and the free market have lost their main legitimation in the collapse of socialism. Authoritarian socialist states represented an external threat to the West, they made socialism an enemy. Such states served as a standing example of why liberal democracy, however flawed, was better than socialist dictatorship and why market-based societies, however unequal, offered the ordinary citizen a better standard of living. Western societies now have to be judged by their own standards and on their own merits.

The results of such judgements are not encouraging and quickly silence most of the nonsense about the 'triumph of the West'. Representative democratic government is failing badly by the standards of liberal democratic political theory, rather than by the easy measure of comparison with inherently authoritarian polities. Even in the most effective and responsive of political systems, modern representative democracy offers low levels of governmental accountability to citizens and of public influence on decision-making. Democracy has become far more a means of legitimation of the centralized and bureaucratic government of the nation state than it is a check upon it. Representative government in mass democracies has become increasingly plebiscitarian in character, the popular vote determining which party or coalition of parties shall have exclusive control of the state machine for a period of years. Moreover, the majority of the West's democracies are far from exemplifying the best of modern democratic practice. In countries like Italy, Japan and the United Kingdom defective electoral and/or party systems have allowed conservative parties to rule, singly or in coalition, for decades. Such ineffective political systems do not ensure the regular succession of parties in office that is essential to the health of representative democratic political competition.

Modern government is more and more difficult to make accountable by the political means promoted by nineteenth-century liberalism, that is, supervision by a representative legislature and the election of the highest executive office holders. The scale and functions of the modern state have developed out of all proportion to the states of the liberal era. Liberal representative democracy presupposed limited government. However, the functions and scale of government grew as the franchise extended, as the state was compelled to meet more of its citizens' needs, and as social liberalism and conservative social engineering sought to stave off socialism with a partial collectivism. Big government is the creature of the drift toward collectivism, a drift strongly resisted by many liberals, by associationalists, and by many in the Labour Movement, but which sapped resistance the more it seemed inevitable. The sheer complexity of the social relations to be regulated, the pressing need to provide more and more services to relieve want and increase national efficiency, and the need partly to restrain and partly to support the activities of the modern large-scale business corporation, drove pragmatic social reformers of differing political hues into moves which steadily extended the scope and scale of government.

The final triumph of collectivism in Britain, in particular, came late. Not only liberals but also many in the Labour Movement feared central state control of social insurance and social welfare. State provision was by no means universally welcomed as the primary source of social insurance, it was opposed by significant sections of employers and unions alike. Even into the 1940s social liberals like William Beveridge continued to support the voluntary principle, and envisaged a continued role for the Friendly Societies and other forms of private insurance. Aneurin Bevan's nationalization of the local authority and voluntary hospitals into the National Health Service in 1947 was resisted not just by vested interests, but also by sincere supporters of voluntarism and anti-centralist advocates of municipal services. Until recently such resistance was portrayed as either self-interested or old-fashioned; anyway it was perceived to be doomed in the face of modernization and the efficiency of uniform large-scale national administration. Now it seems sensible and prescient.

Modern states became, particularly under the pressures of wholesale social mobilization during the two world wars, omnicompetent administrative agencies capable of influencing by their actions the fate of their societies and virtually every person in them. Legislatures typically became the creatures of the executive, and the executive itself became dependent on the administrative machine for advice and information. Laws were and are made to facilitate administration and to extend its powers of regulation. Legislatures turned into engines for what Carl Schmitt (1943–4) called 'motorised legislation', and have thus undermined the rule of law by giving rule-making discretion to officials and by the sheer bulk of the regulations thus created. Elected officials and the leaders of the dominant party have extensive capacities to intervene in society through the policies of the state, which they at least nominally direct, but they have few means of authoritatively determining and responding to citizens' wishes about the course of such policy whilst in office. Just as an election creates and legitimizes their power, so only the threat of failing to be re-elected acts as an effective constraint on politicians. Better that constraint than none at all, yet the electoral threat is infrequent and its influence touches only that small portion of the policies and practices of the state that reach public notice and become a matter for controversy.

The arguments mounted in mitigation of low levels of accountability to the citizens are that they are the inevitable trade-off for the promotion of public welfare through the services big government provides, and that bureaucrats are constrained most effectively by their own professional codes and hierarchical supervision. Neither of these arguments is compelling if the benefits of public welfare can be had without large-scale state bureaucracy. If services can be provided in public, but non-state and effective, ways that are accountable to the ordinary citizen, then there need be no such trade-off. Bureaucracies do not have to be either corrupt or incompetent to pose a threat to the democratic capacities of citizens. Honest and competent administration can close-off citizens' choices and impose its own judgements as to what it deems best for its charges far more effectively. Big government has grown at the expense of individual rights and freedoms. The attempted uniformity of state policy and forms of social provision has meant the imposition of common rules and standard services on the increasingly diverse and pluralistic objectives of the members of modern societies. Imagine a system that combined citizen choice with public welfare. That is what associationalism has to offer.

Associationalism also offers a principle of administrative renewal, a way of restoring the ideal of committed public service in the face of widespread bureaucratic failure and retreat. Voluntarily-based organizations can be tenacious and effective. They tend to endure as forms of organization, where they are supported by the right kinds of laws and institutions. They can combine choice for their members with a more creative role for professional administrators and service providers. Bureaucracies, by contrast, tend to be fragile and rigid. They so easily lose impetus and their officials quickly lose *esprit de corps* in the face of crises of funding and function. Top-down administration appropriates the service from those for whom it is provided, and they have little capacity to redirect a failing bureaucracy toward meeting their needs. Associations, by contrast, empower those for whom services are provided in diverse ways. Voluntary association is an alternative to top-down bureaucracy in the competent provision of services. It is not the case the there is no choice except that between hierarchy and inefficient amateurism in methods of administration today.

By the end of the Second World War associationalist arguments were virtually marginalized. The nation state had become omnicompetent and vital to the welfare of the citizen. This was not merely the result of a political or bureaucratic 'will to power' in building the state machine. The nation state had first become the locus of effective military administration. It then became from the late nineteenth century onwards increasingly the key locus of social welfare provision, and from the 1930s onwards the locus of effective macro-economic management. The intensified competition of states and, in particular, the two great wars of this century, stimulated the growth toward centralization and reinforced the legitimacy of the state's claim to sovereignty. Only the nation state could draw on and mobilize all the resources of society in order to ensure national survival. These international pressures made the 'nation' the key locus for resources, facilities and administration; government and people alike did not want to be without the means to effective national economic and military autonomy in a conflict with an enemy state. Enemies without are a powerful stimulant to, or at least a rationale for the imposition of, social solidarity. 'National defence' provided an unanswerable argument for economic intervention, even in as ideologically *laissez faire* a polity as the USA.

No sooner had the nation state become firmly established as the dominant form of social organization, managing both economy and society, than its primacy began to be threatened. The internationalization of economic relations in recent decades has resulted in the radical reduction (although by no means elimination) of the capacities of national economic management. The changing international conjuncture and the collapse of the Cold War have weakened the military imperatives that sustained the nation state. The national level has lost its automatic primacy in the governance of economic and social affairs, and with that loss much of the rationale for the central state's claims to 'sovereignty' and omnicompetence have gone too. The nation state as a single multi-functional political agency that concedes only such power as it deems necessary to 'lesser' public and private bodies, and that is answerable to no 'higher' power, is now threatened with becoming as obsolete as were decentralized feudal systems in the face of the new national monarchies (Held, 1993). Supra-national and regional institutions and processes of governance are beginning to become more necessary to cope with the complexities of both a more internationalized and a more localized set of economic and social relations. Multi-national companies are less dependent on a given nation state (although the number of truly trans-national corporations located on a global scale is few, and likely to remain so) and international voluntary bodies, like aid agencies and political pressure groups, grow steadily stronger and more influential.

Liberal-democratic politics centred on the nation state are entering a period of growing problematicity, in which their democratic effectiveness and legitimacy are questioned. So too are the dominant methods and doctrines of national economic management. Market-based Western national economies are exhibiting increasing problems of coordination and regulation that prevent sustained growth. Western publics are dissatisfied with existing economic performance, but are currently offered no coherent alternative measures that can address those problems of co-ordination and regulation, and perhaps enable a return to growth and a more widely shared prosperity. A sure sign that the conventional structures of politics that have dominated the past century are in crisis is that the economic difficulties of the late twentieth century have not led to a consistent and widespread return to social democratic pragmatism in countries that have experimented with conservative and economic liberal regimes. Social democracy is closely tied to both state centralization and to liberal collectivism, yet the compulsory and uniform provision of services is less and less popular with more sophisticated and diverse publics. Social democracy has relied on Keynesian national economic management, but, as we shall see in Chapter 4, this is less and less effective as a means of restoring full employment and maintaining growth.

The failure of social democracy is one more sign that politics is moving away from the great left–right oppositions created in the nineteenth century. The creation of a coherent spectrum of political forces from left to right derived from two factors. First the domination of politics by the 'social' question, that is, the politicization of property relations. Second, because the political forces in question struggled for exclusive control in the same political space, each seeking to monopolize power in a 'sovereign' state in order to impose their vision of society and compel others to live as they directed. Within the nation state's exclusive control of its territory, subject to a single sovereign political will, and to a coherent system of national administration, there could be but one 'policy'. Left and right both strove to make their control of the state permanent and that policy irreversible.

Politics is no longer dominated by one great question. It looks less and less like a social war over the forms of property that are to prevail. It is centred less and less on a single structure of authority; supra-national, national, regional and non-state forms of governance are all possible contenders to influence policy. The issues and the forums of political competition are changing. This has resulted in the rise of new political forces that cannot be accommodated on the old political spectrum of left to right. Politics was never entirely dominated by the left–right contest, but it was more important than a superficial glance at the other political issues influential in this century might lead one to suppose. Nationalism qualified but did not alter the dominance of the 'social' question. Many nationalist movements were of the left, most colonial national liberation movements for example. Moreover, once national aspirations were met in an independent state, the 'social' question reappeared with full force, dominating the politics of the new entity.

The new political forces are too diverse, too concerned with different issues, to be placed on a single spectrum. There are new types of nationalist and regional autonomist parties, and ethnic and religiously-based campaigns. There are also new forms of politics centred on resistance to racism, gender issues, the environmental question and on lifestyles. New political problems and new social expectations are ill-accommodated by the old party systems in many Western states, and the traditional parties of both left and right command less and less popular support. In Italy, which is the clearest example, the 'old' parties suffered a rapid and major loss of support following the end of the Cold War. The national state, bloated and corrupt, parcelized between and dominated by the old party cliques, was seen as more the problem and less the source of solutions to Italy's manifold economic and political problems. In the United Kingdom too, both the major parties were and are viewed by substantial sections of the electorate with increasing suspicion, as being incapable of offering real solutions to the economic crisis or social renewal. Throughout the West mainstream electoral politicians have fallen in popular esteem and are widely distrusted.

The main threats to the stability of Western societies are no longer class war within or enemy states without, they are diffuse social problems and sources of unrest. Centralized bureaucratic and repressive structures cope so badly with these more amorphous threats of crime and drug addiction, for example, that these problems can hardly provide the old state structures with a convincing *raison d'etre*. The real sources of these social problems stem from the failure to sustain full employment and from the side effects of collectivist welfare. In the USA, in Britain, even in Germany, we face the growing reality of a two-thirds versus one-third society. The notion of an 'underclass' is both graphic and yet absurd, since its members will not accept their 'place' at the bottom. A differentiated society cannot work if elementary freedoms of movement and association for all are to be preserved. Unless effective work and welfare are offered, in a way that both targets *and* empowers the members of this 'class', then the way is open to an escalating conflict between crime and deviancy and disablingly authoritarian measures which aim at the protection of the majority. This is a new and difficult social question, quite unlike the old. The members of the underclass are not stupid. They know that wealth and success are, in part, capriciously distributed, that is, that they depend on the chances of social position and geographical location. Property will never be legitimate unless it offers real welfare, that is, a stake in society to all in return. The retreat to pure police protection of the property of the 'haves' is ineffective and constitutes the theft of opportunity from the 'have nots'. The disaffected cannot overthrow society, but they can make it impossible to live in.

The only effective answer to this problem is a mixture of social crusading by those 'haves' who care and the empowerment of the 'have nots'. That can best be achieved by adequately publicly funded and committed voluntary associations working in partnership with the poor and excluded. Only by resourcing associations that help the poor to organize themselves and then funding projects to transform ghettos and slums can the state help to reverse this corrosive process of social decline. Socialists have by and large written themselves out of this task, by identifying welfare with state provision, by simply demanding 'more' of it as the solution to social problems, and by spurning the voluntary sector as mere 'do gooding'. Socialists long ago abandoned the task of building security and welfare through mutual institutions in civil society. At present it is not the old political forces of the left, who continue to advocate failed collectivist solutions, but religious and community groups who see the need for activism and cooperation to build a 'civil society' for the poor and excluded.

Many are frightened by this erosion of the old political certainties, by the weakening of the old political forces and the old solutions. Many are frightened by the growth of crime and social disintegration, and many see the source of these social problems in specific groups, for example, in immigrant communities. It is also widely feared that the inheritors of this social crisis will be one of the old political forces, the ultra-right. The fear is that nationalism and racism will become the core of a new politics of protest against the established order and that liberalism and democracy will be rejected as a response to the problems encountered by Western representative systems. It would be foolish to be complacent about the return of the ultra-right, but one must remember that political conditions today are not like those of the 1920s and 1930s when the ultra-right made its political breakthrough to power. Then fascism derived a very significant power of appeal by appearing to offer a 'third way' in the social war between capitalism and communism. Fascism promised to smash the left within, to tackle the Soviet Union without, and yet to cure mass unemployment and to check the powers of big capitalism. Moreover, fascism depended for its appeal on the centrality of the nation state; it would restore national glory, eliminate internal enemies and promote autarchic national economic policies. These claims are hardly a recipe for success today. The experience of Nazism remains rooted in the imagination of Western publics, and will limit the appeal of the most virulent racism. A politics of ethnic homogeneity that led to the gas chambers has, at best, a limited appeal. The barbarity of ultra-nationalism and 'ethnic cleansing' in the former Yugoslavia serve as a timely reminder of what the far right has to offer, and, fortunately, horrify the mass of decent citizens in the West. Of course Germany has its racist thugs, but it also has millions of citizens determined to prevent any return to the horrors of the Nazi era, and who demonstrate in their hundreds of thousands against racism.

The ultra-right will not capture the new political agendas, and we are, therefore, unlikely to enter a new dark age. The problems of ethnic and cultural pluralism in Western societies remain, however, and they will continue to create tension and sustain the far right unless an effective solution is found to them. These problems are not confined to or caused by migrant communities, and, therefore, they will not be solved simply by restricting migration. A positive policy of creating the political and social structures for a truly plural society is the only coherent long-term response, and in Chapter 3 we will consider these issues. In particular, how voluntary self-governing associations might contribute to providing facilities for different communities and also serve as a means of lessening tension between such communities in the public sphere. At present 'pluralism' has become a policy of the state, promoting 'multi-cultural' programmes within uniform structures of provision that satisfy no community and at worst degenerate into a decultured pap.

We have entered an era when the old certainties of politics have dissolved, in which politics and society are more pluralistic and less capable of being dragooned by the ideological programmes of left and right. It would be foolish simply to celebrate the new diversity and to welcome the 'end of ideology', as many of the naive supporters of the importation of Post-Modern ideas into politics do. We are unlikely to escape our manifold problems with-out new political ideas and without new practices of institutional reform. The world is tired of brutal and utopian ideologies, but it cannot either prosper or progress in a state of intellectual catatonia about the possibilities for change in our political institutions and forms of socio-economic governance. Francis Fukuyama in his original essay 'The End of History' (1989) offered a vision of a world purged of ideology, in which history had come to an end because there are no alternatives to the institutions of the present, representative democracy and the market. The future would, therefore, be the endless repetition of more of the same, with no ideological *sturm und drang*, but rather a politics centred in bureaucratic problem-solving, limited social engineering and liberal compromise.

That is to see the future in terms of the 'alternatives' of the past. The old ideologies, like socialism, fascism or dogmatic liberal individualism, are undermined and the pragmatic substitutes for them like social democracy or Christian democracy are deeply flawed and unable to surmount existing problems. An alternative cannot consist in a totalizing ideology that seeks to rebuild the social world anew according to the dictates of a single and exclusive principle. The most readily available alternative, associative democracy, is not of this kind. It is not an idea that involves the wholesale supplanting of existing institutions, rather it provides a vital supplement to them that enables their defects to be meliorated.

Associationalism makes accountable representative democracy possible again by limiting the scope of state administration, without diminishing social provision. It enables market-based societies to deliver the substantive goals desired by citizens, by embedding the market system in a social network of coordinative and regulatory institutions. It is a political idea that is big enough to offer the hope of radical reform, and to mobilize political energies in doing so, but it is specific enough to be developed within and added to

our existing institutions. It requires neither a revolution nor the ⎞
building of a new society, merely the extensive but gradual reform ⎬
of the old at a pace directed by the realities of politics and the ⎟
choices of citizens.

Associative democracy not merely lacks the totalitarian potential of the old ideologies, it is their direct opposite, since it offers
room for the projects of the most diverse social and political
forces. It is not tied to any given part of the old left – right political spectrum. It can appeal to and be used as a guiding political
doctrine by a wide variety of political and social groups subscribing to very different beliefs. The concept of the governance of
social affairs through voluntary associations can enable groups to
build their own social worlds in civil society; for example, conservative religious groups, radical feminists, those seeking a self-
sufficient ecologically sustainable form of life, can all live as they
wish, and compete politically by soliciting the voluntary choices of
individuals. In this respect associationalism is the one great system
of political ideas born in the nineteenth century that is likely to
continue into the twenty-first with real intellectual enthusiasm and
the energy for social renewal driving it forward.

It is not surprising that associative democracy has not generally
appealed to the intellectual left as they have sought to respond to
the collapse of state socialism and the eclipse of Marxism. The
left has discovered democracy and civil society, but in ways that
tend to make it indifferent to associationalism. On the one hand,
a 'new republican' current based on the concept of citizenship,
advocating a return to stronger majoritarian democracy and the
active involvement in common, core political institutions. The
new republicans seek to use democratic ideals against existing
flawed representative institutions and the concept of citizenship to
extend social and political rights. The new republican idea of
restoring a more communal and committed politics is ill-adapted
to current circumstances. It re-emphasizes the idea of a single
effectively self-governing political community at the very moment
when the nation state is being undermined and a complex multi-
focal politics is developing. Insofar as the new republicans
accept existing representative democratic institutions, then they
are stuck with the very real limitations that those institutions
impose on governmental accountability and citizen participation. The ideas of majoritarian democracy and a common ideal of

citizenship are ill-suited to a pluralistic society in which social objectives are increasingly divergent. Citizens need a political community that will enable them to be different, and not one that exhorts them to be the same.

On the other hand, sections of the left have given great emphasis to 'civil society' and to the new social movements, the very forces of anti-racism, feminism, environmental politics, etc. that have contributed much to undermining the old left – right political spectrum. The problem here is the tendency to see those movements in oppositional terms, as a source of renewal against the state and the old politics. Without a change in political institutions, without a state more accommodating to the creation of social communities in civil society, the new movements will be constrained and limited. Moreover, by treating these movements as part of the 'left', as inherently oppositional, this perspective reimposes the divisions of the old political spectrum and ignores the common cause that very different movements may find in gaining the freedom to build their own self-governing communities in civil society.

The intellectual left's embrace of democratization of state and civil society as a substitute for the goal of socialization of the means of production has had little concrete political impact. Movements for political reform in states with defective democratic institutions, like Charter 88 in the United Kingdom, have been successful precisely because they have confined themselves to advocating changes that would constitute existing representative democratic best practice. The only way radical ideas will gain ground is by arguing for new types of institutions and doing so for a constituency that goes way beyond the left. To respond to the changed conjuncture we need political ideas that can cope with decentralization, that are not utopian about the prospects for such change, and that do not confuse decentralization with participatory democracy. Only thus can we hope to promote conceptions of non-collectivist means of ensuring a well-governed and adequately serviced society, open to the aspirations of diverse social groups. Those ideas are most readily developed out of the framework of associationalist political theory.

2
Associative Principles and Democratic Reform

New times for an old idea

Associationalism is not a new idea. It developed in the nineteenth century as an alternative to both liberal individualism and socialist collectivism, and as a criticism of state centralization and the growth of bureaucracy. It was international, and not less intellectually sophisticated than its opponents. It enjoyed considerable success and support. It had several distinct strands, and it was not exclusively a movement of the left. Associationalism had two characteristic features as a social doctrine. The first was the advocacy of a decentralized economy based on the non-capitalistic principles of cooperation and mutuality. The second was the criticism of the centralized and sovereign state, with radical federalist and political pluralist ideas advanced as a substitute. The associationalists believed in voluntarism and self-government, not collectivism and state compulsion. Some associationalists combined the economic and political components of the doctrine, others gave emphasis to one or the other.

Associationalism has several distinct sources. The English advocates of industrial and social cooperation like Robert Owen and George Jacob Holyoake stressed cooperative, self-regulating economic communities. Pierre-Joseph Proudhon combined brilliant advocacy of a mutualist economy, centred on artisan and cooperative production, with alternative non-profit making financial institutions, and the creation of a decentralized state organized on bottom-up federal principles. The English political pluralists, F.W. Maitland and John Neville Figgis, derived from Otto von

Gierke's theory of association, a conception of a pluralist state that would have limited powers in respect of voluntary self-regulating associations. Neither gave great emphasis to the economy, but Figgis supported the autonomy of both the churches and the unions from the state. Figgis inspired the two major English associationalist writers of this century, G.D.H. Cole and Harold J. Laski. Cole developed between 1917 and 1920 a comprehensive Guild Socialist system of economic and social governance. Laski brought English pluralist political theory to its most rigorous level in his *A Grammar of Politics* (1925). Associationalism then went into a rapid and almost total decline, the reasons for which will be considered when we examine the demise of Guild Socialism in Chapter 4.

Other ideas paralleled or influenced associationalism, such as French labour and administrative syndicalism, and some of the French and German corporatist ideas. Most corporatist ideas were authoritarian and, if anti-capitalist, favoured a state administrative or neo-medievalist guild society solution to the problems of modern society. Hegel had developed the idea of a 'civil society' distinct from the state. The corporation was as one of the main agencies of governance of economic relations in civil society. He did not see these bodies as free associations but as compulsory regulative agencies. Moreover, he imposed above civil society a state with attributes that no associationalist committed to voluntarism and individual liberty could accept for a second. The corporatist tradition did contain an important truth, that economic organization and the public power must be brought into coordination. *Laissez faire* ignores this necessity and socialism overcompensates by, in practice, subordinating society to the state. Many associationalists and corporatists argued that representative democracy was a fundamentally inadequate system of representation, that it gave effective expression neither to the actual wills of individual electors, nor to the social interests. Thus they proposed a system of functional democracy based on the major social interests represented through corporatist structures. As we shall see, functional democratic ideas contain important defects and cannot be a substitute for representative democracy. Inadequate as most democratic systems are, few modern citizens would want to lose the vote. There is, however, an important point in these arguments if different forms of representation are not seen as a substitute for representative democracy, but as a supplement to it. Emile Durkheim's work is especially relevant in this respect, not least because he redefined and extended what democracy was. In his *The Division of Labour in Society* (1964), published in 1893, he offered a non-socialist critique of the *laissez faire* principles of economic liberalism, arguing that the idea of a socially-disembedded, purely economic market mechanism was unsustainable. Durkheim rejected socialism as giving all power to the state, and argued that the economy could be regulated by less draconian means. In his *Lectures on Civic Morals* (collected in *Professional Ethics and Civic Morals* (1957)) he argued for corporatist representation as a new form of democratic communication between the state and the key professional groups in the economy.

Associationalism never congealed to form a coherent ideology. It never became a political movement capable of exercising power. It did not lack powerful ideas, but they made little headway against the notions that centralization and the large-scale are the most efficient and historically inevitable ways of organizing social relations. Marx has much to answer for in this respect. Maxists, like other collectivists and unlike most associationalists, were successful because they realized the need to compete for, and capture, state power by parliamentary or revolutionary means.

Imagine, however, that Marx and Proudhon had had a better relationship in Paris in the early 1840s, that Marx had accepted that comprehensive state collectivism must ruin liberty and that Proudhon had accepted greater pragmatism about the need to control political power. Or imagine that Beatrice Webb had been convinced by J.N. Figgis of the virtues of the pluralist state. In that case socialists might have tried to build their socialism in civil society, whilst ensuring, through seeking politically appropriate representation, a state at least not hostile to this enterprise. Such a socialism would have been based on mutual welfare through organizations like the Friendly Societies, on the organization of distribution through non-profitmaking stores like those of the English Cooperative Movement, and on the organization of production either through worker-owned cooperatives or labour-capital partnerships, in which workers took a part of their income through equity.

Such developments were eminently possible, for the Friendly Societies and the 'Co-Op' were very successful. Such a socialism would very likely still exist, since it would have been built in civil society and would have been relatively independent of the state. It would have been non-authoritarian, competing with other institutions for the membership and custom of individuals. It would not have been so threatened by the changes in state policy that have wrecked the nationalized industries and battered the welfare state created by the 1945 Labour Government. The fact is that as the twentieth century progressed, the voluntary and cooperative elements in the British Labour Movement became weaker and weaker. Wage labour and state provision seemed the easier option, especially in the post-1945 period of full employment and the welfare state. Socialism in Britain, once so strong, so pragmatic and fundamentally humane, died through its dependence on the state no less than did the brutal Soviet state collectivist version.

Associationalism was never just the preserve of socialists, however, nor is it trapped in its past. Associative democracy can become a new idea because of the changed political and economic context. Associationalist ideas are no longer compelled to perform the same role that they did in the great contest of systems of social organization in the nineteenth century. They can be reformulated on a revised theoretical basis and in a new political conjuncture. The purpose of this book is not to retrieve and restate associationalist ideas as they were developed by a range of politically diverse nineteenth- and early twentieth-century thinkers. Rather the aim is to draw on those ideas to reconstruct a political doctrine suitable to the present, changing many of the substantive intellectual proposals but also some of the underlying theoretical assumptions of the classic associationalist writers. As this book proceeds, and particularly in Chapter 3, it will be clear that a great deal of previous associationalist argument will either be abandoned or radically redefined. It is hardly possible that an intellectual tradition that was so thoroughly marginalized by the mid-1920s could remain instantly relevant today.

Many associationalists did not see associative democracy as a supplement to existing social relations but as a 'new society'. Associationalism contained strong elements of utopianism, although even apparently highly utopian writers like Proudhon in his economic writings developed ideas that were practical in the context of the relatively decentralized and artisan-based economy of mid-nineteenth century France. Many associationalists did seek to replace entirely representative democracy with a new functional democracy, and also to replace the market-based economy with a socialist system of a non-collectivistic type. I shall argue that neither of these aims is sustainable. Modern associative democracy can only be a more or less extensive supplement to liberal representative democracy, it cannot seek to abolish the individual right to vote on a territorial basis, nor to abolish the state as a public power that attempts to protect the rights of individual citizens and associations. In that sense associationalism extends and enhances liberalism and does not seek to supersede it. Likewise, the introduction of associative forms of governance of the economy and associational forms of welfare provision are designed neither to supplant a market-based economy nor to reduce levels of publicly-funded welfare. On the contrary, associative economic governance is conceived as extending those forms of social embeddedness of markets that enable market economies to work better, and associative welfare is designed to extend individual control and choice, which collectivistic systems fail to do, whilst offering extensive and primarily publicly-funded services.

Associative democracy is deceptively simple in its most basic political claims. These can be stated briefly as follows. Associationalism makes a central normative claim, that individual liberty and human welfare are both best served when as many of the affairs of society as possible are managed by voluntary and democratically self-governing associations. Associationalism seeks to square the aims of freedom for the individual in pursuing his or her chosen goals with the effective governance of social affairs. Individualism is rejected because associationalists argue that in a purely competitive market society many people will lack the resources to achieve their objectives, they will not have the freedom denoted by the capacity to control their affairs, and in consequence many of the dimensions of social life will be ill-governed. Whilst associationalism gives priority to freedom in its scale of values and defines freedom as the ability of individuals to pursue their chosen purposes, it contends that freedom can only be pursued effectively by the majority of persons if they are both enabled and supported by society in joining with their fellows in

A big order
do it ?
possible ?

voluntary associations in order to do so. Associations must, therefore, be protected by a public power that can enforce the rule of law and also, where necessary, be funded by the public through taxation.

Associationalism seeks to combine the individual choice of liberalism and the public provision of collectivism. It is by no means a substitute form of collectivism. Collectivism is opposed because a fundamental contention of associationalist writers like Figgis or Laski is that modern societies are pluralistic, they are composed of different partial societies with distinct objectives and beliefs, and those diverse ends cannot be accommodated by uniform methods of compulsory provision through the state. Associationalists were opposed to the collectivistic schemes of Fabian writers like the Webbs for this very reason. Collectivism is rejected as such, and not just in its totalitarian form in Soviet-style socialism. Associationalism attempts to construct a political framework within which individuals and the groups they create through voluntary association, one with another, can pursue different public goods whilst remaining in the same society. Plural groups share a limited, but common, set of public rules and regulatory institutions, which ensure that their differing goals and beliefs can be accommodated without undue conflict or the infringement of the rights of individuals and associations.

The institutional changes proposed in an associative democratic reform of existing forms of representative democracy and centralized bureaucratic state administration can be summed up in three principles of political organization:

1. that voluntary self-governing associations gradually and progressively become the primary means of democratic governance of economic and social affairs;
2. that power should as far as possible be distributed to distinct domains of authority, whether territorial or functional, and that administration within such domains should be devolved to the lowest level consistent with the effective governance of the affairs in question – these are the conjoint principles of state pluralism and of federation;
3. that democratic governance does not consist just in the powers of citizen election or majority decision, but in the continuous flow of information between governors and the governed, whereby the former seek the consent and cooperation of the latter.

We now turn to examine how associationalist and corporatist writers developed these principles and how they may be given expression today. This discussion is the core of our exposition of the specifically political institutions of associational governance.

Three principles of associationalist political organization

Primary associations as democratic governance

The conception that voluntary self-governing associations become the primary means of democratic governance of economic and social affairs involves two processes. First, that the state should cede functions to such associations, and create the mechanisms of public finance whereby they can undertake them. Second, that the means to the creation of an associative order in civil society are built-up, such as alternative sources of mutual finance for associative economic enterprises, agencies that aid voluntary bodies and their personnel to conduct their affairs effectively, and so on. This is not intended to be a once-and-for-all change, but a gradual process of supplementation, proceeding as fast as the commitment to change by political forces and the capacity to accept tasks by voluntary associations allows. This development can be seen in two ways, as a necessary means of reforming representative democracy, and as a desirable method of organizing economic and social affairs in and of itself.

The principal aim of an associative supplement to representative democracy is to reduce both the scale and the scope of the affairs of society that are administered by state agencies overseen by representative institutions. Existing legislatures and elected government personnel are hopelessly overburdened by the sheer size of modern bureaucratic big government, and the multiplicity of the functions of social provision and regulation undertaken by modern states. The result is to undermine representative democracy, weakening accountability to the people through their representatives of both policy-making and the delivery of services. Associational governance would lessen the tasks of central government to the extent that greater accountability both of the public power and of the devolved associationally-governed activities would be possible.

Economic liberals have attempted to address these problems of accountability and the scale of government by reducing the activities performed by the state, reducing both public provision and public regulation of the wider society. They have sought to privatize and to deregulate activities, but in doing so they have typically handed these activities over to undemocratic and unaccountable bodies, either quasi-public bureaucratic agencies or hierarchically-managed business corporations. Associative democracy is not like economic liberalism, although both advocate that the state should shed certain functions. Associationalism does not aim to reduce either social provision or economic governance, but to change their form of organization. It devolves the performance and administration of public functions to voluntary bodies that are accountable both to their members and to the public power. What would conventionally be regarded as 'private' agencies undertake public functions, but, unlike the agencies created by economic liberal reforms, they are accountable to those for whom the service or activity is provided. The administration of such voluntary bodies is doubly answerable: directly to their membership through their members' rights to participate in, and to exit from, associations and, for the performance of publicly-funded activities, to common political institutions composed of elected representatives and appointed officials like judges or inspectors. Associative democracy aims at a manageable and accountable state, but not an under-governed society. Associationalism does not strip down and diminish the public sphere as economic liberalism does, but actually revitalizes it and extends it.

Associationalists are not the only critics of the present balance between state and civil society, this too is the concern of thoughtful liberal democrats. Thus Noberto Bobbio and Robert Dahl, without doubt the two most accomplished contemporary democratic theorists, argue that democracy is endangered when the pluralism and autonomy of civil society is threatened by unaccountable hierarchically-controlled power. The problem for classical liberal democrats is that democratic government based on accountability to the individual citizen means little if the great bulk of economic affairs are controlled by large privately-owned corporations, and if the great bulk of other social affairs are controlled by state bureaucracies. The space for real democratic government is then small, and 'civil society' becomes vestigial, confined to marginal groups and peripheral areas of social life with little influence over the real decision-makers. If the dominant bureaucratic institutions persist unreformed, then the role of democracy is reduced in the case of companies to shareholders (at least nominally) electing directors and, in the case of the state, to individual citizens electing representatives who have formal direction of public administrative agencies. The problem here for Bobbio and Dahl is unaccountable bureaucracy and the excessive influence of certain groups, not the form and functions of the liberal democratic state.

Noberto Bobbio in *The Future of Democracy* (1987) contends that democracy has stopped short of the 'two great blocks of descending and hierarchical power in every complex society, big business and public administration. And as long as these blocks hold out against the pressures exerted from below, the democratic transformation of society cannot be said to be complete' (p. 57). For Bobbio the acid test of democracy is not just ' "who votes" but "where" they can vote' (p. 56). The central contention in Robert Dahl's' *A Preface to Economic Democracy* (1985) is that effective democracy requires both the widespread diffusion of property and the sturdy economic independence of a substantial portion of the citizens. Excessive control of the economy either by the state or by a small number of private agencies is a threat to the plural society that is the foundation of political democracy. Democracy does not require capitalism, but a market society and a substantial number of autonomous economic units. The concentration of corporate power threatens democracy both because it increases the capacity for influence on government of a small number of unaccountable private bodies, and because it reduces the independence of the citizens, the majority of whom may be employees of such companies. Dahl's answer is the development of a worker-owned cooperative sector as a way of checking the unhealthy concentration of corporate control over the economy, and therefore the polity, that has developed in this century.

These are powerful arguments, and they help to make the associationalist case, but both writers stop well short of advocating associationalism. The reason is that both remain committed to a vision of a liberal-democratic state that is at once a self-governing political community and answerable to its citizens. It is difficult to see how liberal democracy can be restored in an omnicompetent state that is no longer able to function as the sole locus of economic and social regulation, however. Neither Bobbio or Dahl proposes the associationalisation of social provision and the pluralization of the state, but nothing less will suffice to correspond to the complexity of the levels of governance developing in the modern world, and to restore choice and control over their affairs to the citizens themselves. Moreover, if corporate power were as secure and overwhelming as Dahl and Bobbio seem to think, then the prospects for any radical reform would be grim, however, as we shall see in Chapter 5, the large-scale corporation is by no means the inevitable form of organization of economic activity, and hence arguments for the reform of corporate governance and the promotion of alternative means of economic regulation have acquired a new legitimacy.

Modern societies are pluralistic as far as the objectives and beliefs of individuals and the social groups they join are concerned, but not in their dominant forms of service provision and administration. Associationalism aims to make provision correspond more fully to this pluralism. Voluntary associations would thus progressively take over an increasing range of social and public functions and would be answerable in the first instance to their own memberships through their processes of self-government for the administration of these activities. Members would choose the organization they wished to perform a given function for them. As we shall see in Chapters 6 and 7, there would be a variety of associations embodying different conceptions of how the activity or service should be performed. Associative reform would thus gradually change the primary role of government from that of a service provider to a means of ensuring that services were adequately provided and the rights of citizens and associations protected. That is a task representative democratic institutions could perform, given a significant measure of decentralization. The public power would serve both as a mechanism to raise and approve public funds for voluntary bodies to carry out specified social functions and as a means of ensuring that such funds were properly spent, and acceptable standards of service delivered by the voluntary bodies. The representative democratic institutions would have a more limited set of tasks to do than at present in supervising government bureaucracies, not least because associations' members would police and control them themselves, but, in consequence, they would have a greater capacity to carry out those tasks than do overburdened supervisory institutions in omnicompetent public service states. Such states seek to perform simultaneously two contradictory tasks, to provide services and to police the provision of these services.

Associationalism would alter the balance of the public and the private spheres. At present, participation in the public sphere is declining because modern large-scale mass democracies and bureaucratic states are remote, minimize participation, and are ineffective at providing the services citizens require. At the same time the private sphere has shrunk under the dual pressures of state intervention and compulsion, and of corporate power over employees and consumers. Associative democracy by 'publicizing' the private sphere, through democratically-controlled voluntary associations, would not trespass on individuals' liberties, but would enhance them by providing citizens with greater control of their affairs in the economy and in welfare. The point is that unless civil society is given certain 'political' attributes through self-governing associations that perform public functions, then it will be difficult to preserve its autonomy, squeezed as it has been by hierarchical administration. Associative reform would not threaten liberal freedoms by increasing the scope of social governance through voluntary associations, since those associations are independent and self-governing. Thus it is quite unlike totalitarian schemes of compulsory political mobilization of voluntary bodies, or authoritarian corporatist schemes to bureaucratize civil society and to compel individuals to be represented through collective agencies.

One reason why liberal democratic theorists have not adopted associative ideas is because they still see the state as the central political community. Voluntary associations are regarded in modern liberal democratic theory primarily in terms of their role as the social foundation of a pluralistic politics, that is they provide articulation for the divergent interests in civil society and thereby prevent any tendency toward the formation of potentially tyrannical homogeneous majorities. Such voluntary bodies are viewed as 'secondary associations' and as important because they ensure the

democratic nature of the 'primary association', the state. Associationalism turns this relationship on its head. It treats self-
governing voluntary bodies not as secondary associations, but as
the primary means of both democratic governance and organizing
social life. A self-governing civil society thus becomes the primary
feature of society. The state becomes a secondary, but vitally
necessary, public power that ensures peace between associations
and protects the rights of individuals. It also provides the mechanisms of public finance whereby those forms of provision that are
regarded as necessary and available as of right to all members of
society are administered through voluntary associations that those
members elect to join in order to receive such services.

Undoubtedly many readers will be sceptical that this can be
done. Thus I have tried to spell out these arrangements in the
greatest possible detail. How associations can be made answerable to their members and those members' freedoms of choice
preserved is considered in Chapter 3. How the economy could be
governed by cooperative and coordinative relationships between
enterprises, and how those enterprises could be made accountable
to a greater range of stakeholders than just shareholders, will
be considered in Chapter 5. How welfare could be organized
on associationalist lines is considered in Chapters 6 and 7.
The principle of governance through voluntary associations has
been asserted here. The full organizational complexities and the
problems of so doing and how they might be overcome, are developed as the book unfolds.

The pluralization and federalization of the state

Associationalism challenges both the centralization of the state
and its claim to 'sovereignty'. It proposes that authority be as far
as possible divided into distinct domains, whether territorial or
functional, and that authority should be as localized and small-
scale as possible. Associationalism argues that there are fundamental geographical and social divisions that must be respected in
the organization of government. If they are not, then not only is
liberty put at risk by excessive centralization, but those well-
springs of association and cooperation that make a society truly
efficient are also threatened. Harold Laski argued that the art of
good government is to identify, to give appropriate powers to,

and to respect the degree of autonomy necessary to the function of those discrete units.

That art of government is never more needed than at present, since with the relative decline of the nation state, the 'appropriate' distribution of power between different levels of administration is both complex and mutable. It is clear that an explicit theory of how this might be accomplished is now needed. For example, the European Community is seeking to find an adequate distribution of functions between federal, national and regional levels. It has used the Catholic social doctrine of subsidiarity as one of its means of doing so, emphasizing that a function should be performed at the lowest level consistent with competent administration. There is a strong interest in decentralization across the political spectrum: from conservatives who genuinely want to roll back the state in the interests of greater liberty, rather than to make an easy profit out of privatization; on the part of greens who want a less hierarchical and centralized, and therefore less environmentally destructive, economic system; and from the pragmatic left who are desperately seeking some alternative to both big government and top-down planning. This aspiration toward decentralized power has lacked a coherent theory. As a result it is less effectively advocated, and the different parts of the old political spectrum committed to this idea are more conscious of those things that divide them than of what they have in common. Decentralization and localism are strong and widely-shared value preferences, as responses to the remoteness and impersonality of big administrative machines, but they have tended to be dismissed because they have run counter to the apparent efficiency gains of the large-scale in organization. One must show that decentralization and de-bureaucratization can go together, that they are both possible and capable of efficiency (Rendell and Ward, 1989). There is little point in decentralizing if the result is what are still large and bureaucratically administered local authorities or, even worse, managerial quasi-governmental organizations. The pluralist theory of the state can provide the rationale for such decentralization.

Pluralism does so first by showing why centralized and concentrated power is not efficient, in its critique of sovereignty. By sovereignty' the English pluralists like Figgis and Laski meant that a particular political body, typically a legislature, claimed for itself a plenitude of power and the right to exercise control over and to make rules for every person, agency and circumstance within a definite territory. Laski (1925) argued that all power is federative by nature. He meant by that the notion of a single sovereign power, able to govern all social life and centred in a single political will, is a myth. It is a myth that modern states inherited from early-modern royal autocracies. It is a dangerous myth too, in that the claim to sovereignty, while unrealizable in fact, sustains a variety of very different political projects that seek to impose such a will on society. In the process of seeking to realize the unrealizable they inflict great damage on society.

Whilst the powers and functions of the state were limited, the claim to sovereignty posed a limited threat. However, the rise of modern mass democracies, giving government the powerful legitimation of at least formally deriving their power from the will of the governed, and the rise of the omnicompetent public service state, assisted by bureaucracies that could provide the detailed administration of all areas of social life, made this claim doubly pernicious. The propagators or appropriators of this claim could deny the plural interests and wills of a complex society in the name of the majority, and they could use bureaucracy to carry out comprehensive programmes of reconstruction of the 'private' sphere, secure in the state's right to legislate over every circumstance.

John Neville Figgis (1913) saw the danger in the combination of the claim to sovereignty and a mass democratic 'total' state a good decade before the advent of modern totalitarianism in Mussolini's final crushing of the rights of legal opposition. He saw it in the threats to religious liberty posed by French republican anti-clericalism under Emile Combes and in Bismarck's *Kulturkampf*, and in the threats to trade union liberty represented by the Taff Vale judgement. In both cases state policy operated on the concessionist theory of associations, that is, that voluntary bodies in civil society exist only by the licence of the state and with such powers as it choses to give them in law. A centralized sovereign state in a pluralistic and activist society is a glaring contradiction. It may threaten ideas and organizations it opposes by a policy of militant and active suppression, but it can do so less dramatically and no less damagingly by the steady application of common bureaucratic norms and supposedly uniform types of provision.

Power is, of course, limited by the very complexity of the means of its exercise, and, therefore, no single will can prevail throughout the elaborate decision-making and administrative structures that are nominally grouped within the constitutional limits of the modern state. Totalitarian projects have generally failed for this very reason, rather than from active resistance from below. However, this fact of the inevitable plurality of power undermines the claims of those republican democrats who believe that centralized power can be made democratically accountable. It means that however determined they are, the will of elected representatives can only run so far and so consistently within the ramified administrative machinery of the modern state.

American pluralists might argue the foregoing is merely an argument against the tyranny of the majority in another guise, and that modern democracies have means for avoiding these problems. Because modern societies are composed of highly pluralistic and competing interest groups, the threat of majority tyranny is avoided, and modern politics actually consists in the competition of issue-specific minority groups to control policy or influence government on the issue in question. In the process of plural political competition, the most successful and best-organized minorities come to dominate on particular issues, but the capacity of these minorities to influence politics does not cumulate from one issue to another. R.A. Dahl develops this argument very clearly in *Who Governs?* (1961), and against ruling class or power elite conceptions of the distribution of power it has a good deal of force.

What it ignores is the threefold danger inherent in the combination of pluralistic political competition and highly-centralized states. First, there is the danger that highly exclusive and self-interested groups will lobby the state, and either impose extremely partisan and unpopular views on others or secure advantages for themselves through public policy and to the detriment of the public interest. We have seen Dahl (1985) recognizing the dangers of undue corporate influence, but pluralists have woken up rather late to the extent to which the competition to influence big government has led to the domination of the American political process by exclusive and self-interested lobbies. Second, is the danger for policy to swing back and forth or to become incoherent as successive highly-polarized pressure groups gain the upper hand and impose their view on an issue. One side gets enough influence to have its views legislated for or adopted as policy, and then the opposition is either able to repeal the policy or to dilute it. The result is inconsistent policy, and, whoever wins, a large discontented minority on the losing side. Moral issues like abortion or the death penalty show this danger very clearly and indicate a pathological side to the system of minorities' rule. Third, the American pluralist position tends to treat all dimensions of policy as just 'issues', thereby ignoring the structural difference between the old liberal state and the centralized omnicompetent state. Certain dimensions of policy such as national economic management or welfare spending take on a salience for the lives of the majority of the citizens that make them more than just one issue like another. The danger here is that such key policy areas are hijacked by highly partisan and determined minorities, who are able to impose their will through the ruling party which is a complex coalition of interests. Citizens may continue to vote for such a party for reasons that are quite different from those of the influential minority, who may thus have a considerable period in which to impose their policies. The result is both damage to the interests of many citizens and the imposition of psuedo-legitimate policies, that are not successful because they do not call forth real cooperation and consent.

The modern state is too open to the rule of opinionated cliques in economic and social policy, the more so because such policies have become too complex for many citizens to understand fully without considerable effort, and they involve the actions of centralized bureaucracies that are remote from their everyday lives. The management of highly-centralized social relations inevitably produces complex theories about how certain policy instruments will work and how the persons and activities so administered will behave. Far from being certain and efficient in their operation, as their apologists from Max Weber onwards have claimed, large bureaucracies rely on quasi-scientific theories of how society will respond to the actions of agencies that are too remote to have effective local knowledge. In fact bureaucracies can make only their internal procedures certain, and can only do that by making their operations so routine and inflexible that they cease to be truly responsive. Centralized public service states and very large corporations are at the mercy of 'experts' who sell their conflicting nostrums to bemused elected officials and senior managers alike.

English political pluralist thinking anticipated these dangers and argued that the only solution to pathological minorities' rule and to creeping bureaucratization was to change the form of the state. Proudhon, writing in the mid-nineteenth century, argued that the contest for sovereign power between the newly enfranchised masses and the bourgeois strata must lead to an unstable and oscillating contest, but in which the two forces adopted paradoxical political positions. Proudhon argued that all government involves a balance between liberty and authority, and that ideologically the masses are the advocates of freedom and the established strata the defenders of order. However, in the course of their political conflict the masses supported strong rulers who would centralize the state and impose their will, mass political participation led to plebiscitarian leader democracy, whilst the bourgeoisie sought the liberal defence of the private sphere and hence of rights to property.

In *The Principle of Federation* (1863) Proudhon proposed a radically decentralized state that would avoid these conflicts for concentrated power. Proudhon's scheme is not for anarchy, but for a loose confederal state in which communes and counties would retain the basic political powers and would cede less power to 'higher' bodies. The higher bodies would be limited by existing only on the basis of specific contractual relations with the basic communities, and being subject to the assent of the delegates of those communities to any policy. The federal public power would neither possess unlimited legislative sovereignty, nor would it be an administrative machine. It would have no courts and no standing army, rather it would exist merely to link the communities and to provide a means of dealing with particular problems by the decision of delegates from the communes. Proudhon's federation is quite unlike Marx's commune state in which legislative and executive power are fused. Proudhon envisages a decentralized economy based upon contractural relations between free individuals, not the dictatorship of the proletariat to impose socialism through class war. As is so often the case with Proudhon, his arguments against the centralized administrative state are more developed than his own institutional proposals. His federation is a sort of super Swiss Confederation that compliments a decentralized mutualist economy.

Laski in 'The Problem of Administrative Areas' (1921) proposed a more realistic system of federation, recognizing that the public power could neither be as vestigial as Proudhon envisaged, nor could it actually depend on assent from the bottom up, since in existing centralized states power could only be properly federated if it were to be devolved downwards by explicit public policy. Laski argued that the state should be pluralized, and power federated on two principles. First, that each level of authority or administration perform only such functions as are absolutely necessary to it, and that its powers of jurisdiction not exceed those functions. Central state institutions would exist solely for certain particular purposes and would have no general power of legislation over, or intervention in, the affairs of 'lesser' authorities. Those lesser territorial or functional bodies would not exist by its *fiat* alone, and would enjoy autonomy in performing their own specific functions. Figgis (1913), who Laski followed in this argument, maintained that the primary purpose of the central public power was to police and protect the pluralist system, ensuring that self-governing voluntary bodies did not damage one another or the rights of citizens. In matters of internal concern, the associations were free to arrange or conduct their affairs as they saw fit, without requiring either the sanction or the specific legal concession of certain powers by the state.

Second, Laski argued that alongside territorial authorities, central and local, there would be the self-governing domains of social authority. Laski argued 'the railways are as real as Lancashire; and exactly as the specifically local problems of Lancashire are dealt with by it, so could the specifically functional problems of the railways be dealt with by a governing body of its own' (1921: 70). Activities would be answerable to their own constituencies of interest, and within that domain would make their own policies or rules. Like G.D.H. Cole in his *Guild Socialism Re-stated* (1920a), Laski assumed that self-governing domains would voluntarily (or contracturally in Proudhon's terms) establish mutual relationships of cooperation and coordination where these were necessary. Decentralized self-government would thus both reduce the scope of regulation of the public power (it would not intervene directly in distinct domains of authority) and reduce the range of activities for which it was responsible. The classical English political pluralist arguments did not involve a complete rejection of a central legislative and regulative agency; a public power. What they did entail was that the scope of such legislation and regulation be reduced and circumscribed. Some pluralist formulations (like the early work of Laski before the 1920s) did seem to place the public power on a parallel with private associations, claiming it had no higher authority or right to demand loyalty, but, as we shall see in Chapter 3, this is not necessary to, and indeed contradicts the fundamental associationalist argument.

Associative democracy is thus not merely a doctrine of devolving power to voluntary associations, since it is accepted that not all social affairs can be administered in this way. Associations require a common framework of regulatory rules if they are to interact satisfactorily with one another and their members. Internal self-government needs to be answerable to minimum but non-optional standards to ensure that it is fair and does not infringe the freedom of individuals through unequal forms of authority or undue group pressure. Associations may need public funds to perform their functions, and must be answerable to the funding body for them. Further, there are certain affairs common to all members of society, and that cannot be devolved to the governance of associations chosen by their own members, such as the defence of the territory, certain police powers, certain environmental and public health provisions, and certain forms of compulsory control of individuals (such as mental health regulations).

The public power in an associationalist system, even given federal decentralization and the devolution of many functions to voluntary bodies, would not be a marginal entity. Whilst power should be as localized as possible, and where possible individuals should be able to choose the form of the governance of most social activities they prefer, there must be a common public power. Such a power should be based on representative democratic principles, deriving its authority from a federal constitution that prescribes and limits its powers. It would consist in a legislature elected on a territorial basis by universal suffrage and an independent judiciary appointed on legal merit, with autonomy to enforce the laws. Such a public power would be, in effect, a liberal constitutional state, but with limited functions. Associationalism and liberalism are not inherently in conflict. Indeed, given the self-government of most activities by voluntary associations and a federal state, liberalism would become a reality. At present classical liberal ideas are in contradiction with centralized, bureaucratic public service states that substitute state for society and circumscribe the 'private' sphere of individual liberty.

Democracy as communication

Most associational thinkers have seen representative democracy as an inadequate political mechanism. G.D.H. Cole in *The Social Theory* (1920b) argued that it is impossible to represent the actual wills of the electors and so, while elected assemblies act in the name of the people, they substitute the will of the representatives for the represented. Functional democracy will overcome this problem because the interests involved in the performance of a function are directly represented on the organizing or coordinating bodies for that function. Power is dispersed by function, and so representatives have specific tasks, unlike the representatives of the people in a sovereign legislature, who may make decisions on any aspect of life. Cole stands in here for the entire tradition of functional democratic and corporatist thinking on this issue. He is explicit in his assumptions and no less coherent in his arguments than any other critic of representative democracy, including Hegel.

The difficulty with the functional democratic critique of representative democracy is that it sees the problem with the latter primarily in terms of the inadequacy of its form of *representation*. Therefore, it is argued, a change in the *form* of representation will permit the *real* representation of actual interests and will solve the problem of the gap between representatives and represented. This is a false argument. There can be no *real* representation. All systems of representation have specific problems and construct the 'represented' in particular ways (I have argued this case against Cole at length elsewhere – Hirst, 1989: 30–9; Hirst, 1990: 12–15 – and will not repeat the argument here).

The problem with representative democracy is different: it is the type of democratic decision process and the scale of decision-making which is at issue, not real versus artificial representation. The sovereign representative democratic assembly combines a conception of democracy as the exercise of the majoritarian principle with decision-making in an omnicompetent centralized state.

Such a democracy tends to degenerate into the plebiscitarian legitimation of administration. Majority decisions are infrequent whereas administration is continuous, and majorities are often artificial, the 'majority' is a coalition of disparate interests. As we have seen in discussing the new republican radicals, emphasizing democracy as majority decision is hardly likely to answer problems of government accountability. Part of the answer is found in decentralization, limiting the scale and scope of decisions, and part in creating institutions that emphasize a rather different conception of democracy, that is democracy as effective governance based upon an adequate flow of information from governed to governors, and the coordination of the implementation of policy through ongoing consultation with those affected by it.

This conception of democracy as communication defines it not in terms of the rule of majority parties or popular majorities but in terms of the quality of decision-making that results from the interaction between the governing agency and the agencies organizing the activity being governed. This conception is the foundation for most neo-corporatist conceptions of social governance (Schmitter and Streeck, 1985), and was probably best expressed by Emile Durkheim in his *Lectures on Civic Morals* (1957). Durkheim does not treat the majoritarian principle and representative democracy as the most significant phenomena in defining what is or can be democratic about the modern state. For him democracy is, in its most important aspect, a process of effective two-way communication between an independent public power (the state) and organized social groups representing the main occupational interests. The state is an organ of social coordination not a mere medium for the registration of the wills of social majorities: 'the state is nothing if it is not an organ distinct from the rest of society' (1957: 82). Only the independence of the public power can ensure that the state does not become merely a medium through which conflicting social interests struggle for supremacy, in which the majoritarian principle enables one set of interests to prevail over others. But the separation of the state from society cannot be too complete, for then the state loses the capacity to coordinate social activity. Hence the hallmarks of an effective democracy are accurate information, objectivity and rationality in policy-making: 'The more deliberation and reflection and a critical spirit play a considerable part in the course of public affairs, the more democratic the nation' (1957: 89). Hence the interaction between organized interests and the state is only effective if it enables public policy to be made on this basis. The state is coordinative for Durkheim, and effective communication is the foundation of coordination. Communication enhances social solidarity because it enables social groups to know each other's expectations and objectives, and to begin to act together. Enhanced solidarity promotes effective government, because groups are able to act together, and the state can expect both consent and cooperation because its actions will be based on information and discussion.

It is often assumed that Durkheim's conception of 'democracy' leads inevitably to a form of centralized corporatism. Such intense state–society communication is possible, but only where both state and society are dominated by elites, and the core of social decision-making involves small numbers of professional decision-makers. The state elite and the elites of the major organized social interests – typically big business federations and organized labour – are cohesive and relatively closed. The corporate organizations are disciplined enough to transmit coordinated and agreed policies to their memberships. Elite communication, state access to societal elites, and social compromise are thereby attained, resulting in low direct state coercion, high compliance of affected interests and effective coordination between them. These are the benefits of an effective corporatist system. The question is whether they actually represent any kind of 'democracy' at all, or rather a system of interlinking hierarchical management that is meliorated by elements of consultation with the grass roots of the distinct organized interests. Durkheim presented his ideas in a corporatist mode, he conceived of his doctrine as a form of 'solidarism' not of associationalism based on the voluntary principle. One might ask whether this system of quasi-compulsory corporatist consultation has much in common with the voluntarism and activism of associative democracy.

In response I would contend that Durkheim's conception of democracy as communication need not be delivered solely in the form of centralized corporatist consultation between a public service state and highly-concentrated forms of interest group representation. Neo-corporatist theorists (Schmitter, 1988), and associative democrats (Cohen and Rogers, 1992), have both be-

gun to question whether existing systems of corporatist intermediation of an inclusive kind (or more exclusive forms of interest
group competition) can function effectively, and whether they do
not require some form of democratizing supplement that will open
up interest group representation to excluded groups and make
corporate bargaining more accountable and representative of the
wider society. The need for democracy as communication is not
questioned here, but the corporatist forms of its delivery have
begun to be dogged by problems. As we shall see in Chapter 5,
economic and social changes are making corporatist systems, such
as Germany or Sweden, less representative of, and centralized
bargains less acceptable to, the wider society.

The answers proposed by Schmitter and Cohen and Rogers are
ingenious and turn on measures to increase interest group formation and effectiveness. Such measures are to be effected by interventionist policies of the central state. Cohen and Rogers, for
example, argue that associations representing social interests
are 'artifactual', that is, 'there is no natural structure of group
representation that directly reflects the underlying conditions of
social life' (1992: 30). The state, therefore, can intervene to craft
associations and by deliberate public policy can encourage 'those
qualities of groups that contribute to democratic governance'
(1992: 37). The aim of such intervention would be to increase the
inclusiveness of group representation and to reduce the obstacles
to weaker groups influencing public policy.

The problem with such views is that they impose a task on the
central state that it increasingly lacks either the legitimacy or
the competence to carry out. Such reforms will be rejected by
exclusive and influential insider groups. Given that such crafting
will be conflictual, since the aim is to improve social efficiency by
equalizing group representation, it is difficult to see how it can be
accomplished by disinterested state officials acting in the common
good. Such changes can hardly be neutral.

It is also the case that while groups and associations are to a
degree artifactual, they are neither necessarily nor desirably the
malleable objects of social engineering by the state. Associations
that depend for their capacities on crafting by the state are likely,
as a general rule, to be weaker than those formed and sustained
primarily voluntarily. They become dependent on a benevolent
state policy and will tend to falter if it is withdrawn due to a change

of government. The aim must be to promote policies by the state that empower associations generally and devolve activities from the state to associations, rather than retaining the central state as a service provider and trying to rejig the conditions of access to, and influence of, associations upon it. Such intervention by the state on the conditions of associations' formation and functioning will tend to empower the state and not the associations. Traditional associationalism failed because it neglected the state. It would be foolish to repeat that mistake again. But the concept of state 'crafting' relies too much on the state, too little on associations' own active response, and gives too little emphasis to a politics of changing the state by decentralization and devolution of functions.

The fundamental problem with the state's crafting associations is similar to that of schemes for formal functional representation through associations; it is one of legitimacy. Which organizations are to be taken to need extra support or are taken to be representative of a fundamental social interest or perform a vital social function? Corporatist systems have presented less of a problem since their activities have tended to be confined to the specific role of economic coordination, to depend on bargains between the assenting parties, and to involve a small number of widely-recognized large organizations – union or employers' federations. Corporatism has acted as a supplement to and not a replacement of representative democratic institutions. Even so, critics have challenged it from contrary directions, either as undermining parliamentary sovereignty, or as bringing oppositional voluntary associations like trade unions under state control. Most people can agree that there are major social functions, but there would be extensive disagreement as to which organizations are representative of such functions and should be included as part of a scheme of formal functional representation in a national parliament or other such body. Representative democracy has the advantage that it is flexible – it can accommodate social change, and changes in the composition of the electorate, the voting system, in political ideas, and in the party system.

Democracy as communication does not require the supplanting of representative democracy with a formalized and centralized scheme of functional democracy, nor does it require the central state's re-crafting the conditions of associational representation. It can operate best in a decentralized system, where local knowledge makes processes of consultation easier, in a system where a great deal of the tasks of government are ceded to associations, and where coordination depends on the cooperation of these associations.

There are two ways of beginning to change the balance of power between the different kinds of associations and for promoting new patterns of coordinative governance between associations and the decentralized state. The first is to advocate a process of building-up associations from *below*, not state crafting from above. This involves political campaigning and voluntary action in civil society, and assistance from stronger associations to weaker. The resources to form and sustain associations are far from equally distributed, but they do not prevent efforts to construct or to rebuild means of campaigning on behalf of the poor, the excluded and the unpopular causes. Trade unions have so far made poor efforts to develop or to help representation for the unemployed. Churches are possessed of considerable resources and great public influence, and often accept a social mission. They might become more effective in campaigning and in aiding marginalized constituencies if they saw the value of an associationalist strategy. The list can be extended to cover a large part of civil society. Given such action from below, then it makes sense to press for tax and other concessions to associations, and for the voluntary sector to begin to take over public tasks.

The second would be to work at the regional level, to build-on and to attempt to widen the efforts of regional and local governments to promote programmes of economic revitalization, and to promote a coordinative politics for the economy at subnational levels. It may well be that more collaborative relationships *within* firms, between management and labour, will develop from partnerships *between* firms, organized labour and local public agencies to develop and sustain the local or regional economy. Greater economic democracy involves recognizing the importance of the conception of democracy as communication, building up two kinds of partnership, one between employees, managers and external providers of capital in the firm, and the other between firms themselves, creating a public sphere of collaborative economic governance of the locality or region.

Such methods of building both associations' capacities and

democracy as communication have the advantage that they side-step the central state, they are objects of citizens' and local initiatives. However, in certain societies like the United Kingdom, a substantial measure of central political reform is necessary for this to happen. Britain has become so centralized that local authorities lack the fiscal or policy autonomy to create institutions of effective local economic regulation; it has also developed a structure of restrictive legislation on union rights and public order, so as to frustrate action in civil society by marginal groups and to render much activity oppositional. Britain is, however, very much the exception. In its case constitutional reform and political reform of the main institutions of central government is the pre-condition for any form of radical politics, not just an associationalist strategy of reform.

An associationalist reform strategy

In the long run an associationalist strategy for reform cannot become widespread unless it has a state at least not actively hostile to such a strategy. Voluntary action in civil society and at local levels can initiate such a strategy, but for the devolution of tasks to associations and for the decentralization of the state to take place significant legislation would be required and a commitment of a substantial section of representatives to the growth of associational governance. That can happen only if politicians and officials see that associations are succeeding in pursuing such a strategy and that it had large-scale public support. Associationalists traditionally ignored the state in favour of action in civil society, we can now see that action in civil society has, in part, to be directed toward winning over the state.

How might that happen? In the economic sphere, as we shall see in Chapter 5, if industrial districts, organized regional economies and collaborative interfirm relationships that balance co-operation and competition can survive competitive pressures from large firms, then they can serve as a political model. The hope would then be of the gradual diffusion of localization and mutuality through its regional success stories, promoting both emulation from below and pressure for the reform of national laws to permit the diffusion of such developments. Similarly, in the welfare sectors, the gradual growth of voluntarism as a remedy for and a supplement to state collectivism may create models to be emulated and diffused.

Above all what is needed is a concept that ties these various, potentially popular, ideas together and shows their practicality – political decentralization and governance through associations, new regional economies and federalism and voluntarism in welfare. That concept has been missing, not because it was not available, but because political activity and circumstances have only just caught up with long-neglected ideas. The only route to the success of associationalism demands a clear concept, because that will tie together organizationally and attitudinally separate efforts working in different localities and social spheres toward similar ends. Local unionists and the owners of small firms, Christian or Muslim voluntary workers in the inner cities, disadvantaged ethnic groups seeking to develop their own businesses and services as a way to promote employment and community control, feminist and gay groups attempting to escape from discrimination and wishing to create social relations according to their own values, ecological groups seeking both a more human scale and a sustainable environment, and many other diverse groups, may all profit from this knowledge.

The model of them all coming together in a single political party that attains power by persuading the electorate of the virtues of its programme and then enacts that plan into the simultaneous reform of the whole society is quite inappropriate. That is possible as a dream for collectivists and for those who wish to decollectivise through deregulation and privatization – both accept centralized sovereign state power and do not wish to change it. Associationalists have to rely on the multiplication of diverse efforts. Associationalist relationships have to begin to be built by citizens' initiative and bodies freely formed by committed individuals. Unless such relationships arise from genuine cooperation they will be of little value. Success in civil society, through municipal and regional initiatives and cooperation, and through specific campaigns directed at the central state, will gradually show associational relations to provide a viable strategy of social and political reform. Then it may be possible to persuade the central state to begin to legislate to make associative development more easily available and more widespread. However, the role of legislation must be permissive and gradual, not prescriptive and peremptory. Fortunately there is some hope that this process of diffusion of the associational model may begin to happen: if nation states continue to become less effective loci of economic regulation, if highly concentrated corporate power becomes less legitimate to citizens as it seems less and less the only route to industrial efficiency, and as the secret of supply-side success comes to be seen as a diffuse set of public and private commitments to the effective functioning of firms, networks and supportive public institutions. The ultimate legitimations of the large-scale are now economic; if they falter then the case for more decentralized institutions will grow in strength.

But it would be foolish to talk ourselves into a process of transition to an associationalist utopia. The associational principle can democratize and reinvigorate societies as a supplement to, and a healthy competitor for, the currently dominant forms of social organization: representative mass democracy, bureaucratic state welfare and the big corporation. Not all economic activities can be carried out by cooperative small- and medium-sized firms (however efficient), nor can all economic regulation be collaborative or regionally-based. Some elements of public welfare cannot be entrusted to voluntary agencies (however sophisticated the mechanisms for devolution of functions and funding): in the last instance, rights of entitlement, standards of service and principles of equity must be maintained by the public power at the federal level.

It is best to envisage associationalism not as a social system complete in itself, but as an axial principle of social organization. That is, a pattern of organizing social relations that can be generalized across sectors and domains of social activity. In this it resembles the market and bureaucratic administration. Such principles compete for dominance in modern societies: a mixture of the prevailing social conditions and the availability of a credible and effectively-presented political model decide whether a principle will play a major or a subsidiary role in a given period. The role of a political model is to show how the axial principle in question can be elaborated as the practical and credible basis for social organization. Associationalism needs elaboration to show its widespread applicability and effectiveness. What it has too often been is a blueprints for the turning of models into utopian actualities. Whether associationalism can act as a supplement to our failing institutions now depends not on restating the principle, but in working out the detail of credible models of associational governance in the economy and the welfare sectors. This is the task to which the bulk of this book is devoted.

3
Associationalist Ethics and the Logics of Collective Action

Associationalism has always been an explicitly normative political theory. The propositions it makes about states of affairs are connected with the normative claims of the theory. The key proposition of this kind is that if human actors are given the greatest possible freedom to associate one with another in voluntary bodies to perform the main tasks in society, then the affairs of that society will be better governed than if they are left either to the isolated activities of individuals or to the administrative organs of a centralized state. Associationalism makes a set of claims about how actors ought to behave, and those can be simplified into three main claims:

1 that human beings ought to associate one with another to fulfil common purposes, and that they should be able to do so on the basis of free choice;
2 that, as far as possible, such voluntary associations ought to be allowed to develop freely and that their internal affairs should be a matter for their members to arrange as they please;
3 it therefore follows that the state or public power may only abridge the freedom of an association either in order to preserve the freedom of individuals or to prevent harm to the freedom or interests of other associations.

Associationalists have distrusted the centralized state because it was both a compulsory community and one that made omnicompetent claims to regulate social life. They argued that the most genuine communities are those freely formed of citizens, and that the rationale for the state is as a limited and artificial community necessary to preserve the freedom to associate. Associationalists have never accepted the claim that simply because the state has a 'democratic' decision procedure, its claims upon the citizens and their associations were thereby justified.

Four unwarranted assumptions about associations

In this chapter the aim is to state the normative case for associationalism in a way that is defensible in the context of modern styles of theoretical argument, and that does not make extravagant or unjustified claims about human nature or the properties of associations. Here we find many of the early associationalists' arguments less than satisfactory. Associationalists have made a series of unwarranted and unjustified propositions about states of affairs to sustain their normative claims:

1 that there is a spontaneous and natural will to associate or 'spirit of fellowship' in all human beings, thus association is a natural human propensity and should be respected as such by the institutions we construct;
2 that associations, because they are voluntary and organic products of social life, truly enjoy the loyalty of their members and thus may make claims upon them not less strenuous and yet more justified than those of the compulsory state;
3 the state is an association just like any other and its claims to obedience are of no higher moral order than those say of a church or a trade union, therefore, the member of such associations may in good conscience deny obedience to the state if its demands clash with those of their association;
4 that associations have real corporate personalities independent of their members as individuals and that those personalities must be allowed freedom of organic development without external constraint.

P.-J. Proudhon, G.D.H. Cole and J.N. Figgis all more or less strongly supported the first proposition, from different theological and theoretical viewpoints. Cole and H.J. Laski strongly supported the second point with regard to trade unions, and Figgis did so with regard to churches. Laski in his earlier writings strongly advocated the third point, and at different times so did Cole. F.W.

Maitland, Figgis, Laski and Cole all strongly supported the last point, on the basis of a reading of Otto von Gierke's convoluted statements on this issue.

These four propositions, so important to the historical development of associationalist doctrine, and so tied in with the mode in which associationalists developed their discourse, are not merely unnecessary to the associationalist moral argument, they are each fundamentally defective and are actually destructive of that argument. I shall make the case against each proposition in turn.

Against the first claim, that human beings are animated by a natural and spontaneous 'spirit of fellowship' one may reply on two counts: first, that there can be no ready proof of this assertion, there are no strong arguments for it in the pluralist texts, and the rise of voluntary associations implies definite social and historical conditions rather than any natural propensity among humans; second, even if it were true it can, of itself, give rise to no ethical claim. For example, an individualist ethical theorist might deem it to be a sign of a primitive herd instinct that ought to be repressed by institutions in the interests of the self-development of the individual.

This proposition derives from a loose and careless piece of philosophical anthropology that need not detain us. Associationalism can be sustained without recourse to assumptions about a natural inclination to fellowship. If we accept that human capacities are largely constructed under definite historical conditions by social processes and by practices of training and formation, then we can see that the way human beings are motivated to join and to cooperate in associations is anything but natural and spontaneous. It also follows that we should not treat the previous history of associations, such as the medieval guilds, as part of a continuous natural tendency of humans to associate. Medieval institutions like the guilds do not resemble the modern associations which are models for the contemporary argument for associative democracy; they were compulsory for most of their members and highly undemocratic in their decision-making procedures.

However, the naturalness or otherwise of the propensity to associate is at best a secondary matter. Against this conception of an inherent 'will' to association is the more important point that it is actually contrary to the logic of associationalism. Associationalism treats organizations as being freely formed by the voluntary choices of individuals. Therefore, it is the individual as a being capable of intelligent choice, rational enough to follow his or her own perception of what his or her interests are, that is the precondition for voluntary association. The choice and the right to choice of the individual are prior to any attributes of the associations that these choices may create. Associationalism therefore supposes individuation and a degree of rationality, not some instinct to band together.

Against the second proposition, that associations may demand of their members unconditional loyalty, it will be obvious that the powers of a voluntary organization over its members are limited by the fact that they have freely chosen to join. Therefore, they can be required to submit to no obligations or discipline that are contrary to their right to make a subsequent free choice to leave the association. Members cannot be compelled to remain in a voluntary association, that is simply contrary to the logic of associationalism and is no more justifiable than Rousseau's notorious proposition that those who defy the 'General Will' must be 'forced to be free'.

Against the third proposition, that the state be considered as an association like any other and has no higher claim upon the individual, we may argue that if the function of the state is primarily that of the preservation of individual rights, among them the right to associate, and, therefore, the protection of the right to join or not to join an association, then the state does have one purpose which is higher than the claims of any given association, and that is to preserve the conditions of the voluntary associational order itself. Faced with a threat to the individual right to associate the state may sanction an assoication and, if necessary, punish those responsible for its policy in violating individual rights. In fact by no means all associationalists went along with this dubious proposition of ethical pluralism with regard to the state. J.N. Figgis in particular recognized clearly that a society composed of voluntary associations required a public power that was paramount in one respect, that it regulated the interactions of associations and preserved the conditions for such a society founded on the voluntary membership of its groupings.

Against the last proposition about the corporate personality of groups, it is not necessary for the associationalist to claim that the groups formed by the choices and actions of individuals become entities distinct from those individuals. The corporate personality of groups is a bit of bad metaphysics standing in quite needlessly for a far simpler and more effective argument. Contrary to the thesis of group personality, the group is not an entity, but a relationship between individuals. Put at its simplest, the group cannot continue to exist if the individuals who comprise it choose to dissolve it, for example, when the members of a joint-stock company pass a motion for its winding-up. That the group is a relationship and not a new entity separate from the individuals who form it was the point pressed by Morris Cohen (1919) against Harold Laski's early stumblings into group metaphysics. The point about the difference between an association and the individuals who compose it can be made quite differently and in a way that does not incur methodological individualist strictures. The choice made by individuals to create a certain form of ongoing relationship between them alters the conditions of their interaction. They can no longer be treated for purposes of explaining their actions in this context as if they were merely individuals acting severally, for they all have the facts of their own relationship and the new interactions it makes possible to contend with when making decisions. They have collective property, institutionalized decision procedures and issues relating to the collectivity to decide upon. All these features stem from the fact that they have chosen to create and to participate in a collectivity.

Even given the methodological individualist hypothesis, corporate personality becomes a fact created by the actions of definite individuals and one that cannot be ignored in the subsequent explanation of their actions. The law in establishing the corporation as a legal person distinct from its individual shareholders that can hold property, that can sue and be sued, has taken recognition of this fact. Corporate personality as a legal status need be treated neither as a mere fiction entertained by the law to attain certain ends, nor as a real entity. The distinction between real or natural and artificial persons is hardly useful once we have rid ourselves of the metaphysics of the real personality of groups. Individual's legal statuses are 'artificial' too, they change and evolve with changing views of the individual and his or her rights; women, for example, have rights in law they did not have 100 years ago. The problem here turns from the metaphysics of real personality to an obstinate tendency of some methodological individualists to talk about corporations or associations as if they were somehow less real because they are artificial, and that they were somehow secondary in explaining social action because they are not 'natural' persons. Thus does anti-metaphsics often breed its own metaphysics – in refusing the corporation as an entity they turn the individual into one, ignoring at the same time the historicity of the attributes of the person and the role of social construction in making individual's actions. Groups are not entities that can exist independently of the actions of human individuals, but they are quite different from those individuals *qua* individuals and they do have certain *sui generis* properties as products of the actions of associated individuals.

Communities of choice and communities of fate

This exercise in clearing away bad arguments and unjustified ethical claims from the associationalist doctrine has its point, and that is to show that the core of the theory is the freedom of the individual to associate. What then is the difference between this theory and conventional liberal individualism? It consists in the argument that individuals cannot satisfy certain of their needs and aspirations by private actions alone, and that there are certain freedoms the pursuit of which requires individuals to associate. Take two classic examples from associationalist theory. The worker as an individual cannot influence his or her employer about wages and working conditions as well as he or she can as a member of a trade union. Joining a trade union gives the worker both greater security and greater control over his or her affairs. The Christian can only truly seek salvation as part of the community of the faithful and by service to others. Such membership can only be voluntary, for religious belief enforced by state compulsion is contrary to true faith.

Associationalists have tended to see membership of an association as modelled on something more than a subscription to a body for merely utilitarian convenience, like joining a railway season-ticket holders' association. It is seen as a chosen means to pursue some common purpose and that in doing so, through fellowship with others, the individual enhances his or her personal capacities. Freedom is thus not merely the negative liberty to choose what one will, upheld by law, but it also follows *from* association and from the type of purposes that are chosen. The argument here is that association – through the interaction of individuals, through them giving of themselves in service to others, and through striving to attain some common purpose – enhances the individual both in some specific sense related to the objectives of the voluntary body in question (the worker enjoys more liberty as a consequence of union membership because he or she has more control over their work and also a higher wage) and as a person, developing their capacities through running or participating in the work of the group.

Association thus has two positive outcomes in this view, both of which can be expressed in terms of individual freedom. The first is that by banding together individuals attain some purpose or govern some activity defined by them as important to their interests, and do so in a way that they could not unless they associated. Thus the superior social governance associationalists see being achieved through the extensive control of major activities by voluntary bodies can be expressed in terms of the benefit it brings to individuals. The second is that in the process of banding together individuals develop themselves; they are further individuated by associating with others. Therefore, the core ethical claim of associationalism, that individuals ought to associate and should be free to do so, is justified on essentially individualistic terms, that it both enhances the freedom and the individuation of the individual. Essentially, therefore, associationalism can be said to be about the pursuit of individuation, and its distinctive contention is that this is more effectively accomplished by cooperative rather than by purely private individual action.

Associationalism is thus opposed neither to the category of negative liberty, nor to the specific individual rights to choice and to privacy. Those latter rights are seen as the necessary conditions for the strictly voluntary basis of cooperation and collective action. Likewise associationalism subscribes to the fundamental principle of liberalism that, as far as possible, the law ought only to intervene in the affairs of individuals to prevent harm to others, but extends this category of 'others' to include both individuals and associations. Associations should be as free as possible to govern themselves and their own purposes, and any engagements they enter into should be determined by their own internal

decision-procedures. By accepting the necessity of certain fundamental negative liberties as a starting point, associationalism
retains the core of liberal individualism, and by accepting that
positive freedom can be pursued through voluntary collectivities it
goes beyond classical liberalism, but without falling into the problems of compulsory collectivism. This is not to pretend that there
are no conflicts between what can be claimed to be part of the
negative liberty of voluntary choice and the positive freedoms
sought through cooperative associations. There are many potential sources of conflict, particularly over property and taxation.
The point is that these two forms of freedom are not in irreconcilable conflict in associationalist doctrine.

In developing the institutions of an associationalist theory in
the spheres of politics, economics and welfare, we should be
guided by two ethical claims:

1   that association must be justified in terms of their benefits for in-
    dividuals, those benefits being as perceived by the individuals in
    question (and not imputted to them as being in their real or objective
    interests) and where the association providing them has been chosen
    by those individuals for this purpose;
2   that all associations should be communities of choice and not of fate,
    and that compulsion in an associational commonwealth is only justi-
    fied in order to preserve the condition in which individuals can freely
    choose associations and enjoy the benefits of cooperating with others.

From the right to be a *voluntary* member of an association we
derive the most basic right in an associative society, that is, the
apparently paradoxical right of exit, to be able to leave an association within a relatively short and specified period of time and
without a significant fine or equivalent financial loss. The negative right to leave an association at one's choice, and the legal
defense of that right by the public power, is more important than
any positive interventions by the public power to ensure that
the association is democratic. The danger of seeking to ensure
the freedom of individuals and associations by prescribing their
internal rules and procedures is that in trying to do so the public
power is actually taking them away. Thus the rules applied to the
governance of associations must be as few as are consistent with
preventing them oppressing their members and denying them

choice. In practice these amount to guaranteeing the right of exit, to ensuring that one member one vote (or one share one vote) rules are followed, and in requiring the annual publication of audited accounts. Associations in receipt of public funds will be subject to stricter regulation, but associations are free to eschew such funds and be subject to nothing more than the minimal rules of associational law and the civil law.

The unquestioned right of exit ensures that associations are communities of choice. However exalted their purposes, however much voluntary commitment they happen to be able to extract from members, associations are open communities that individuals may join and leave. Thus, despite the facts of moral pressure and the difficulty of rearranging one's affairs on leaving an association, if it covers a good deal of one's daily life, associations cannot compel loyalty in the way that states or 'existential' communities have done. All communities in an individualistic society must accept that – in form – they are no different from a railway season-ticket holders' association. The grander and more exalted purposes are supposedly closer to the pursuit of freedom than the more utilitarian and mundane, but since they are pursued voluntarily the associations fulfilling them have no more ultimate claim on their members, save what those members choose to accept. It should by no means be imagined that this fact somehow diminishes community or cooperation, nor should we accept that the utilitarian and the mundane are somehow inherently secondary and trivial in associationalist terms. Quite the contrary, the need to build a community out of choice, to win members and to keep their trust is not merely a fundamental discipline or a protection of individual rights, but also helps to make real the cooperation that is built-up and the trust that is created. The utilitarian and the mundane make up by far the greatest part of life; governing the ordinary affairs of life well is as important as anything else. From that governance, from participating in running the season-ticket holders' association, can come a schooling in the arts of freedom and an enhancement in the political capacity of the individual as real as leading a major strike or being a bishop.

The view that a society can be built on communities of choice is often disputed. Carl Schmitt (1930), for example, challenged the English pluralists, and Laski in particular, on this very point. He argued that pluralist communities could not survive because as public powers they were like the season-ticket holders' association: limited bodies of limited loyalty. People ultimately would not identify with and, therefore, die for them as they would for the state. Schmitt's position was shaped by his view of politics as friend–enemy relations (1932), but his conception of the limitations of communities of choice is widely shared. A state whose major purpose is to service and secure a society of voluntary associations has a limited function and can claim neither the universal role nor the unlimited loyalty enthusiasts for state power would desire of the highest collectivity. The answer to this is, 'so what?' It only matters if states are beset by enemies. At present, Western advanced states are not. Moreover, should enemies arise, then Schmitt's logic of the political will take its course, the pluralist state will acquire extensive powers over life and property, the season-ticket holders will endorse their community and raise funds to support its fight with the enemy.

Schmitt's critique made sense in the 1930s and it would have force in a world of widespread international or intercommunal tensions. Another criticism, which develops Schmitt's logic, is that the pluralist and associationalist system is threatened not from without but from *within*, that it is too weak to contain the pressures that arise from conflicting associations. This critique applies to liberalism too. It contends that in a multicultural society of conflicting identities, of communities *as* identities, the public sphere and the freedoms of civil society become nothing more than a medium for different groups to seek to capture the public power for their own purposes. This view supposes that existential communities will predominate and that they will enclose the life of the individual; far from being voluntary associations, they will become communities of fate. Thus to be black, for example, will be an all-defining identity. In such an antagonistically pluralistic society of competing communities liberalism would have little place and associationalism no hope. Only a Hobbesian state, where the public power so overawes society that it can ensure civil peace, could protect the individual against the communities. It will be the 'New Leviathan' and not just the association of associations. The point to emphasize here is that such views see society as fragmenting into competing existential communities and, therefore, argue that a society based on voluntary association is impossible. But so ultimately, in that case, is one based on choices for individuals. Liberalism and associationalism are both challenged by such views. Individuals in this analysis would be trapped in communities they cannot leave and unaware that exit is possible: they are stuck with an identity imposed by fate. We shall return to this issue of competing communities when we consider the idea of 'Ottomanization' later in this chapter.

The point to make here is that most communities of fate are, in fact, created and sustained by force. The state as a compulsory organization claiming exclusive possession of a certain territory is the most obvious example, especially states that limit the right to leave. Here compulsion is inescapable and depends ultimately on force. The sub-state community that claims to regulate every aspect of the life of its members, that seeks to demand complete identification and complete loyalty, is another attempted construction of a community of fate, and here the compulsion is primarily internalized by the individual and amounts to denying any identity or experience inconsistent with the community. Such communities bind their members by limiting their individuation in the interests of a pre-written community 'script' of conduct and belief.

Genuine communities of fate are few and far between; most are created by force and by community pressure. Thus classes, ethnic and religious groups are ideological categories that rely upon forms of social closure, to convert them into communities. Classes existed, over and above the multiform differences in wealth and occupation, because certain social forces, political parties or trade unions, claimed a certain primary identification for their members and claimed that they could only escape their condition collectively. If communities of fate are forms of social closure then they are inconsistent with individuation and are difficult to defend as necessary in a world peopled by literate, at least minimally informed individuals who have the desire to shape their lives by choice. It is difficult to assert that the populations of the World are becoming less aware and less individuated. Many of those who have suffered from political projects based on social closure identify freedom with representative democracy and legally-guaranteed human rights. As points of departure in the creation of a free society, those institutions are essential, but they are not enough to ensure either the full development of individual freedom or an effectively governed society. In a world where individuation and educated choice are almost universally valued, associationalism has more of a future than the attempted construction of communities of fate. That associationalism must be sharply distinguished from any form of communalism as will now be obvious, but was seldom so for the early associationalists who drew inspiration from churches, classes or unions conceived as communities.

The point to be made here is that Schmitt's objection and the criticism based on plural communalism rest on the assumption that an associationalism founded on the ethics of individualism and choice is weak, and unable to face political conflict. I have tried to show why this is not so and why association based on consent fits in with the dominant trend of modern human aspirations. An ethic based on choice assumes that the majority of individuals are rational pursuers of their own interests, and are intelligent enough to submit to limits placed upon them in the interests of the freedom of others, and, therefore, of their own freedom. But what of those who will not accept such a rational self-limitation or subscribe to ends which encompass the subordination of others? Is associationalism not based on rationalistic and providentialist assumptions about human nature?

It need not be. It only needs to assume that people are rational enough to know their own interests and to desist from certain actions faced with the threat of sanctions. In Kant's terms it assumes that the majority are rational devils. But what of the irrational devils? They pose no greater problem to an associationalist society than to any other. Associationalism provides, through the ethical principle of the preservation of the conditions of choice, ample grounds to use sanctions and force if needs be against individuals or associations determined to pursue goals that cannot fit in with a liberal and pluralistic society. Similarly, state pluralism or federalism as a theory of political power fits more squarely with the proposition that there is the potential for human evil in all of us than does the concentration of power in the sovereign state. To disperse power, and to limit both its geographical and functional scope, is to accept the dangers of the conquest of power by evil persons far more squarely than any other doctrine. Faced with an external threat, voluntary cooperation and a loyalty of necessity will bring the groups in a society of voluntary associations together, the better to resist an aggressor.

Liberal societies have proved more tenacious and efficient, and capable of prosecuting war more successfully, than have totalitarian ones. Thus associationalism can easily deal with Russell's refutation of anarchism in *Roads to Freedom* (1918), that such a defenceless and disarmed a society will fall prey to the power-hungry. This is because it both retains a public power, whose task is to ensure freedom, and it helps to create the conditions of voluntary cooperation between the associations that could create a strong solidarity against the aggressor.

Associations and public regulation

We have argued that the state in an associationalist commonwealth should intervene as little as possible in the affairs of associations and should do so primarily to preserve the conditions of individual choice. But how and on what terms would it intervene? We assume that the primary general regulation of all associations would be legal, that the core of this regulation would be a Bill of Rights, securing fundamental human rights, and an Associational Law, specifying certain general rules all associations would have to comply with.

In this sense associationalism is not greatly different from the liberal conception of the state's regulation of civil society: that is that citizens may pursue any activity not forbidden by law, laws should be as few as possible, and should exist only to prevent harm to others. The common public morality of an associationalist society is, therefore, like that of liberalism, thin and procedural. It consists of a limited statement of fundamental human rights, all of which are at least designed to preserve the autonomy of the individual, and a number of constitutional provisions that are designed to ensure the integrity of the public sphere. This common morality is thin because it is formal, it protects choice and does not prescribe what is to be chosen, and is procedural, that is, it provides mechanisms for the protection of rights or the relief of harms. The 'good life' is defined privately by each individual citizen, and quasi-publicly by the associations he or she chooses to join. Nevertheless, this minimum common morality is capable of generating strong common support. As the glue that holds a voluntaristic society together, it need not be thick, just strong. People are capable of a strong common identification with human rights and constitutional standards, accepting that these are the core of a civilized society. The view that liberal or associationalist societies are weaker than those with a common and thickly prescriptive morality is largely unjustified.

Associationalism allows for a certain kind of value pluralism. Citizens may pursue their own conceptions of the good life. But associationalism is definitely not committed to a comprehensive moral and epistemological relativism that would follow from a complete policy of *laissez faire* in matters of group belief. On the contrary, associationalism must give primacy to the ethical principle of the protection of choice, and if such a voluntarism is at the core of its public morality, it must be able to prescribe actions contrary to that principle. It must, therefore, know what such actions are and be able to demonstrate why they are contrary to that principle. The common public morality of an associationalist society cannot just consist in the assertion of values, there must be justifiable and demonstrable grounds for abridging freedom in the name of freedom. It is only an apparent paradox that an associationalist society, far from being committed to the most pluralistic and relativistic view of human belief and conduct, will have to hold certain principles and truths in common.

This common moral core is connected to the principle of choice and to the legal defence of that principle. Therefore, the society will have to accept that legal argument and reasoning, the assessment of evidence through the courts, is sufficient to establish the truth about whether a certain policy or practice of an association is or is not contrary to the principle of choice. Such an associationalist society will seek to reduce the mass of legislation, to simplify rules and to allow associations a large measure of self-governance. Despite this it will in the end be no less dependent on law to establish its common compulsory standards of conduct than are existing liberal societies. Thus an associationalist society cannot dispense with formal legal procedures, it cannot rely on informal justice or arbitrary ajudication. In that sense the public power, as the means to assure the autonomy and security of associations, must be exactly defined, its powers and their limits must be specified in a written constitution.

If we apply the principle of choice to associations then we find certain very basic public requirements for the policies and conduct of associations:

1   as we have seen, individuals must be free to leave an association, but they must also be free to join it – individuals cannot be excluded from associations except on the conditions that they can choose to accept or reject, thus subscribing to Catholic doctrine is a choice, one may or may not accept the doctrines of the Church, whereas being black or being female is not a choice, one cannot decide to be white or to be male (some proponents of fashionable social constructivist doctrines about sexuality and race would dispute these propositions, and, of course, there are exceptions to them – however, for the great majority of blacks or women facing institutionalized racial or sexual discrimination, the problematicity of these categories at the margin could hardly be a great comfort);
2   children are, until some point in their lives, both highly impressionable and not fully capable of making an informed choice. If the principle of choice is to have any force then, children must be educated to be informed that choices are possible, and they cannot be forced to commit themselves to some course of action that will bind them for life – parents and the communities they join do not own their children, they have a conditional social stewardship of them and this gives the public power the right to set minimum eductional standards, to enforce certain items on the curriculum, to prevent physical and mental abuse, and to remove children from their parents if needs be;
3   associations may not be founded for purposes that are designed to abrogate human rights or that are subversive of the constitution. Thus an associationalist society would not permit racial or sexual discrimination, it would protect children and enforce a fairly prescriptive curriculum, and it would possess fairly strong public order laws. It would do these things not merely because it inherited them from classical liberalism but because they are concomitant of its core principle, than an individual must be free to join and to leave an association.

So far we have been dealing with the basic principles of an associationalist society. We have established a thin procedural morality and a set of legal limits on the pluralism of values and practices that is established by the public power. This thin common morality is compulsory because it is consistent with the maintenance of choice for the widest possible range of individuals. It does prohibit some choices, as any set of rules or standards must. It prevents people joining a whites – only club because an entire category of persons is excluded from membership, who have no choice in the matter of the attribute selected for exclusion. It suppresses the Fascist Party, bent on overthrowing the associationalist system by force, and thus prevents choice to fascists. If either of these choices were granted, then the principle of choice would be violated, and there is no greal moral difficulty with making such exclusions by force if needs be and even if substantial numbers of persons wish to exercise these choices.

An individual or an association may find this thin common core sufficient and, for these purposes, those will be the only public functions that need concern them, other than taxation. The laws and taxation will be made and approved by a legislature elected on a universal adult franchise and, if votes are to be of equal weight, by a system of proportional representation. However, for other functions and by agreement of the associations involved, a far thicker system of 'public' cooperation between associations, and between them and those functionally relevant aspects of the public power, could be created. This is outlined in the chapters on an associative economy and welfare state later on. Such a system would be cooperative and many of its governing arrangements consociational, some would be quasi-public, and some strictly public – varying with the purposes in question. The citizens who wished to avoid this structure would be free to do so, except that it would impinge on them in matters of taxation, and to the extent that social activities were governed through such methods, and the abstaining citizen or association was confronted with the consequences of cooperative regulation between associations. Certainly, citizens would be taxed to support activities that stemmed from associational cooperation and from the consociational machinery; if, that is, those activities commanded the support of the legislative assembly, and the budgets proposed for public and quasi-public functions by the consociational machinery were approved. In that case, those budgets and policies would have the support both of a large number of associations and a majority of individual voters. The private citizen who disapproved of publicly-funded health care would be taxed to pay for it, but he or she would be in no way different from the pacifist who contributes to the defence budget in a liberal-democratic state today.

No citizen can avoid the consequences of the vast majority of his or her fellows following a certain public policy and making it binding upon all. No society has been devised that lets each do exactly as he or she will, contribute what he or she wishes, and yet have the enjoyment of the security and common advantages of a community.

This thick quasi-public cooperation of associations appears to violate the principle of choice. I cannot choose to avoid its consequences, even if I refrain from joining any association committed to cooperation with others and to participation in such associational governance. Yet one is free to not join such associations, and free to vote for representatives who oppose such a policy of public-private collaboration and who favour a rigid division between state and civil society. Such cooperative relationships will only exist if they have majority support and are voluntarily entered into by associations and the individuals who join them. To strike such relationships down because they involve certain social constraints on other individuals would be to deny a power of choice to the majority and would be inconsistent with the purposes of associationalism, which in no way seeks to prevent cooperation between associations. Such individuals who are hostile to cooperation could not be compelled to join such relationships, although they would suffer some of their consequences in the area of regulation. They would have a case in law if such regulations were in some way discriminatory, but otherwise they would have to face the consequences of the common formal rules of the society being relatively thin. In an associative system a great deal of law would consist in framework legislation, that is, the law sets the parameters within which associations may make more detailed regulatory norms. A great deal of rule-making thus becomes quasi-public because – at least in theory – it affects only those who have consented to it by reason of joining an association. If the dissenting individualist cannot prove that such local norms infringe basic rights and yet refuses to participate in associations on principle, or accept their regulations, then he or she would be in a difficult position. As a dog in the manger, the only option for the ultra-individualist would be to argue for giving greater powers over legislation back to the state, and thus they would be faced with the contradictory prospect of the binding rules of a compulsory body rather than the agreed norms of a voluntary one.

The logic of collective action and its impact on associations

An associationalist society is at the mercy of the purposes that the individuals who compose it choose to band together to pursue. One argument would be that highly exclusive interests that are central to the concerns of small groups with substantial resources will be strongly organized, and that inclusive interests of large groups without significant resources will be weakly organized, or not organized at all. In other words associationalism is actually a society that favours the self-interested, the rich and the resourceful. It will favour them because they can make most use of the principle of voluntary association, and in such a society the state will be far weaker than in a collectivistic one.

This means that the ideas of a rich culture of associations, of evening-up disparities in power and wealth through associations, and of a strong form of social governance through the cooperation of associations and the construction of an associational machinery are just naive. They are desirable outcomes that are unlikely to occur. To answer this objection we cannot rely on assumptions of a higher level of altruism than at present, or that people on average will be willing to spend greater amounts of time than they do at present in conducting the affairs of voluntary associations. The one assumption we will make for the moment is that the taxation system and the system of public funding of associations described in Chapter 7 is already in place.

The problem described above is outlined in Mancur Olson's *The Logic of Collective Action* (1971). It can be overcome. If an activity can be sustained by public funds proportional to membership, then the difficulties of creating and sustaining an association for an at best moderately involved, large and diffuse membership are simplified. In the long-run, organizing to obtain these benefits makes the front-end load of effort required in cooperating to build an association worthwhile. Assuming the opportunity for citizens to donate a portion of their tax revenue to a limited number of organizations, as Schmitter (1988) proposes, then associations can be built-up to the point where they can effectively claim public funding and without too much effort or expense by the public. This work would be undertaken by salaried officials of the associations in question, who would stand to gain from growth and could be regarded as associational entrepreneurs. Thus associationalism does not necessarily require more altruism or citizen effort than other political systems. It could work through no higher motivations than the self-interest of members of the public who choose to support an association and the self-interest of its officials, whose livelihood is connected with building it up. The argument would be that both the individuals involved and the wider society gain from this public support of associations, activities are governed through associations, and needs are met.

Olson sees all associations as potentially self-interested and, if they gain access to political or social power, dangerous, since they can distort the market and impose rents on the whole society that reduce its flexibility and efficiency. In *The Rise and Decline of Nations* he argues that those societies like Britain and the USA that have enjoyed both political stability and political cultures open to the influence of organized interests, have failed economically because of the gradual accumulation of protectionist and rent-seeking measures on behalf of organized and exclusive interests. In both books (1971 and 1982), Olson makes it clear that it is exclusive and rent-seeking rather than encompassing organizations that are the problem. He recognizes that in certain societies like Germany or Japan encompassing organizations have contributed to effective economic governance. Such organizations depend on definite and relatively difficult to attain social and institutional conditions. In particular, he tends to see Germany and Japan as exceptional cases. Owing to the fundamental disruption of their interest group structures during their periods of authoritarian rule, and their reconstruction in the post-1945 period, they have been able to avoid the steady accumulation of rent-seeking lobbies. Britain and the USA have not suffered such discontinuity, and because they are liberal market societies and because their governments have accepted a limited role in public economic coordination they have been more open to the accumulation of particular and self-interested causes lobbying for and retaining benefits from the public power.

Olson's analysis is coherent, but limited. It is not the place to dispute here his comparative analysis of post-1945 economic performance, although as we shall see in Chapter 5 there are other, more compelling reasons for German and Japanese manufacturing success. My main point is that a system in which voluntary associations compete for members introduces real competitive disciplines and also allows the evening-up of associational influence. Associationalism achieves by a different route some of the accountability to consumers and social fluidity that economic liberals seek through markets, but without the social side effects of weakly-regulated markets. I shall also show in Chapter 7 some of the means whereby voluntary institutions could be prevented from becoming conspiracies against the public interest.

An associationalist society need not become inefficient and dominated by exclusive rent-seeking conspiracies against the public. There is no general reason preventing an associationalist system from being as constructively collaborative as (West) Germany was, the associations combining to provide coordinative and cooperative support for an efficient market economy. Such an economy might be all the more efficient because its institutions would, in the main, be smaller and more democratically governed than the large, hierarchical and rigid corporations of today. Moreover, collaborative government would tend to provide a more even spread of public support between firms, trade associations and other organized interests, and leave less room for purely self-interested lobbying.

The core of Olson's argument rests on seeing the market ideal – typically as a neutral, impersonal and efficient allocative mechanism and other organizations, voluntary or otherwise, with some exceptions, as flawed actualities – as rent-seeking and self-interested. We cannot operate on the same logic, and idealize associations whilst criticizing the faults of actual market relations. The kind of associational commonwealth we are considering in this book does not need to make extravagant or providentialistic assumptions about human motivation. It could work on the assumption of narrowly self-interested behaviour. An individual joins an association, whether or not it is in receipt of public funds, in order to obtain certain definite benefits. He or she chooses whether or not to play more than a minimal role in its governance, at least not to exit and to pay dues. Associationalism can survive with the bulk of society's members as 'passengers' and on the strength of an activist elite, who are rewarded for running the voluntary bodies in question.

This is not a desirable outcome, nor is it likely. Existing societies have far higher levels of involvement in voluntary bodies than this. The point is that even on very bleak assumptions about human motivation the system would work. It could also avoid, even on the assumption of purely self-interested behaviour, a descent into plunder by the associations' elites and generalized rent-seeking by the associations. In fact an associationalist system retains some of the competitive disciplines that are ascribed to markets. Voluntary associations will be in competition: they will either prevent others gaining undue advantage, or, if they fail, self-interested members will flock into the successful organizations and defeat the advantages of membership to those who sought a privileged deal. Associations will have to deliver at least the minimum of goods their self-interested members seek and this sets a limit to the power of their elites. Through their power of exit, individuals can ensure that an association does not become hopelessly corrupt or that its elite act entirely contrary to the members' interests. This can be accomplished without any great effort on the part of the ordinary member, simply by saying 'I quit'.

The market is a very different case when we start explaining how little we need to expect from human motivation. The idea of a market society is a virtual impossibility. Social relations cannot be sustained by buying and selling alone, even if we assume an elementary non-commercial solidarity in the natural affinity between the members of the family. Intelligent economic liberals from Adam Smith to Hayek have known that the market can only work in a context of social institutions that supply it with a distinctive morality for its participants. Even if we assume near-perfect competition and reasonably available market information, we find that the market requires, even with public regulation, strongly moral and self-denying individuals if it is to be equitable. Honesty, fair-dealing and a respect for law are essential to an efficient and impersonal market, but they are not supplied by it and they cannot be bought at any price. They are a gift from society and its moral order. That 'society' is the product of individuals and their choices does not alter the case. The market relies on the non-market motivations, beliefs and behaviours of individuals.

We need to thicken this social embeddedness necessary to an efficient market economy under modern conditions; individual morality is not enough. A market economy can function well if it is embedded in a society that is complementary to the market principle, but, in being complementary, uses non-market calculations and forms of resource allocation. In particular, such a society is cohesive enough and collaborative enough to judge market performance substantively, that is, the market system will be expected to produce acceptable levels of employment, investment and a suitable composition of output. If it does not, social actors will intervene to correct it, and provide the appropriate means of regulation and inputs to achieve the substantive outcome desired. The market system is thus a viable economic mechanism in the right kind of social context.

But the claims of many modern economic liberals are that the market is the sole effective means of resource allocation and that all interference with it by the public power or by society at large will reduce its efficiency. Therefore, all other social institutions must be restricted in their capacities and purposes in order that they do not interfere with the market. This claim simply does not hold water, although it has the tenacity of folklore among Anglo-Saxon economists, politicians and central bankers. An associationalist society, as we shall see in Chapter 5 is the most effective route to combining a market economy, with all its advantages for liberty, with a coordinative and redistributive society that provides the means to ensure the market's continuing effective performance in meeting substantive economic standards. However, the argument for an associative democratic society does not rely on best possible outcomes or upon emphasizing ideal-typical conditions. Such a system could exist and could function even if its worst flaws were to be allowed for and if the majority of its members all had no higher aim than pure self-interest.

An answer to Ottomanization

We have considered the dangers of antagonistic pluralism in the abstract, now let us look at them in a concrete example. Most Western societies have been subject to a process of pluralization of social norms and styles of life. This has been carried farthest in parts of the USA, where the radical divergence of ethnic, religious and lifestyle groups has produced a virtual re-creation of the Millets system of the Ottoman Empire in which plural and semi-self-regulating communities co-existed side by side, with very different rules and standards. One could call this process the 'Ottomanization' of America, and construct a 'dark future' scenario in which the common morality of the USA had worn paper thin and political power at state and federal level was largely divorced from the communalistic private governance of most aspects of most peoples' lives.

There are extremely radical differences between groups in the USA and one notices this most when such groups clash over the prevailing laws and mores: Gays versus Christian fundamentalists, pro- and anti-choice campaigners on abortion issues, blacks versus Hassids in Brooklyn, etc. The centralized state does not prevent and cannot check this process of pluralization. Indeed, it is hardly able to contain the violent antagonisms arising from it. Such tendencies toward divergence are almost inevitable in societies in which the range of social and personal choice is extended by mass affluence, by geographical and social mobility, and by the decline of prescriptive community standards in the face of the personal autonomy that the former factors make possible. At the same time old and new foci of identity compete to bind individuals' choice of communities of association – religion, language, lifestyle, gender and ethnicity. For those left at the bottom, these foci of identity may appear as classes used to, as communities of fate and resistance. For others, however traditional and communitarian they may claim to be, old and new identities are re-shaped to be sources of social solidarity around *chosen* standards.

Communities of choice and the associations representing them may be no less disruptive for being recent social constructs than are ancient feuds between traditional communities. Common national standards of personal conduct may be fewer and thinner, groups may have divergent mores and ideals of the good life, but most groups act in and make claims on the public realm in remarkably similar ways. Groups make similar claims to freedom of action, seek to have their own chosen objectives made into rights and also seek to criminalize or deny public funding for behaviour of which they disapprove. This applies to both the 'born again' and the 'politically correct'. In the end, such antagonisms between groups and attempts to annex the public power to their own exclusive interests are corrosive of the public sphere and of any common political life. This is exaggerated in the USA by weak and non-ideological political parties.

Surely in such circumstances associationalism is a cure that is worse than the disease, it just endorses an entirely negative pluralism and permits groups to opt out of a common political culture? I believe the opposite to be the case. Associationalism offers the only clear way – in the absence of enforced common standards – to make such pluralism a going concern. That way is to reduce inter-group antagonism by the acceptance of a substantial measure of self-regulation, at the price of mutual tolerance. No group could impose its vision on all, most groups could regulate themselves. Clearly, there would be limits to this process, a common morality is not *that* thin – paedophiles are unlikely to enjoy rights of self-regulation, nor are rich white neighbourhood associations that exclude black residents. In other cases the likelihood of mutual tolerance is small. Pro- and anti-choice lobbies on abortion issues can hardly by expected to agree to co-exist, even geographically in separate states, any more than could slave and free states. Outside of such irreconcilable and competing claims to rights and moral regulation, the parallel and socially-competitive social governance by associations would be more often possible than not.

In an associationalist society, given sufficiently varied and overlapping planes of social identity and cleavage, most conflicts between groups could be contained by being parcelized. The co-existence of standards would allow the associations representing groups to regulate those members who choose to join them. Most groups would have a strong interest in preserving the associationalist system because it would secure them the chance of public funding for their welfare activities, an enhanced role in social governance within their own sphere, and protection of their legitimate autonomy from predation by other groups by the defense of group and individual rights by the public power. Laws regulating all persons and groups would remain, and so would certain common core standards. This core would be narrow but strongly subscribed to – the born again and the politically-correct alike abhor armed robbery, embezzlement of charity funds and child beating.

The advantage of a measure of localized regulation by groups and associational self-governance is that it would permit the reduction of the extent and complexity of the laws and regulations of the central public power. Framework legislation might be sufficient, if it set the goals of, and the standards to measure, self-governance. This is true not only of associations in the social and moral sphere, but also, for example, joint management-worker safety committees in the area of occupational safety and health. The result might be that laws might once again become almost comprehensible to the citizen, rather than filling kilometres of shelf-space. A society that spews forth more and more regulations because its political institutions are centralized and it purports to cover all aspects of life, does not attain comprehensiveness and uniformity in regulation, quite the contrary. Hence it may be just as well to accept the inevitable diversity that will come with self-governance. Provided the institutions in question are reasonably democratic and that there are protections for basic individual rights, such diversity can be healthy. A legal system whose rules are by their very bulk and complexity unintelligible to the citizens, and whose regulatory processes often seem opaque even to specialist lawyers, is in danger of undermining the rule of law in its search to perfect it.

The basic checks imposed on such self-regulating associations are that they must submit to certain minimum common standards of democratic self-governance and that they must not prevent exit by dissatisfied members. Exit is a powerful solvent of oligarchy, it also limits the extent to which groups may sanction the loyalty of their members. There is no point in pluralizing the state, only to create totalitarianism potentialities and authoritarian practices at the level of associations. Associationalism is a vital supplement to liberal democracy and *not* a substitute for it.

Our discussion above is a negative thought experiment, it has envisaged an extremity of group divergence and value pluralism. In doing so it has drawn on tendencies that are evident in the USA. Other societies are more cohesive, but even here there are strong reasons for decentralization and associational self-government other than the dampening of inter-group conflict. Moreover, even in circumstances of strong pressures toward group divergence, associational governance may actually help to rebuild ties between groups, and facilitate the construction of national, regional or social foci of common identification. Associationalism hands over great powers and responsibilities to groups.

But most associations will not be exclusive groups that enclose the whole of their members' social lives. A self-governing association cannot stand against all the world – if it did it would be de facto a sovereign state. Associational law, as we have seen, would enforce choice. In other respects it should be as thin as possible in the constraints it imposes on associations in general. However, certain associations will exercise quasi-public powers and receive public funds, and the laws regulating them, as we shall see in Chapter 7, would limit certain acts as *ultra vires* – in particular it would forbid labour unions to own firms directly and it would compel associations to create special organizations for each domain in which they were in receipt of public funds (e.g. schools, hospitals, etc.). The members of most associations will also be members of others too. Furthermore, for many purposes associations or their organizations will need to coordinate and collaborate with others in like spheres of activity – if only to build coaltions of mutual convenience when funds are distributed or common standards set. Associations may thus gradually create a network of formal and informal relations, which enables society to enjoy both diversity in social governance and a substantial measure of coordination.

As far as individual citizens are concerned, associational institutions may actually reduce the negative sources of identification with groups and dispose them to regard neighbouring groups in a more tolerant light. Greater democratic governance through voluntary associations means greater control over her or his affairs by the citizen. The possibility of diverse standards of social governance on the part of associations representing groups at least ensures that among those with whom one has chosen to live certain values will prevail. The combination of a reduction in powerlessness in the control of one's own affairs and the removal of the fear of being at the mercy of hostile moral legislators may well promote more widespread feelings of security on the part of citizens, and a consequent lessening of hostility toward others. Fear of others' moral politics can be acute where the state is both centralized and claims a plenitude of power in the recognition and regulation of groups and their actions. In such a state moral minorities compete to control or influence power and then compel others to live in a certain way: the state is then either for or against

Gay rights, either militantly anti-clerical or the upholder of a compulsory religion.

Associationalist ethics and the limits of the political community

This book is explicitly addressed to problems of the reform and renewal of democracy and social governance in Western societies. However, there are a number of problems, theoretical and political, that concern the boundaries of an associationalist system and that require an answer in a chapter on the normative basis of associationalism.

The first is theoretical and takes the form of asking whether or not associationalism is merely another attempt to resuscitate the myth of the 'self-governing community'. This idea, central to neo-republican and other left radical attempts to renovate democracy, has been devastatingly criticized by Barry Hindess (1991). In essence the arguments against the idea of a self-governing community are threefold: first, the social and geographical boundaries of the community are not subject to political legitimation or choice, 'citizens' are defined by criteria of inclusion and exclusion that mean that 'the people' is some contingent or exclusionary sub-set of persons in a particular territory; second, the state is not an all-powerful agency of decision, capable of making policies for all and every dimension of causality that effects the lives of its citizens, thus states are limited by international phenomena – economic, political, cultural, etc. and by their inability to govern social relations comprehensively; third, there is no decision-procedure that can make the actions of government the choice of the 'community'; policies are always made by a small sub-set of actual citizens and legitimated by the endorsement of a somewhat larger sub-set.

These are all devastating criticisms of the idea of the modern state as a new *polis*, complete within its boundaries and whose citizens are free collectively to choose the good life. But these criticisms do not apply to the associationalist theory of social governance. First, as will be evident, the structures of authority in an associationalist commonwealth are federal and pluralistic. Powers may be divided both territorially and by function, and the powers that a public body may have are specific to a definite role.

like Samuel Beer describes

An associationalist society, therefore, has no problems about a complex match between territory and authority: it is not like a centralized sovereign state that claims a monopoly of power and regulation within a given territory. An associationalist commonwealth need have no problem in accommodating functionally specific domains of authority that are part of its polity, and yet not confined to operating within its borders. In addition to submitting to international agencies or signing treaties making ongoing commitments as sovereign states do today, an associationalist commonwealth could easily accept sharing certain functions either between a group of states or with international agencies. A 'state' need not have a given set of attributes in associationalist theory. It can accept a good deal of its law from without, accept an externally-controlled currency, and accept pooled and collectively-controlled military forces. The logic of federation and of pluralism finds no difficulty with this lack of a rigid boundary between the state and other forms of authority. Such agencies at a higher confederal level, or outside the territorial membership boundaries of the political entity altogether, may be subject to diverse forms of control and decision-procedure. In a federal system democracy does not mean exclusive control by a single citizenry, rather it means accountability and some form of checks and balances. Decision must be subject to discussion and some check by an agency subject to the decision and heteronymous to the 'will' of the decision-maker.

An associationalist society can cope better with such fluidity in the entities forming the political system. It is designed for an open-textured and federal system of power. There is no reason why the associations citizens will want to join will all be local or 'national' ones. Citizens will be free to create and to join international associations. They will be free to donate funds to them. There is at present a relatively strong international civil society. It includes major charities, sporting bodies, business organizations and political agencies like Amnesty, PEN and the International Federation of Jurists. It could be a great deal stronger and there is no reason why certain problems should not be governed through this international civil society – its organizations being answerable to their local memberships. Obviously, world poverty cannot be tackled by Oxfam alone, nor all human rights abusers by Amnesty, but many areas of regulation or cooperation could be handled in this way. Voluntary agencies have a good record in the post-1945 world. They have drawn attention to and tried to address problems that national governments have preferred to ignore.

The last problem is the most difficult. Why does a given political entity have the membership that it does? Here the theoretical problems merge with the political. The response might go like this, 'Within your associationalist commonwealth you make the whites – only club illegal, but on a world scale that's what you are advocating: a better deal for the Western, rich and predominantly white countries. Indeed, how can you be so concerned about problems of entry and exit to associations, when people wait in detention camps at the boundaries of states, live illegally without rights as economic migrants, or simply suffer at home because they are too poor and weak even to get to the borders of the wealthy world'.

The wealthy world lives with the hungry eyes of the World's poor upon it, and it will not do simply to say one is addressing one's own political community. Associationalism has no specific answer to this, it will hardly suffice to tell the World's poor to go and form associations. Until the populations of the West see the division between rich and poor in the World as intolerable, it will continue. Whilst it continues Western states will continue to shut their borders and try to stem the flow of economic migrants. Even if the populations of the West were to see things in this way, there is a limit to the possible results. Who wants a new colonialism of enlightened aid?

Socialism allied with national liberation, autonomous economic development through modernization of agriculture and self-sufficient industrialization, these were seen by many in the Third World as an answer – until the disasters of Stalin's successors like Pol Pot and Mengistu. Socialism and autarky are defeated political creeds, even in hungry countries where the survivors at feeding stations literally have nothing to lose. The death of socialism is the death of one kind of hope, hope for the World's poor that they could leave their condition by armed struggle and their own efforts. The populations of the rich countries have other options, fundamentalist socialism never became more than a minority creed there. Associationalism cannot be peddled as another kind of hope for the World's poor. That would be an obscenity, rhetoric loosed from the limits of reason or compassion.

But the problem remains. If we do accept that all human beings are fundamentally equal, essentially in their inevitable weakness and the necessity of their death, then despite all differences of strength, intelligence, skill or inherited wealth, they are the same, and deserve to be treated as such. If human beings are mortal, then their lives are precious to them and may not be taken from them, save *in extremis* to ensure the lives and liberty of others where they have taken or threatened the same. Human beings have the right to life because they are equal and are destined to die. Having accepted that we each have an obligation to aid and preserve others, at the very least to prevent unnecessary deaths. The question is, does this stop at feeding the hungry whatever keeps them alive and giving a little miliary aid occasionally to topple the most oppressive regimes? If we accept that all people are equal, if we also accept that wealth is social within our own communities, and that membership confers certain rights to share that wealth, how can we pretend that those arguments stop at a border?

We cannot in all conscience, and yet, the citizens of the West will continue to follow the logic of pragmatism and comfort, and their leaders will draw their own conclusions. Associationalism would certainly transform Western politics. Within the boundaries created by wealth and comfort it would increase the accountability and effectiveness of the mechanisms of social governance. It might well make citizens more benevolent to the less fortunate in the world beyond the boundaries of wealth. It would, however, remain unjustified and unjustifiable while a world of gross disparities of wealth and poverty remain, in which some enjoy a good life as of right and others live a short while in wretchedness. This is a flaw in our morality and in our world. The absence of an easy solution is no excuse to ignore the problem. It would be foolish to abandon advocacy of reform and renewal in Western societies, as if the World's poor would gain by our maintaining the imperfections of our current institutions. That is self-defeating, but such advocacy of associationalist reform can only be honest if we do accept that in doing so we are better arranging the affairs of the rich and we know what lies beyond, in the world of the poor and that to its questions we have no ready and effective answers.

4
Associative Democracy and Economic Governance

In this chapter and the next we shall consider the ways in which associationalism can contribute to improving the organization and the performance of Western industrial economies. We have seen that associationalism is best conceived as an axial principle of social organization, and thus partly a supplement to, and partly a substitute for, other forms of social organization. It cannot claim to be a solution to every social problem, and it certainly cannot claim to provide an entirely new system of economic institutions and management that will cope with every problem of producing and distributing wealth.

Associative democracy has two fundamental distinctive features: that it bridges and transforms the division between state and civil society, 'pluralizing' the former and 'publicizing' the latter; second that it promotes the democratic governance of corporate bodies in both public and private spheres, aiming to restrict the scope of hierarchical management and offering a new model of organizational efficiency. How can these features contribute to solving modern economic problems?

Associationalism is not a regime of technical economic management; it is a system of social governance based on a conception of democracy as informed decisions by public bodies through the continuous seeking of the consent of the governed. Many of the most pressing problems in economic management turn on the relative decline of the nation state as an effective agency of regulation on the one hand, and the problematicity of the relation of state and civil society in the main doctrines of economic governance on the other. Associative democracy, by transforming structures of authority through its supplemental institutions and practices, offers a more effective link between state and civil society, nation and region, and between the firms in the industrial sectors. These links, even in the best governed national and regional economies, are at present neither strong enough nor systematized and this lack inhibits the coordination of the economic actors and public agencies essential to effective economic performance. Associative democracy allows cooperation and competition to be effectively balanced in market-based economies. Enough cooperation to ensure adequate levels of the essential inputs like investment, training, etc. without which firms cannot function as effective competitors in markets, and enough competition to ensure consumer choice and productive efficiency without, at the same time, destroying the social foundations of the market economy itself. These are large claims, yet they are put forward for essentially modest institutional and social changes that pale in comparison with those that have been required to construct a centrally-planned economy, or that would be needed to build a pure, free market economy.

This chapter is organized as follows. In the first section we consider why there is a problem to be solved, arguing that, in general, modern economies are not performing well and that economic liberal apologetics are now unable to present convincingly the experiments of the 1980s as success stories. In the following section we shall consider why the main doctrines of economic governance – central planning, Keynesianism and economic liberalism – have all failed in different degrees and in their different ways. We shall trace a core aspect of this failure to the separation that each has been compelled to maintain between state and civil society in order to have the power to function in reordering the priorities of civil society. Then we shall consider briefly what the associative democratic supplement would prescribe as general goals for economic governance. We shall then answer the claim that associative democracy has already been tried and found wanting as a doctrine of economic organization in the form of Guild Socialism. In the following chapter we shall consider what lessons can be learnt for the future of associational governance from the most successful contemporary market-based industrial economies. We shall then go on to consider the specific associative reforms proposed here: improving regional economic governance, giving it greater salience and scope within federative structures at national and/or trade bloc levels; developing public–private partnerships to provide collective services to industry and in order to regulate markets; developing diverse forms of social and mutual ownership, and promoting the democratic account-ability of the business corporation to the wider society.

Economies in crisis

The post-1945 long boom in the West ended in the early 1970s and since then growth has been very unevenly distributed between nations, and has been volatile and uncertain at the national level. National Keynesian policies have become more difficult, if not impossible, in a more international and yet relatively weakly governed world economy. Those states with the strongest manu-facturing sectors, like Germany and Japan, have been, until recently, able to avoid most of the constraints that made Keynesian reflation desirable. Somewhat weaker economies, like France, have failed when they have tried an ambitious expan-sionary policy, as did the Mitterrand government in the early 1980s, because they suffered simultaneously from intense pressure on their exchange rates and foreign import penetration. The USA, which has exploited its unique position as the World's largest economy, practised through the 1980s a substitute for expansion-ary policy in 'Reaganomics'. Even in a continental-scale economy it has led to unsustainable budget and trade deficits.

Unless the key advanced nations of the 'G3' (USA-Canada, Japan and the European Community) decide on a common regime of domestic expansionary policy and large-scale inter-national aid to the ex-Soviet world and the Third World, this dismal situation will continue. What inhibits them from doing so collectively is fear of a really large-scale expansionary policy: fear that it will be inflationary, and fear that there will not be the social resources of cooperation and coordination between nations and within them to sustain expansion. Western politicians are cynical and so are their publics. In the 'post-Keynesian' era both have diminished expectations about what public policies of economic management can accomplish.

Associative democracy cannot pretend to reform the world economy. What it can offer in the medium term are means for ensuring the effective response of regional and national economies to the turbulent and increasingly competitive international economy. In the longer term, if associative democracy were to succeed in promoting the effective economic governance of key regions and nations then it would provide a basis of security for more generous and less fearful policies by the advanced countries in the international economy.

This fear of risks is in large measure dictated by the prevailing mood of the absence of hope and the failure of the previous alternatives to the present market-based corporate-industrial system. It is now becoming clear that there is no such thing as capitalism *per se*, that can either be advocated as the model for economic success or opposed as a form of unequal and irrational economic system. There are radically distinct national and regional variants of capitalist economies, some far more successful than others. The sources of such success seem complex and debatable, but they are not to be found in the generic features of the market economy. Rather, they seem to lie in specific cultural and institutional inheritances that are difficult to replicate or to impose by political reform. We shall see that such patterns of success tend to simulate the cooperative and coordinative features of associative democracy and that, therefore, associative democratic reform might be easier to generalize than, say, directly trying to copy specifically and distinctively Japanese institutions and cultural practices.

The failure of economic liberalism

Economic liberals are committed to the view that the market, when freed from as many regulatory restraints or distortions as possible, is the best and most efficient of all possible economic mechanisms. Some like Hayek are honest enough to admit that the market cannot be judged by the standard of 'social justice', that fairness with regard to outcomes has no place in the lexicon of economic liberalism. Many economic liberals are not so cautious and appear like Panglossian fools in claiming that free markets will secure widespread prosperity and will ensure a trickle down of spending from the wealthy to the benefit of the poor. The problems with economic liberalism as a kind of mundane theodicy are all too evident. Market economies, unless suitably directed and regulated by public agencies, and embedded in appropriate social institutions, cannot be expected to deliver substantive social outcomes like a healthy environment, an acceptable level of employment, a desired composition of output, or the means to reproduce and expand existing levels of economic activity.

The Keynesian critique of economic liberalism, that a market economy may well settle down to an equilibrium that is well short of full employment, remains valid. The institutionalist criticism that free markets cannot ensure, by their own workings alone, adequate supplies of key inputs like capital investment, trained labour and competent management remains powerful. This is especially so after the massive over-investment in the UK and the USA in the 1980s in commerical property and the service sector to the detriment of the manufacturing sector. The market system is indifferent to the concept of the national or regional economy. For economic liberalism a dollar is a dollar, whether it is earned in the financial dealing sector, in the marketed services sector or in manufacturing. That the manufacturing sector is the core of an advanced industrial economy, and that it needs specific institutional support to advance its market performance, is a claim of institutional economics that is being gradually and painfully relearnt after the economic liberal excesses of the 1980s. The question is how to ensure the cooperation between the economic agents and public bodies necessary to support the manufacturing sector in order to preserve its long-run competitiveness.

Economic liberalism relies on the proposition that free markets are efficient because they are able automatically to equate supply and demand – that they are coordinative mechanisms in and of themselves which are only distorted by unwarranted social intervention. The evidence of market failure is so widespread now that this proposition cannot be seriously entertained at the level of national economies, and not all of this market failure can be attributed to political interventions in the market, to imposed administered prices, or to other 'distortions'. The myth that the market fails because of non-market factors, that as markets approach perfection they will become more efficient, remains the core of economic liberalism and the means of shrugging off every difficulty. The lessons of the mixed economy need to be relearned, but they can only be effective if we can find the institutions of a new 'mix' to replace those of the post-1945 long boom.

Furthermore, the Panglossianism of economic liberalism becomes absurd when it confronts the problem of poverty, and argues that as the market is the best of all possible allocative mechanisms, even the poorest would be worse-off under another system. Pointing to the wealth of such countries as a measure of success of the market-based system merely exacerbates the stupidity of the response. Wealth is the product of the whole of society, and markets are merely one of the many ways in which such societies are economically organized. Moreover, if such wealthy societies fail effectively to succour the poor we must face the fact that far less wealthy and less developed societies have managed to mitigate the worst effects of poverty. In fact, the wealth of the advanced countries, whether derived primarily from the market or not, has not abolished poverty and wretchedness, nor has it brought security to the well-to-do. Even the successfully employed and the prosperous now live with uncertainly and nagging fear – dreading unemployment, worrying about their savings, and feeling anxious about the prospects for their children.

During the post-World War II boom in the West people did feel secure, and poverty was seen as something that could and should be eradicated. These were years of Keynesian interventionism in some countries and interventionist industrial policy in others, and in most they were also a period of expanded welfare provision and attempted redistribution – they were not years of economic liberal complacency. The problem today is that there appear to be *no* alternatives – economic liberalism has failed too, when in the mid-1970s it was presented as a source of a new prosperity. This absence of hope is a serious problem when both Western publics and a large part of the rest of the World's populations define the aims of life in material terms and have been conditioned to expect progress in the form of rising prosperity. It is the combination of uncertainty and the absence of clear remedies that makes the mass of the 'haves' self-interested: they behave like *rentiers*, seeking to preserve their own assets against an uncertain future, resistant to taxation because they doubt the efficiency of state spending, and unwilling to spend more than the barest minimum on aiding the unfortunate.

In the 1930s those who were disenchanted with capitalism or appalled by the waste and suffering of the Depression had clear political alternatives. They could either support state socialism or Keynesian demand management as ways out of the crisis. The latter was then effective, but largely untried, and the former a monstrous mirage. What ways are there today? Keynesianism remains the one major economic doctrine that is not simply irrelevant, but it cannot deliver at the national level what its more sanguine ideologists promised in the 1950s – full employment and sustained growth. At best at the national level it can, if the national macro-economic circumstances are propitious, stop a depression turning into a self-reinforcing slump. Keynesianism needs an effective political context in which it can be one part of a policy for prosperity. It is neither a panacea nor can it of itself supply that context. One can see this most clearly at the international level, where a coordinated expansion tied to large-scale aid and trade credits would simultaneously promote employment and exploit under-utilized productive capacity in the West whilst helping the ex-Soviet world to avoid collapse and the South to avoid accelerating poverty. The problem is that none of the major nations' leaders really believe in it. They are risk-averse, in part because they know they would not have their publics behind them, and the reason for that is that they lack the means or the inclination to appeal to these publics in convincing terms.

Why economics has failed

Why has economics not offered an effective solution to this crisis? Because the answers to most current economic problems are not narrowly 'economic', rather they concern the socio-economic governance of market-based economies. The sources of alternative policies are not primarily in the realm of technical economics, in new theoretical models, different approaches to econometric calculation, or in a new policy 'fix' for national economic management. Many of the existing policy instruments would work well enough if they were set in a different political context, in which the social institutions that regulated the economy produced different responses from economic actors so that those policy measures could work. If governance were different economic actors would be able to behave in less defensive and cynical, more cooperative and trusting ways because they faced less risk in doing so and they could expect a significant number of other actors to behave the same way.

Economics has acquired its place as the central discourse of modern public affairs not because the societies in question are mainly market-based, but as an outgrowth of a certain relation between state and society that has made national economic management possible. If one could imagine a truly *laissez faire* economy in which free markets predominated, then economics would not matter very much. It might teach a version of neo-classical economics as a kind of intellectual introduction to the market system, but very little would turn on this knowledge for the entrepreneurs and dealers who would acquire and practise their actual skills as economic actors without much need for theory. To reverse Keynes's remark, in such an economy practical men could afford to remain the slaves of some long defunct economist.

Modern economics, by contrast, is concerned with the central state's management of, or transformation of, national market economies. Central planning, Keynesianism, and the economic liberal practices signalled by the label of 'Monetarism' all attempt to manipulate macro-economic aggregates by policies that are designed to provide constraints on, and information for, the decisions of economic agents. Econometric forecasting, national income accounts and mathematical planning models have been devised as frameworks for generating the data necessary for such manipulations through various policy instruments. Modern technical economics in its various versions is thus the rationalization of types of policy that are the outgrowth of certain forms of state. Those states have certain capacities of control over, and mobilization of, the wider society, and those limitations set constraints on economic management. Economics is thus constrained by political relations that are the preconditions for its existence and determine in the main the degree of its success or failure.

The 'nightwatchman' state of the supposed *laissez faire* era was largely a fiction – states always accepted, willingly or not, greater responsibilities for intervening in economic and social affairs than the mere preservation of property and civil peace. The liberal era created a state with far greater capacities to intervene in the economy than that of the old absolutist monarchies of the *ancien régime*. These powers were enhanced for two reasons. First, the liberal state could claim greater legitimization for its actions through representative – if not fully democratic – government. Second, with formal equality before the law, economic capacity no longer depended on privilege or status. Economic actors could thus be treated as if they were all equals, and be subject to common policies. However unreal in fact the latter equality may be, it gave the state great power because it had no need to try to justify a policy that depended on specific discrimination and privilege. Liberal states indulged in the fiction that civil society was an homogeneous realm of legally equal actors.

For such a civil society to exist, there must be both a clear boundary between it and the state, and the state must abrogate exclusively to itself those public and regulatory powers necessary to those interventions it does make in the economy. Under absolutism and mercantilism, the space between the public and the private spheres was confused by status privileges and the ceding of public powers to entities like monopoly companies, licensed municipal corporations and aristocratic landlords. Liberalism is thus one of the principal sources of the modern centralized nation state with a monopoly of public legislative and executive power and able to impose its sovereign will on civil society. It will be obvious that the liberal state's power depended on its distinctiveness from what it regulated, on a definite separation between the public and the private spheres. The modern, twentieth-century state inherited this centralized sovereign power from liberalism (or autocracy modified by liberalism), and was able to turn it to a wider and wider range of purposes, becoming in effect a public service state with an expectation that it would make provision for each and every circumstance that might affect its citizens. Without the modern state's inheritance of the claim to a plenitude of legislative power from liberalism, and the transformation of the scope of that power by the acceptance by the state of its omnicompetence in the legitimate objects of policy, it would be difficult to manage the economy in the modern sense.

Modern states, whether socialist or otherwise, accept the widest possible range of objects of policy because they are basically demotic, that is, at least formally they claim to execute the will of, and to provide for the needs of, the people. This may be a fiction, as those dying in Stalin's camps or in famine zones found out to their cost, but it provides the fundamental legitimation for economic management and intervention. Socialist central planning, and those relatively diverse packages of institutions and practices that may loosely be labelled 'Keynesian macro-economic management', appropriated sharply different versions of the sovereign nation state's claim to legislate for, administer and make provision for society. In both cases the states in question had limited capacities for economic governance that constrained, and – in the state socialist case – utterly undermined the objectives and outcomes of such governance. These limitations were built into the state–society relation in question. The very effectiveness of these interventions depended upon a definite form of separation from, and dominance over, society by the centralized state. These forms of separation were at once the basis for the state's capacities to intervene, and the sources of the failure of its interventions.

Three doctrines of economic governance and their failure

Central planning

In the case of socialist central planning in the USSR and the nations dominated by it or modelled upon it, this separation took the form of an authoritarian dominance of the state over the existing society. Many of the earlier Soviet economic planners viewed the process of socialization in quasi-technocratic terms. They saw planning as a rational process. They relied on the active consent of workers. Stalin ignored technical planning constraints and brutally ignored the widespread popular resistance to the state's forced transformation of property relations, in particular of the peasants' effective possession of the land. However, even had the building of a planned economy not been accompanied by forced collectivisation, planning would still have required a monopoly of state power over society. For the state socialist re-volutionary, the existing society was viewed both as flawed and as plastic, as an object to be transformed into a new social sys-tem. The separation of state and society was both extreme and unidirectional in a socialist autocracy in that the state enjoyed a wholly autonomous power, and that society was something to be remade in its own image by the state. This task was legitimated by the ideology and revolutionary rhetoric of the activists of the dominant party. The very idea of 'civil society' was denied. Society could have no autonomous existence. The extreme form of separation of the state from existing society was the pre-condition for the apparently paradoxical process of the fusion of society with the state as the latter succeeded in its aims.

Comprehensive planning was claimed to be a complete alternative to and replacement for the market system. However, planning involved an economic formalism to rival the economic liberal's belief in the allocative efficiency of free markets. The planning process, like the market which it sought to replace, was to be the dominant allocative mechanism. It was to be guided by rational calculation, and assigned the factors of production to their optimum uses and combinations to meet plan goals. Just as in the economic liberal view of the market, socialist planning regarded the existing structure of occupations, enterprises and industries as fluid, to be made and re-made as economic rationality dictated. Enterprises were simply a means of realization of planning decisions. They were a geographical and administrative convenience and were subordinate to the decisions of the centre, their function was to obey orders and to relay information to the centre. Central planning was no more capable than the theory of the perfectly competitive market of viewing the production and distribution of wealth as a *social* activity. That is, an activity in which individuals made commitments to, and identified with, the institutions whereby production is carried on, in which individuals possess norms and expectations about work, exchange and consumption, and in which individuals seek non-material satisfactions as well as wages or profits.

In this formalism, and in the specific relationship between centre and enterprise, lay the fatal flaws of central planning. It could neither create stable, autonomous and social institutions nor a sense of community at work. Many market-based societies have been able to do this because in them the market has not been sovereign, but has been embedded in an ensemble of institutions of social governance. To that extent some capitalisms have created greater security and control over work for both the worker and manager than did centrally-planned socialism. Central planning could utilize the separation between centre and enterprises authoritatively to command the productive activities of society. What it could not do was motivate either managers or workers, except by crude sanctions and incentives externally imposed on the enterprise. Given the target directives of the plan, the performance measures and compliance incentives, then enterprise directors had every reason to comply with them – irrespective of local conditions or the desirability of other courses of action from an enterprise perspective – and every reason to present information to the centre in a way that confirmed its own expectations. Central planning thus involved a fatal perversion of both the flow of information necessary to its working and the attitudes to work of those who carried out its directives.

Hierarchical authority in non-socialist societies often mirrors this perversion, because it constructs its own smaller version of a 'command' economy. Business corporations that are run autocratically from the centre and on the basis of accounting data, and public services run through top-down management and performance indicators, share in lesser degrees the inefficiency of central planning. It is one of the reasons that, for example, the UK is becoming an ever more inefficient economy and society – with remote boardrooms ignorant of the realities of work and ignorant public sector managers indifferent to the necessities of service.

Keynesianism

In considering Keynesianism we face a fundamental problem, the extreme variability across nations of the forms and rationales of economic management aimed at expansionary policies. There is no archetypical Keynesian programme, because states differed in their institutions, in their possibilities of winning consent from social actors, and in the economic conjunctures they faced. The two most successful economies post-1945, Germany and Japan, did not practise Keynesian demand management policies and sought to avoid deficit financing as a key aim of policy. Swedish-style counter-cyclical investment policy was very different from the 'stop – go' cycle of British intervention. Having said that, there are certain fundamental features of Keynesianism as a doctrine of economic governance, and these can be illustrated by considering it in the context of the society for which that programme was shaped, the UK.

Keynes aimed to save the market-based private property economy from itself, and to do so with the least possible disturbance to the fabric of the liberal-democratic state. Hence both the means and the extent of state intervention in the economy were to be strictly limited. Keynesian measures could be accomplished by means of the existing system of state administration and law. It was a change of *policy* – not of the constitution, not the relation of the citizen to the state, and not of the basic forms of property ownership. Civil servants were to steer the economy at the behest of their elected masters, neutrally and efficiently. They did so using the existing powers of the liberal state transformed into an interventionist tool with an expansionary purpose, that is, monetary and fiscal policy. This intervention was predicated on preserving the autonomy of civil society, of influencing economic agents by general measures that did not abrogate their own independent powers of calculation and decision.

In the Keynesian case the separation of state and society derived from an objective opposite to that of state socialism: the preservation of civil society as an entity distinct from the state; including private ownership of the means of production and discretion to respond to market signals by firms. Keynesianism used the liberal state and its specific forms of separation from civil society to act upon that society. But manipulating macroeconomic aggregates through policy instruments, like the money supply, public expenditure, government borrowing and taxation, the central government could alter the conditions in which economic actors made their decisions and lead them to act differently, to the overall benefit of the economy and the vast majority of individuals. The principal exception to the beneficent logic of the multiplier was the unproductive *rentier*. Keynesian policy was to be accomplished without undue coercion and without the excessive exercise of administrative discretion by officials between one citizen or firm and another. It thus preserved the core of liberalism in that respect, *pace* its dogmatic economic liberal critics. Keynesianism did not damage the autonomy of civil society, despite the growth in public expenditures as a proportion of GDP. Keynesian policies exploited the state's potential as a revenue raiser and public spender. They could only be effective in a state whose fiscal and spending powers were large enough to substantially affect the performance of the economy, that is, in a post-nightwatchman state. Keynesianism was thus an effect of the transformations of liberalism toward liberal collectivism, and not its primary cause.

In order for such macro-economic manipulation to take place the central state had to have exclusive control of fiscal and monetary policy, to be able to use it independently to steer the economy as circumstances directed. The national economy had, moreover, either to enjoy at least a minimum of autonomy in relation to the international economy, or an international economy governed by similar objectives. Keynesianism supposed both the liberal state's sovereignty and the effectiveness of economic governance at the level of the national economy.

Once the classic Keynesian conception of counter-cyclical policy had succeeded, and created full employment and sustained growth, it was then threatened with failure if it could not go beyond the existing form of separation between state and civil society and build a link between government and the major organized social interests. Classical Keynesianism did not greatly concern itself with the composition of civil society, it looked upon it externally as a realm of economic actors that could in substance be taken for granted. Get the macro-economic aggregates right and the appropriate forms of calculation by actors would follow. But civil society did not resemble the heterogeneous mass of individuals and small firms of classical liberalism – it was organized by large firms, labour unions and collective organizations of employers. Keynesian policy encountered two obstacles that required it to go beyond the use of liberal policy instruments – wage push inflation and the failure of management decision-making in large enterprises. To handle these required moving beyond classical liberalism into a new form of state–society relation. Britain suffered both from wage inflation and from manufacturing failure, yet failed to develop effectively either corporatist social governance or an industrial policy.

Neither corporatism nor an industrial policy is an inherent concomitant of Keynesianism, both are specific practices of economic governance that can be pursued in a non-Keynesian context and, indeed, their pursuance may avoid the need for Keynesian measures as the main form of governing the economy. 'Steering' the economy by monetary and fiscal policy alone is both too hands-on and too hands-off: it implies careful and judicious macro-economic management by the central state, putting a huge burden on the wisdom and coherence of policy framers, and yet ignores those forms of social cooperation that might ease that burden and serve as a cushion when policy fails, as it must from time to time.

Keynesianism tended to promote corporatism, since consultation of the social interests provided a means of handling inflationary pressures in particular. However, such consultation is a two-way street, and, if effective in ensuring compliance, would promote the influence over government policy of the organized social interests and in doing so restrict the autonomy of the state in fiscal and monetary policy. States have been unable consistently to control domestic inflation given a high level of employment, whether pursuing Keynesian policies or not, unless they happened to enjoy, as a specific political and institutional inheritance, a highly centralized, disciplined and economically-responsible union movement that could adjust current wage demands to those concomitant with the long-run growth of real incomes. Countries like Germany and Sweden have, until recently, benefitted from such union movements. Britain has not: its unions were both powerful and subject to weak collective discipline at the peak association level of the TUC. The unions have remained strongly committed to a form of *laissez faire*, 'free collective bargaining', and that has gravely limited their capacity to cooperate with government policy and to play a decisive role in economic stabilization.

The Keynesian state was required to perform the balancing act of maintaining a high degree of centralization and autonomy on certain dimensions of policy in order effectively to manipulate macro-economic aggregates – thus maintaining the classic separation from civil society of the liberal state – and yet developing a close and ongoing connection with the major organized interests in order to check inflationary pressures and to ensure consent for its policies. This relationship was inherently unstable. In certain states like the UK, that continued with the 'arms' length' policy of state intervention, this instability was particularly evident and led to a series of ever more unsatisfactory outcomes, each of which set the terms for the next crisis. The UK was Keynesian enough in the 1950s and 1960s to practise a limited form of demand management that produced full employment, but not Keynesian enough to continue to enjoy sustained and rapid growth. Short-term expansions of demand had to be choked-off by deflationary measures; this led to fitful 'stop–go' growth and to a volatile pattern of short-term macro-economic fluctuations that inhibited major capacity-enhancing investments. The UK was corporatist enough into the 1970s to give considerable influence to organized labour, but not corporatist enough to create a collaborative political culture. The British political parties and organized social interests could not ensure sustained cooperation between industry, labour and the state to control inflation and to promote industrial policy. British incomes policies were either wage freezes imposed by the state relying on its separation from civil society, or short-term bargains in which the unions reserved the right to return to the free collective bargaining of industrial civil society.

Keynes made the assumption that if one could get the macro-economic conditions right then firms would behave like rational actors and markets would ensure the right signals about performance and profitability were sent. In that sense he remained an economic liberal. Management would be on average as efficient as the disciplines of the market could make it. Hence the failure of UK economic policy-makers to attend to the institutional structures of manufacturing finance, industrial organization or management training. In the post-war period Birtish firms failed to make the right decisions in industry after industry. Restrictive union attitudes were coupled with *fainéant* managements, who failed to innovate, to ensure productive efficiency, to upgrade products or to ensure quality.

It has become fashionable to blame the City for this, and to explain success elsewhere by the superior structures of industrial finance and corporate governance. There is no doubt that in both respects British institutions have many defects, but British manufacturing in the post-1945 period has got the financial sector it deserves. Had British manufacturing been internally expansionary and successful it would have been able to re-shape the priorities of the financial institutions or at the very least press government for reform. British manufacturing enjoyed good trading conditions during the 1960s and 1960s – stop–go cycles apart – and generally had substantial retained profits with which to re-shape and re-structure its products and performance. In general it did neither.

When the consequences of British management failure became evident in the 1960s, both Conservative and Labour governments tried to create an industrial policy. These policies did not succeed. Unions and business were unwilling to limit their own powers and prerogatives. The state had neither the capacity nor the political will to force a solution upon them, it remained bound by the limits of liberalism in the case of business and fear of electoral defeat with the unions.

An industrial policy was neither inherently impossible nor doomed to failure in the UK had the political parties and organized social interests attached enough importance to the goal. The problem is that peacetime politics in the UK is not a matter of widespread cooperation and collaboration toward a common goal, but is a competition for exclusive party governments. Such party governments are able to exploit the highly-concentrated and largely unaccountable power of the British state to do things *to* society, so much so that British government has been called an 'elective dictatorship'. What the Westminster model of government finds most difficult to do is to get beyond the separation of state and civil society, to act through cooperative mechanisms rather than through formal legislation and administration.

Britain is a specific instance of the failure of Keynesian policies, but it is also paradigmatic since its failure to develop effective institutional supplements to Keynesian demand management (or more specifically, since policy was often more orthodox than Keynesian, centralized macro-economic 'steering') revealed the inherent limits of such a regime of economic governance. Britain's Keynesian failure was not unique. The tendencies toward inflation and to the growth of public expenditure as a proportion of GDP were widespread even before the crisis of the early 1970s.

Economic liberalism

It was in this context that the third doctrine of economic governance, the new economic liberalism, found the conditions in which to ally itself with governments with new and changed political priorities in managing the economy. The 'new' economic liberalism was not simply a re-statement of the old, it relied on the classics and Adam Smith in particular, but it was a doctrine of active steering of the national economy. That steering was toward the market and in the interests of the private corporate sector, but it was still national economic management, not pure *laissez faire*. The new economic liberalism should not be confused with the Monetarist theoretical fatuities and policy nostrums that accompanied it into power. The new economic liberalism consisted in essence in new priorities for policy: in giving greater autonomy to monetary policy and not viewing it as a mere means to promote employment and output: seeking to reduce direct taxes on higher income earners; seeing inflation as more important than unemployment as a regulatory problem; aiming to reduce public expenditure as a percentage of GDP; and loosening or abandoning the dialogue with the major social interests of organized labour and the major manufacturing employers.

It was in the UK that the unstable Keynesian synthesis of economic steering and quasi-corporatism was first and most radically broken. The Thatcher government gave priority to asserting the autonomy of the state to govern, in spite of and against the views of social interests if needs be. Thatcher ruthlessly excluded organized labour, but increasingly her governments revealed themselves deaf to the pleas of, and apparently indifferent to the fate of, manufacturing industry. Conservative ideologues argued into the later 1980s that Britain's comparative advantage lay in financial and other marketed services, not in 'metal-bashing'. If industry were to be aided it was by sound money, low inflation, weak unions and the state's defence of the prerogatives of top-down management. Centralized power at Westminster was to be coupled with the 'right of management to manage' in public services and private industry.

The UK has exhibited this combination of priorities most clearly. Australia's Labour governments of the 1980s embraced many aspects of economic liberalism, but combined this with an active corporatist dialogue with organized labour in the successive accords on pay and conditions. The USA talked economic liberalism, and practised such priorities in de-regulation and tax breaks for the rich, but it practised a deficit-based expansionary policy under Reagan. The reason for this difference has a great deal to do with the differing levels of autonomy of the central governments in question, and the possibility of imposing such policies without an effective check by other public bodies or by public opinion and by fear of electoral defeat. The UK could reject social cooperation because a combination of Westminster centralism and an unrepresentative electoral system enabled it to ignore the losers.

The principal devices for steering the economy increasingly reduced to two: cuts in direct taxation and the manipulation of interest rates. The aims of policy in fiscal and monetary policy were modified by the need for 'electoral Keynesianism' and by the expansionary consequences of financial deregulation on credit creation and in stimulating the housing market. The effects of this ensemble of policies were supposed to produce sustained growth and lower inflation, but they produced accelerating inflation, unsustainable growth with consequent sustained deflationary measures and the gradual collapse of economic activity into a policy-induced slump. The results of the Thatcher years were, as Keynes would have predicted, to give short-term benefit to the rich, to the *rentier* sector, and to the financial institutions at the expense of the public sector, the low-paid, the unemployed, welfare recipients generally and capacity in the manufacturing sector.

Economic liberals have not proved themselves political libertarians. Economic liberal national economic management and policies toward the wider society continue to rely on the centralized state, and they further emphasize its separation from, and sovereign capacity to act upon, civil society. The state–civil society division of classical liberalism, inherited by Keynesian economic management, is in substance altered by the new politics of economic management. Economic liberals are state activists in a way analogous to central planners because they seek to reconstruct a society structured by the state–social interest exchanges characteristic of the mixed economy toward their ideal image of a market-based system. The means by which this transformation of both state and society are achieved are centralization, a mixture of de-regulation and re-regulation, and privatization.

The state is thus a regulator. It intervenes to break its links with inconvenient social interests, to subject their activities to ever-tighter checks, and it asserts its regulative dominance over all lesser public bodies and prevents them from challenging its priorities for managing the economy. The aim of such regulation is to free markets, which in practice means the major corporations and employers generally, from social pressures and from the substantive demands of political lobbying by organized interests. Only centralized and exclusively-controlled state power can create the space for 'free' markets by deregulation and privatization, but this involves imposing controls on certain social agents. To do this the state must ignore large sections of its people, to treat their views as of no value, and it must ruthlessly discriminate between different components of civil society, favouring some and coercing others. In doing so it acts quite contrary to the image of the classic liberal state as a neutral public power, that treats all citizens equally through general laws and their neutral administration. The state has to be partial and autocratic if it is to use its sovereignty to re-shape civil society, to build a 'spontaneous' market order by deliberate planned action.

If the state regulates in order to de-regulate, what is the defining feature of the latter process, since it cannot just be simple libertarianism? It is in fact the destruction of the social embeddedness of markets, on the belief that thus unsecured by social institutions they will approach closer to perfection and therefore to true allocative efficiency. This measure is, of course, formal; it defines efficiency as the equation of supply and demand by means of sales and purchases. The advocates of the mixed economy assumed, quite rightly, that sales and purchases could not accomplish these things except in contexts of considerable institutional simplicity and if one attached no substantive expectations to the outcome. The mixed economy concept is not anti-market, but is based on the proposition that markets are merely one part of the complex process of the production and distribution of wealth in a modern industrial economy.

Economic liberalism, however, challenges the general proposition of social embeddedness and regards the institutions of the 'mixed economy' as contrary to the efficient working of markets. Chief among these is public ownership, and hence the special role for privatization within economic liberal strategy. Privatization aims to restore the disciplines of independent management and the market, chief of which is the equities market – since failure to perform profitably will be reflected in stock market prices. That certain industries, like public utilities, are not best suited to effective price competition in supply is not of great interest, since profitability is the ultimate measure of efficiency. Here privatization has inevitably meant re-regulation; even economic liberals cannot give private monopoly utilities an unlimited power to raid the public's purse. Hence the rise of a series of regulatory agencies in the UK after privatization.

Britain is the paradigm case of economic liberalism as a sustained political regime committed, despite all the surface shifts in policy, to the new mechanisms and priorities of economic governance. The ruinous state of the British economy shows that economic liberalism is ineffective as a device of national economic management, it can neither protect the economy against international shocks by technical policy instruments nor mobilize the social cohesion and cooperation necessary to cope with them. If the future lies with those regimes and nations able to ensure effective domestic cooperation in policies to enhance economic and, in particular manufacturing, performance, then economic liberalism is a non-starter since it undermines such cooperation at its roots, in the forms of political authority that it requires. If a market economy needs to be coupled to non-market social institutions that regulate its performance, it is in order to be both competitive and socially sustainable in the long run. Social cooperation and the diffusion of political power are routes to market efficiency, not obstacles to it. A 'market society', that is a social system where the fate of the social fabric hangs on the outcome of purely private sales and purchases, is unsustainable. Such a society is at the mercy of the short-term and anarchic performance of markets and the calculations of immediate profitability by the strongest players in those markets. It has no capacity to respond to unfavourable conjunctures. Economic liberalism sought to make this absurdity real, to create by political will the socially denuded space in which market forces can act unchecked.

All the major doctrines of economic governance that have competed to determine national economic policy since the 1930s have failed in their own specific ways: state socialism catastrophically; Keynesianism after a long period of considerable success and only in terms of its most ambitious goals of full employment and sustained growth; and the new economic liberalism by its dual failure to achieve its macro-economic objectives and its damage to the social fabric that sustains the market economy. Common to each of these species of failure is the relationship that each has established between state and society. Common, too, is the reliance of public policy on a belief in the efficiency of a definite species of economic 'formalism' – that is, that policy can impact externally on the economy as a distinct realm of interacting causal variables. If that economic sphere is steered adequately it will, of itself, deliver the appropriate states of affairs as outcomes.

Economic liberalism's formalism consists in believing that the market mechanism works best when it is most autonomous, and that the measures of its efficiency, for the economy as a whole, are the nearest approximation to general equilibrium in which supply equals demand across the distinct markets at a given price structure and, for the individual enterprise, the best approximation to profit maximization. Keynesianism's formalism is a modification of this: it sought to steer the market economy by giving economic actors general signals and incentives to behave in a certain way, and assumed that those actors' otherwise autonomous decisions would produce not merely adequate aggregate outcomes, but appropriately efficient micro-level consequences too. Central planning's formalism consisted in seeking to substitute a state-controlled rationalized economy of contrived information flows for the actual decisions of the agents in the real economy. In each of these doctrines the externalizing of state action and the concept of the economy as a distinct realm with its own intrinsic causality fit together. Each of these doctrines as techniques of economic management has foundered because as they each relied on a specific form of separation between state and civil society, they could not build a close and ongoing dialogue between the institutions that govern the economy and the economic agents.

The prevailing doctrines have failed because their forms of economic management have been too remote from what is to be regulated: too remote to ensure quality decision-making, in which actors' capacities and commitments are known and built in to the intended outcomes. Economic management has been remote of necessity, because from the separation of state power from society has come the capacity for national governments to act on society. This 'power' of centralized and exclusively-controlled techniques of economic management has now become their undoing, for to remoteness has been added the fact that the nation state is less and less effective as a sovereign economic regulator. Economies now have no single centre, no given point of locus between international, national, regional, institutional and corporate powers of regulation. A more decentralized doctrine of economic governance that relies on political mechanisms of seeking coordination and compliance in regulation through the cooperation of economic actors now seems to be more appropriate. Until recently, pursuing the logic that societies are federative in structure, and that markets are socially embedded in complexes of institutions that are not the exclusive property either of formal political bodies in general or of the nation state in particular, would have seemed naive. The reasons are that almost all political forces have been mesmerised by the objective of manipulating state power, and because they have been schooled by economists to reject the view of the economy as itself a set of social institutions, that operate as much by the political logics of negotiation and cooperation as by the economic logics of exchange and competition. Considering the economy as a set of social institutions, accepting that it no longer coincides with the boundaries of nation states, means that economic governance can only work as sufficiently detailed and appropriately located coordination.

Associationalism as the supplement to modern economic governance

Economics has become the dominant discourse of the social sciences and the model for explaining all processes of social action. The hegemony of economics has become so complete that a great many non-economists accept that political and social processess should be analysed in terms of concepts based on assumptions about the behaviour of rational actors derived from economics. The result, as Charles Sabel [1993] has argued, is a new 'science of suspicion' in which non-hierarchical institutions and non-market cooperative relationships become at best unstable, and at worst impossible, in the face of the inherent tendency toward narrowly-constructed calculations of self-interest on the part of social actors. We need to approach the economy with a new set of expectations.

Economic relationships need to be judged by a suitably complex set of criteria that capture the relevant dimensions of substantive performance and that concern and involve the full variety of economic actors. Until one assembles these criteria, it is difficult to have a conception of why and, therefore, how the economy should be governed. The standards of judgement of the three dominant schools of economic governance we have considered have all been one-dimensional and formalist. That is, they have viewed the economy from the standpoint of a very specific type of social actor, and one embodying a socially de contextualized calculative rationality. This is most evident with economic liberals who view the economy from the standpoint of the consumer and the entrepreneur, on the demand and supply sides of the market, respectively, and who measure success in purely abstract quantitative terms, as the lowest possible prices for goods from the consumer's calculative stand-point and as the highest possible profits from that of the entrepreneur.

Associationalism tries to view the economy from the standpoint of the interests of a wide range of economic agents including those who are economically inactive as well as the active, the consumer and the producer, the worker and the manager – and does so in terms of a wide range of substantive goals. It is democratic in that it seeks to incorporate the widest possible range of actors as full participants in economic governance, and not just as the objects of decision-making and management. It is concerned primarily with ensuring that the basic institutions of economic governance are sound rather than starting from a concern with specific forms of economic calculation or techniques of economic management. It is not that associative approaches need reject the latter, but rather the argument is that the latter will be able to work better if the basic forms in which the economy is organized are appropriate. Associationalism is dominated by substantive economic standards of judgement, but it is not a 'substantivism', that is, it does not seek entirely to replace the market or monetary economic calculation. The argument that the economy is a social institution, that both production and markets are embedded in social relationships, is not part of an anti-market mentality. Rather the aim of attending to such social embeddedness is to enhance the substantive performance of markets by appropriate social governance.

The substantive economic goals of associationalism are as follows:

- that the economy produces an adequate level of wealth, and that wealth is distributed in the form of a widely-shared prosperity, but not a strict equality of outcomes;
- that in producing wealth the social processes that govern the economy also ensure a reasonable level of security of employment and consumption to the widest possible range of participants. Wealth is not the exclusive goal and it is clear that ceaseless change in its pursuit does not produce well-being, especially if it is accompanied by continuing insecurity and frequent unemployment for many economic actors;
- that it is important that as many economic actors as possible have the highest level of control of the assets that are necessary to their livelihood, this control may be either direct, as with the artisan who owns his or her own workshop, or through some representative system in the case of enterprises that depend upon external capital;
- that the interests of consumers and savers are represented in the main structures of economic governance, as are those of local communities that may be affected by the actions of a particular enterprise or economic association.

These goals require both democratically-governed firms and methods of cooperation between firms, public bodies and organized interests at local, regional and national levels. We shall consider the ways in which such governance may and does take place later, in Chapter 5. The point to make here is that this view has always seemed naive to economists, both because it lacked a suitably abstract theory to defend it, and because they have treated the actual institutions whereby economic activity is organized as, at best, secondary. It is worth re-emphasizing that different national experiences post-1945 seem to show that long-term manufacturing success has belonged to those firms, regions and nation states that have simulated in their institutions the forms and goals of an associatively-organized economy.

Security, stability and the capacity to have a measure of control over one's affairs are part of human well-being. They enable the mass of people to enjoy those economic conditions that are necessary to advanced individuation. It is only an apparent paradox, that security and stability make individuals more willing to contemplate, initiate and adapt to change. One will accept changes in methods of working, or even contemplate an entirely new activity, if the risks of doing so are minimized by security in one's employment status and livelihood. A high level of technical and even institutional change will be tolerated by those who are socially secure, in that they have both no need to fear for their prosperity, and a measure of say in the changes in question. Contrary to economic liberal conventional wisdom, insecurity and ruthless competition may not be the best stimuli to effective change and competitive advantage. The pursuit of quality and the continuous upgrading of both production processes and products appears to be the core of competitive success in manufacturing. As W.E. Deming's ideas have shown, and Japanese best practice has confirmed, this is not achieved by pitting worker against worker, nor is it achieved by employment insecurity and rigid status hierarchy in the enterprise. As modern economies have developed, they have placed more emphasis on broadly-skilled workers with some level of autonomy over their immediate activities, not on the management-manipulated human automata of Taylorism. In economies where success in research and development, and in intelligent responsive production and marketing, come to be the keys to competitive advantage, participation will demand a relatively high level of education and individuation from most core workers and not just the managerial elite. It is foolish to imagine that such individuated and accomplished populations in the successful advanced economies will accept either unlimited management prerogatives at work or environmental damage and corporate pillaging as consumers and residents. It is also foolish to imagine that less successful advanced manufacturing economies will regain competitive advantage by downgrading the skills of their labour forces or promoting the power of hierarchically-controlled corporations in weakly-regulated markets.

We shall see that contemporary evidence thus reinforces the credibility as well as the ethical worth of the substative aims of associative governance of the economy. Associationalism is not naive about the economic advantages of decentralized governance by the cooperation between self-governing economic associations and public bodies. Such a system, however, has to meet some demanding conditions if it is to work. These conditions are:

- that the institutions of economic governance are able to create sufficient levels of solidarity and trust between the members of economic associations, and between those associations, such trust both overcomes the pressures toward increasingly self-interested behaviour that are inherent in competitive markets and by doing so enables the market economy to work in a way that ensures its continued survival at a high level of economic success;

- that the institutions of economic governance are able to strike an acceptable balance between the cooperation and the competition of economic associations, enough cooperation to ensure sufficient regulation – thereby providing key inputs like trained labour, research and development support and capital at acceptable terms for investment to enterprises and providing the monitoring and supervision of their product quality and distributive practices – and enough competition to ensure a spur to efficiency in the interaction of enterprises one with another and with consumers;
- to create a coordinative partnership between public bodies and economic associations and enterprises, one that allows the latter sufficient autonomy to ensure economic motivation and innovation, and one that also allows the former a close enough degree of relationship to make informed decisions, but not too close as to lose all independence and become subject to the lobbying of special interests;
- to involve the more general organized interests in the process of economic coordination – such as the 'peak' organizations representing firms and organized labour, for example – but to reinforce this highly-restrictive national-level corporatism, with strong practices of public consultation and involvement at regional, local and industrial sector levels;
- to achieve a satisfactory balance between the conflict of, and the cooperation of, organized social interests representing individuals and associations – too much conflict will undermine the possibility of coordination, too little contestation will lead to ossification and the neglect by organizations of their members' interests in their pursuing ongoing accommodations with other organizations; too much and too centralized corporatism can be undemocratic and safe for organizational elites.

The specific ways in which such conditions are met by complexes of institutions in specific national and regional circumstances cannot be directly prescribed by associational theory. Associationalism cannot offer simple models of governance aiming at the same level of abstraction with which neo-classical economic theory has presented its ideas, in which the specific is merely contingent. Here the specific is central, and this has always made the advocacy of associationalist economic governance more difficult, however ingenious and complex the ideal-typical models of possible institutions might be. It is not enough to invent plausible institutions or, for example, to defend the possibility of trust with elaborate theoretical rationales. Such ideas will only be believed and be more widely accepted if they are already being practised to some degree already – if there are actual models of such institutions that we can adapt and generalize to provide new forms of economic governance. Thus associationalists should work by uncovering the current equivalents of associative economic governance and generalizing these experiences into clear institutional models, that derive credence from their being abstracted from working examples. The questions we shall have to answer are thus messier than those addressed by most economic theorists, since we have avoided the advantages of abstraction in the interests of starting to reason from definite institutions. Can the separation of the liberal state and civil society be bridged by specific institutional supplements that do not attempt to eliminate either term? Can such forms of melioration of the public power–private agency division achieve the social coordination of market-based economies without themselves creating new forms of regulatory paradox or imposing new limits to economic performance that are inherent in these new forms of social governance of the economy?

The failure of the Guild Socialist 'third way'

In order to answer these questions we must overcome two obstacles. The first is that associative democratic ideas and economic institutions have been around for more than a century and they have been defeated and pushed aside by the very doctrines of economic governance whose failure we have just considered. How can the supplement to our currently failed economic doctrines be forged out of ideas that failed in political competition with them in the 1920s? The second is that the predominant associationalist ideas about the economy were *socialist*, in the sense that they were oriented toward the workeas' movement and aimed to achieve a strong measure of equality of outcomes. As presented in a general form in the last section, associationalist goals for the economy are neither capitalistic nor socialistic. The political context and also the social structure of modern societies has changed in such a way that a purely worker-based social doctrine has no hope. The majority of society's members are no longer, and indeed never were, full-time male factory workers. Thus associationalism has to be given a broader appeal and a new content of social objectives relevant to the modern economy, but also the aspirations of diverse social groups – not merely waged workers.

Associational socialism's failure did not appear a foregone conclusion to many contemporary observers. To some acute observers and participants it had won the battle of ideas. Bertrand Russell in *Roads to Freedom* (1918) took it for granted that capitalism was finished, and compared socialism, anarchism and syndicalism as possible replacements for it. His judgement was that English Guild Socialism was the best alternative on offer. How could an idea have appeared so promising to an intellect like Russell's and yet fail so completely?

Britain in the early twentieth century was particularly rich in attempts to find a 'third way' between the collectivism of state socialism and the unbridled egoism of *laissez faire*. C.R. Ashbee and the Arts and Crafts Movement, sought an alternative to big industry and wage labour through high-quality craft production and self-regulating cooperative colonies of artisans (Crawford, 1985). A.J. Penty's *The Restoration of the Guild System* (1906) argued for the viability of medieval guild organizations as an answer to the market and the factory of mass industry. G.K. Chesterton, Hilaire Belloc and the Distributivists argued that the prevention of poverty and the preservation of freedom could only assured by the most widespread distribution of productive property possible, especially the land (Barker, 1978). Collectivism would destroy freedom in the attempt to cure poverty, whilst modern monopolistic industry and great landholdings would cut the poor off from the means to independent livelihood.

All these movements had some popularity, especially among intellectuals, artists and craftsmen. They were doomed because they appeared to have very little to say to the industrial working class. They sought to abolish or ignore large enterprises, and they sought to build the future on handicraft production and the small-scale. As such they could make no headway against the mainstream economics of the defenders of the market or the alternative economics of the state socialists.

Guild Socialism of the National Guilds League sought to avoid these defects and in the hands of their most prominent intellectual, G.D.H. Cole, it was brought to a high level of theoretical elaboration and institutional credibility. Cole's *Guild Socialism Re-stated* (1920a) was his blueprint for the new social organization. Cole started from the position that political and economic power should be as divided as possible, and that no social interest could claim a monopoly on power. Thus Cole sought a structure of economic governance in which the prevailing division between state and civil society would be overcome. The existing state claimed a sovereign plenitude of power – claiming to regulate all society from a single centre with a sole source of legitimacy. But society is not an entity, it is complex grouping made up of many specific associations and institutions with particular functions. This complex cannot be regulated by one body, nor can that body ever have genuine legitimacy in attempting to do so – no scheme of representative democracy can ever sum up the diverse wills of society on a whole range of different and functionally distinct issues. Hence Cole's support for the pluralization of the state, giving each territorial and functional grouping the autonomy to act within its sphere of competence but in no other. If the 'state' is thus dissolved into a multi-centred plural public power, so 'civil society' is transformed from a private domain governed by competing individual wills in the market into a federative structure of social cooperation between quasi-public bodies, the guilds. Cole argued that the existing division of state and civil society meant that the state was supreme in one sense, it had legislative primacy over individuals and associations, and yet abdicated all responsibility in another, in the market it left individuals to follow their own devices provided they obeyed the law.

Cole sought to transform the division of state and civil society, reducing the power of the central state and increasing the scope of middle-range institutions of social governance, subjecting them to democratic control. As he said of the medieval guilds: 'Industry was carried on under a system of enterprise at once public and private, associative and individual' (Cole, 1920a: xiv). That is what Cole sought to achieve through a modern 'guild' system, that in practice would have nothing to do with neo-medievalism. The new guilds were like the old in their objectives, in that they sought to regulate production as a social service, but were not to be like them in their actual organization, scale of operations or industrial methods. Cole argued that the nation would be the ultimate owner of all major productive property and land. However, the national guilds would hold that property in trust, and have effective possession of it while they provided a service to society and the consumer. The dangers of collectivism in which the state monopolistically owned and controlled the major industries were thus avoided.

Society is not the state and the state cannot substitute itself for society:

> With society, the complex of organised associations, rests the formal more or less determinate sovereignty. We cannot carry sovereignty lower without handing it over to a body of which the function is partial rather than general. We must, therefore, reject the three theories of state sovereignty, theocracy and Syndicalism, the theories of political, religious and industrial dominance. All these mistake a part for the whole ... (Cole 1914–15: 157)

Sovereignty is thus something that can be appropriated by no single agency or institution – it emanates from all the complex and divided governing powers that compose society. Both the market system and central planning require that should happen; the market system because individuals can only compete fairly if there is a single neutral public power to which all have access. The market requires the state if it is to be given neutral rules of the game and if it is not to be made imperfect by unjustified accumulations of private power. Under central planning, the state claims a monopoly of ownership of productive property *and* the right over the direction of its use. Cole seeks to end the anarchy, unfairness and inequality of the market, and the concentration of power in the sovereign state. His self-governing public–private associations provide a service and in order to do so they are governed by higher bodies representing both producers and consumers. These bodies are coordinative rather than directive, they rely on cooperation not imperative control, and on widespread agreement between distinct agencies rather than hierarchical planning.

Cole sought to find a 'third way' in more than one sense. He sought to avoid the three great social and economic antimonies of his time: that on the left between state collectivism and workerist syndicalism; that between free market and centralized planning; and that between labour and management in the enterprise.

First, Cole tried to avoid the opposed doctrines of state socialist collectivism and syndicalism. Cole argued presciently that the ownership and control of industry by the state would lead to the authoritarian concentration of power and the subordination rather than liberation of the worker. Syndicalism, on the other hand, sought to subordinate political power to the industrial power of organized labour and, therefore, neglected the interest of the consumer. Both systems aimed to socialize property but at the expense of concentrating the control of all social functions in the hands of one agency or social interest.

Cole, as a political pluralist, believed that power must be dispersed into specific functional domains and controlled primarily by those directly involved in those domains. An inclusive political organization was necessary only to deal with those very general and common circumstances of living together in a community. This was to be a political regulatory body, but not a sovereign state. Alongside this political organization there would be another inclusive organization representing the general interests of consumers. Industries, however, would be organized by their own active members. First in self-governing factories and, then, representing all factories in national guilds for each major branch of production. The guilds would both organize production and serve as the basis for coordinating the industry's activities with those of other guilds. The guilds would control industry, but they would have limited powers and would require the cooperation of other guilds outside of their immediate sphere of activity.

Second, Cole tried to create a system that would offer a third way between the opposed doctrines of the free market and centralized planning. Guild Socialism was not to be like modern 'market socialism', in which worker-owned firms trade in conventional markets and compete with one another to make profits. The unit in Cole's scheme is the National Guild which controlled and coordinated production within the whole industrial sector, the specific enterprises taking their part in an agreed schedule of production. The guild is thus a coordinative body, having both representative and organizing functions. Consumers would purchase the goods produced, expressing preferences in market terms, and also they would do so politically, and the guilds would respond both to market demand and organized consumer opinion. Furthermore, the relation between industries would be developed by elaborate networks of negotiation and voluntary coordination between the different guilds. Such a system may sound quaint, but it had real strengths. It avoided both the allocative discretion of state officials characteristic of central planning and the effects of unregulated market forces characteristic of the more extreme forms of market socialism.

Third, Cole emphasized the need to overcome the antagonism between labour and management. He believed passionately that industries should be controlled by those who work in them, but also that they should be organized efficiently. The different levels of decision-making in an industry should not be collapsed and conflated, as they are in the simple-minded versions of syndicalism – where the factory council is all-powerful. Cole recognized the need for specialist management functions, for co-ordination by higher-level bodies, and for the social assessment of investment priorities. These tasks could not be undertaken by the direct democracy of ordinary workers in factory councils, but by the complex indirect democracy of the guilds and their national machinery of negotiation between the guilds. Cole never forgot that the guilds were functional bodies, whose job was to provide a service to society. The ethic of such a service-based system depends on the recognition of reciproal obligations: the worker owed the consumer, and society generally, a good service; whilst society owed the workers the security and the respect to which they were entitled for providing it. Labour should not be regarded as a mere factor of production, to be hired and fired, used and discarded as the need arose.

Cole believed that factories needed creative leaders and that such leaders required authority. In a democratic factory, workers would vote for managers, but that fact would give managers democratic legitimacy for their decisions and make them powerful in a way conventional salaried managers in capitalist enterprises faced with a powerful and hostile labour movement on the one side, and a profit-oriented board on the other, were not. Cole claimed:

> Only under the free conditions of democratic industry would the leader find real scope for leadership, and we would find it in a way that would enable him to concentrate all his faculties on the development of his factory as a communal service, instead of being, as now, constantly thwarted and restrained by considerations of shareholders' profit. (Cole, 1920a: 57)

This may seem naive, but in fact it is tragically prescient. The view of industry as a service has all but vanished in countries like Britain and the USA. Managers regard themselves as dominated by the pursuit of profit, and workers seek the best deal for themselves.

Why, given its theoretical subtlety and its high level of attention to avoiding the problems of other schemes of economic governance, did Guild Socialism fail? We shall look at the political and contextual reasons in a moment, but first we must consider the intrinsic problems in his Guild Socialist scheme.

To begin with it will be obvious that a commitment to pre-industrial technologies or a small scale of operations were not among them. Guild Socialism was designed to cope with large-scale industrial production. The real intrinsic problem with the Guild system was that because it envisaged given industries being governed through national guilds, it found it difficult to accommodate the possibility of rapidly-changing divisions of labour and entirely new technologies transforming and rendering obsolete whole existing industries. It was designed to satisfy existing needs through known methods of production of established products. Its coordinative methods could cope with fulfilling static functions, but, being national and industry specific, the guilds were relatively inflexible. How could new capital for wholly new industries be mobilized? How would existing industrial guilds that would be made obsolete by new processes, and the skills of their members made redundant, cope creatively with change in a system that gave them great coordinative but also, therefore, obstructive power?

The answer to these questions is that Cole tended to view functions as the provision of given services. Guilds were functional to the extent that they provided one of a mix of services within a complexly-governed, but relatively rigid, whole. Cole could not escape this because he wanted to avoid giving control of the economy to dynamic and all-powerful 'purpose'-oriented agencies – like central planners or entrepreneurially-directed large firms. Purposes are different from functions – they are general and loosely teleological open-ended pursuits, like that of the maximization of profit or the socialization of the means of production. Guilds could be democratic, and collaborative because what they did was largely given in the existing pattern of activity and assets, their task was simply to manage going on performing this service in roughly the same way as efficiently as possible.

A guild is thus a self-governing association, subject to internal democratic controls and external coordinative ones from higher-level bodies in which it collaborates. The authority structure of the guild is not hierarchial, but a carefully-structured balance of constitutional powers, of limited authority based on consent. The firm in conventional economics is by contrast an open-ended agency: it is an organization wholly subject to the top-down control of those appointed by its owners to manage it. It is independent and free-standing, its sole relation to other firms being through the market and through competition. Its internal institutional arrangements may be re-structured as the economic calculation of the managers dictates. The firm is thus not a constitutionally-defined association with finely-balanced powers of democratic governance for each level within it. Firms may be made or remade organizationally, the better to attain the objectives the directors determine. Hierarchy is needed in the conventional view of the firm in order to ensure the flexibility to pursue open-ended purposes. Undivided and un-checked managerial power is capable of rapid re-direction to new avenues of advantage, whereas divided power and governance by consent are not.

Top-down management looks at first glance efficient by contrast with Cole's cumbersome distributions of power and authority. Open-ended goals like profit maximization also look more economically dynamic, more able to enhance new processes and products, more able to respond to competitive pressures, and more able to practise that 'creative destruction' that makes capitalism in the eyes of its defenders truly the most efficient economic system. The problem is that the view of the firm as a black box, open to be given any form by the creative entrepreneur and directed toward the abstract goal of profit maximization, is a gross simplification of what complex organizations are like and has nothing much to do with the explanation of industrial success or failure. The contrast between Cole's constituted economic association directed to fulfilling a given function and the goal-oriented open-ended firm is too simple, the defects of the former can hardly be said to reflect to the benefit of the latter.

As we shall see in a short while, it is possible to create structures of industrial governance above the level of the firm that do most of what Cole envisaged the guilds as doing, whilst being far more flexible in structure and more capable of accommodating change. Any successful organization must strike a set of balances, between providing a service and efficiency, between given needs and future possibilities, and between imperative control and motivation through consent. The simplistic theory of the firm as a profit-maximizing black box entirely at the will of an entrepreneur will hardly do to explain successful modern industrial enterprises. Yet it has been used politically as a legitimation of top-down control and as a substantiation for the claim that such control promotes 'efficiency', i.e. profitability. The contrary tends to be the case, that hierarchy tends to de-motivate those subject to it, and it tends to disorganize the effective cooperation of teams within the firm. Firms that cannot accommodate their workers as something more than automata, that are not really committed to providing the public with a service through the goods they make, and that do not renew and upgrade their products with an eye to the satisfaction of new wants, will not continue to succeed and make profits.

The annals of British and American industry are littered with examples of firms that became moribund through the dual obsession of maximizing profit and maintaining management prerogatives. The most successful firms have combined the search for profit and ultimate management control with institutional forms that allow their members involvement and that give incentives to motivated service. This is now a commonplace of the best of management theory. Successful firms have sought to make money through making things well – approaching profit from a perspective in which manufacturing quality and sales success through good service are the means to attain it. Cole was far from naive in his aims, even if his structures were too rigid. A new associative economy will inevitably be different from Cole's model. It will combine some of his aims with new and more flexible structures of governance. It will combine his concern for the worker with more modern views about how to combine involvement with effectiveness, such as those of the 'apostle of quality', W.E. Deming. The new associative economic democracy will be neither 'socialist' nor 'capitalist'; it will be able to accommodate very different forms of enterprise ownership and control within the same scheme of social governance. It will, nevertheless, seek to accomplish the same tasks that Cole did – to make the economy simultaneously democratically accountable to its participants and efficient from the stand-point of the consumer.

Guild Socialism did not fail politically in the 1920s because its proposed structures of national economic organization were too inflexible, and unable to promote or respond to social and technical change. Indeed, many workers would have liked just that; to preserve Britain's declining staple industries – coal mining, cotton textiles, iron-making and shipbuilding – and employment in them. Britain could not be isolated from international competitive pressures, since much of this industry had grown up to serve world markets that were fast vanishing. However, Guild Socialism had failed before it became clear how radical a rationalization of Britain's declining industries would be necessary.

It failed in part because it could not attract a distinctive enough and large enough constituency. In one sense it was 'workerist', in that it was primarily developed for and was aimed at improving the lot of the manual worker. It was, however, proposing changes that appealed to neither the conservative nor the revolutionary wings of the post-1918 Labour Movement. Conventional trade unionists concerned with defending wages and conditions were uninterested in a doctrine that aimed with the revolutionary socialists at abolishing the current system of wage labour. Revolutionary socialists and syndicalists regarded it as a 'middle class' diversion. Not surprisingly, given the importance thinkers like Cole attached to managerial authority in the new system and to the interests of the consumer. Some guildsmen became revolutionaries and joined the Communist Party; some gravitated to the Labour Party. Guild Socialism was too radical for the gradualist instincts of orthodox Fabians and was too committed to political change for the constitutionally conservative and statist Labour Party mainstream.

Guild Socialism also subscribed to a doctrine that it held in common with Syndicalism, that, as economic power is primary, economic struggle takes primacy over parliamentary activity. The guilds could, in fact, only survive and succeed as industrial experiments if they could enter into partnership with a government at least not hostile to their aims. The National Building Guilds, the most successful practical venture of the movement after 1918, depended on the availability of public finance to advance them working capital. When that was withdrawn in 1921 they collapsed.

The political pluralism of thinkers like Cole was viable only if they could face the fact that the existing state was not a pluralist state, and had to be dealt with by conventional political methods, such as winning majorities for legislative reform in favour of the guild principle.

After 1926 Guild Socialism became an irrelevancy. During the General Strike the state asserted its sovereign power against the miners and their allies. Labour opinion centred more and more on getting a majority in Parliament and using the state to promote reform in the interests of the workers. Pluralism and Guild Socialism could only seem like a diversion. After the 1929 Great Crash opinion swung decisively in favour of state intervention and 'planning', whether of a socialist or Keynesian kind.

5

Current Realities and Associative Economic Reform

Lessons from current practice

In 1959, when G.D.H. Cole died, associationalist ideas looked dead too. The future still belonged to big corporations, large-scale mass production and efficient managerialism. National economic management would ensure steady growth, secure in an international regime of fixed exchange rates and free trade. The dominant logic of industrial organization was standardized mass production, utilizing capital-intensive special purpose machinery and predominantly unskilled or semi-skilled workers to produce long runs of standardized goods. Manual workers enjoyed in the main low autonomy and identified very little with the enterprise or its goals. The archetypical modern industrial employee was the alienated assembly-line worker. Mass production conferred competitive advantage on the large corporation that could fully exploit economies of scale and acquire a sufficient share of the market so as to be invulnerable to competition from all but a few comparable firms.

One can overestimate the extent to which industrial organization conformed in fact to 'Fordist' stereotypes either at the beginning of the sixties or in earlier periods, the point is that the large corporation and standardized mass production were the prevailing ideal-typical forms of industrial efficiency. Economists and managers believed that these were the routes to competitive advantage and acted accordingly. These models were also applied to the public services – and still are. Large-scale and managerial public administration legitimates itself by reference to the success and the inescapable economic logic of industrial efficiency. If there was a political and institutional supplement to this economic logic, it was also large-scale and top-down. The big labour unions organized and represented the relatively homogeneous mass labour force of 'Fordist' industry. Corporatist bargaining between the representatives of industry, organized labour and the state ensured the framework within which distributional coalitions could be constructed and wage settlements adjusted to sustain economic growth. Effective corporatist interest intermediation relied on the 'peak' organizations representing the social interests in question being able to make the bargains stick with their own member organizations, and those organizations in turn being able to impose the deal on their own rank-and-file.

This world was shattered in the early 1970s. At the level of the international economy, four major changes occurred at an accelerating rate from the late 1960s onwards, and had become well-established by the 1980s.

First, the stable and fixed exchange rates that were the primary object of international monetary policy in the Bretton Woods system broke down when the US dollar ceased to be convertible into gold in 1972, and, therefore, could no longer act as the lynchpin of the system. The result was to promote the internationalization of currency markets and intensify speculative dealing in them, leading to volatility and uncertainty in exchange rates. This volatility was checked by the formation of the EMS in 1979 and by the Louvre and Plaza Accords between the G7 advanced industrial countries in the 1980s. Exchange rate imbalance remains a continuing threat, however, as the difficulties of the EMS in the autumn of 1992 and early 1993 indicated.

Second, financial deregulation in the 1980s strongly reinforced the trend toward the internationalization and interlinking of the major equity markets – London, New York and Tokyo are linked by continuous interactive trading, and the exchanges are vulnerable to rapid movements of large volumes of footloose capital.

Third, the dramatic increase in the volume of trade in manufactured goods between the advanced industrial economies. Most markets for major industrial products are now international, and major industrial economies now both export and import significant proportions of such goods, whereas before the 1960s home sourcing was dominant and export markets between the major industrial nations were specialized.

Fourth, the formation of supra-national economic and trading blocs, the two most important being the European Community and NAFTA (including the USA, Canada and Mexico).

The result of these developments has been a rapid change in the nature of competitive pressures and the forms of industrial organization that are appropriate to respond to them. Growth in the international economy has become more volatile and uncertain. Markets for manufactured goods are now internationalized, less homogeneous and less predictable, leading to firms being confronted with changing patterns of demand on a world scale and the complex differentiation of local markets. This has dramatically undercut the previously dominant company strategies of mass production for steadily growing and standardized mass markets. Hence it has been more difficult for firms to exploit long runs or to enjoy major economies of scale in manufacturing.

The most obvious consequence of these developments since the 1970s is, as we have seen, that Keynesian strategies for national economic management have failed to maintain their effectiveness in the face of both the internationalization of the main macro-economic variables and their increasing volatility. Another obvious consequence is that a centralized national industrial policy that aims to promote industrial concentration in the interests of productive efficiency in exploiting the advantages of economies of scale is also less and less effective. Building 'national champions' has less and less rationality, as the processes of competition become more diverse and favour different types of firm. The same problems affect a policy of 'picking winners', of national policy-makers determining the technologies of the future and mobilizing both R&D resources and major firms to meet them. Technologies are less certain and more diverse, and the errors of a centralized industrial policy can magnify those of the misjudgements of firms.

The result has been a series of major changes in both public policy and economic organization, as states and firms have both had to adapt to new forms of production, responding by seeking strategies that cope with uncertain and turbulent markets. Public governance of the economy is by no means entirely defeated by such changes, rather adaptive advantage has shifted to new institutions and forms of economic management. There are six major changes in forms of organization and policy in the post-1973 period.

The first is a shift from Fordist standardized mass production to new manufacturing strategies that emphasize productive flexibility – these are first and most coherently described by Michael Piore and Charles Sabel in *The Second Industrial Divide* (1984), and I shall use their concept of 'flexible specialization' to describe these changes, in preference to the variety of other labels on offer. Standardized production claims to exploit the economies of scale inherent in long runs and large production units, but it is able to do so only when there is a predictable pattern of demand for goods with a high degree of commonality. Flexible specialization is production for changing and differentiated markets, that require diverse quantities of varied goods over relatively short periods of time. It can be defined as the production of a changing range of customized or semi-customized goods by broadly-skilled workers with a substantial measure of autonomy using general-purpose machinery. The production process can adapt rapidly to different compositions of output through the skills of its workers and the responsiveness of its management structure.

Many firms have had to learn the consequences of this shift in the conditions of effective competition the hard way, and the larger and the more committed they have been to large-scale standardized production the more difficult it has been for them to adapt. Firms that relied on market dominance through sheer size like IBM or US Steel have suffered badly. Firms like General Motors in the USA have tried to introduce elements of flexibility into their lines and product ranges, to win deals for more flexible working patterns with unions, and to flatten their management hierarchies to make them more responsive, laying-off whole levels of middle management and dispensing with much of their routine administration. Other large firms have responded to these changes in a more innovative and dynamic ways: emphasizing the autonomy of their subsidiaries, divisions and product groups; restricting the role of central group management; developing partnerships with other firms; and encouraging ongoing relationships with sub-contractors that are inherent in shared R&D toward new products and just-in-time servicing of components. Many innovative firms have emphasized in the course of their decentralizing the need for a less authoritarian and *dirigiste* management style, recognizing that their core workers are their key asset and that the workers should enjoy the greatest level of autonomy consistent with effectiveness.

Small and medium-sized firms, far from being confined to marginal sectors or merely being the subcontractors of the subsidiaries of larger ones, have taken on a new lease of life in these changed conditions. In many sectors they can exploit niche markets or product areas unsuitable to large firms, however flexible and diversified the latter may be.

Such firms are most effective and competitive when they are to be found in industrial districts – that is constellations of firms in the same or related or complimentary industries that typically share a common regional location. Such districts are highly diverse in their organization but the most effective ones are those where firms have some ongoing collective and cooperative form of organization, and especially where that organization enters into partnership with a public body. Industrial districts provide firms with the equivalents of economies of scale in the provision of many key inputs and capital goods. Examples of such collective services and common facilities are: contributing to training local and suitably-skilled labour; providing common-use facilities like CAD centres that firms can rent; in providing access to low-cost capital through local industrial credit banks; and providing access to common marketing and trade information services. The small firm in a well-organized district can enjoy facilities and collective services, at a modest cost, that compare favourably with those of a large company and that it could not afford were it to try to buy them on the open market.

Industrial districts and the scale-mirroring advantages of collective services show that social governance of the economy has not collapsed, but that it has shifted in emphasis from national management of macro-economic aggregates to the regional level and to the orchestration of cooperation and the provision of facilities by regional public agencies. Regional government has grown in salience partly because industrial districts tend to be clustered in this way, but also because this level of government has certain definite advantages in the new economic situation. Regional governments are of a scale where it is more possible for them to know in some detail the capacities of local industries and firms; they can develop, in the words of Alfred Marshall (1919), an 'intimate knowledge' of what they must regulate and sustain. The can both make well-informed decisions and seek consent from those prominent members of local firms and trade association leaders known to them. Regional governments also tend to be concerned with the success of *local* industry, with the pragmatic ends of local wealth and local employment, far more than with the ideological goals that national governments or major-interest organizations frequently pursue. In Italy, for example, 'red' regions like Emilia-Romagna and 'white' regions like the Veneto have both developed local collective services for industry and the co-operation of local business, labour and other interests. Prosperous business people do not find it odd to be dealing with a Communist-controlled municipality like Bologna, for example.

The nation state, however, is far from loosing all capacity in economic governance – despite the re-emergence of regional economies and the formation of integrated trading blocs (of which the EC is the first example) with a confederal governmental structure and specific regulatory powers to create a common regime of trade, industry and competition policy for the bloc members.

Old and new patterns of social cooperation

Nation states remain political communities and many have and will retain extensive powers to influence and sustain economic actors within their territories. Even within a strongly-developed trade bloc, like the EC, national states will have key economic integrative functions and they will retain military, cultural and legal functions and powers that are specific to them and give them certain capacities of economic intervention and regulation, and that both the trade bloc and the regional levels lack. Even if the technical powers of national economic management have declined with the internationalization of key variables, the political role of government is still important, but as the facilitator and orchestrator of commitments by economic actors. The national state remains effective if it can draw upon and reinforce bases of cooperation and consensus among social actors. The national state has three key functions in this respect.

It must construct and sustain a *distributional coalition*, that is, an acceptance by the key economic actors and the organized social interests representing them for an ongoing distribution of national income and state expenditure that promotes economic effectiveness generally, and competitive manufacturing performance in particular. Such a coalition will embrace the portion of national income devoted to consumption and investment respectively, the level of taxation required to sustain state investment in infrastructure, training and other collective services for industry, and institutional arrangements for controlling wage settlements, credit creation and dividend levels, in order that inflation is kept within tolerable limits relative to international competitors.

Such a coalition will only be sustained if the state gives ongoing and active attention to another function, the *orchestration of social consensus*. Such coalitions can only be sustained in a collaborative political culture in which the major organized interests accept both the need to cooperate and the primacy of the nation, that they view the nation as a community of fate in which they share success or failure. Consensus does not imply the absence of conflicts of interest, rather that a balance be struck between cooperation and competition, and that the national state acts as a medium wherein specific resource allocation mechanisms, such as the system of wage determination and the operation of capital markets, are able to operate effectively.

That the national state achieves an effective distribution of its fiscal resources and its regulatory activities between the national, regional and local levels of government. Those national states are most effective that can give autonomy to, and sustain, the kind of regional governments that promote local industry. National states are thus effective when they are either the constitutional architects of decentralization or where they at least tolerate a de facto federalism in economic governance.

Organized labour has the strongest interest in continuing and in promoting such consensus policies at national level. As Scharpf (1991) shows in a remarkable analysis, labour is collectively less mobile than capital and must regard its national situations as a community of fate. Thus where organized labour is cohesive enough and can adopt the appropriate policies of restraint in its demands, it can offer the conditions for an ongoing pact with employers. Where employers have the minimum of solidarity and the national commitment to respond, then the conditions are created for an effective economic partnership of the major social interests. Organized labour has to accept responsibility in wage bargaining, a commitment to improve productivity, and tax levels on wages high enough to support infrastructure spending. These commitments are difficult to sustain on the part of organized labour, even where a strong social democratic tradition and the inheritance of the appropriate structure of industrial relations institutions make this possible. Effective corporatist bargaining continues to be a means of achieving economic stabilization in a post-Keynesian period, but it is exceedingly fragile, subject to default by self-interested sections of business and workers alike.

If corporatist bargaining at the national level were available to most countries as a strategy of economic stabilization, then economic governance could easily be restructured without the need for associationalist reforms. An accommodation between industry, labour and the state, and a periodically redefined distributional coalition would provide a sufficient bridge between state and civil society. Corporatism did function in this way in countries like Germany and Sweden during the long boom, and proved robust enough to cope with, and adapt to, the turbulence of the 1970s. However, changes in social and industrial structures of the kind we have outlined above have begun to undermine the possibilities of satisfactory corporate representation and, therefore, of the conditions for corporatist bargains to stick with the wider society. This seems to be beginning to happen in Germany, and it is well advanced in Sweden.

Swedish corporatism is in dire trouble. The distributional coalition that has been solid for fifty years is breaking down. Large-scale internationally-oriented industry perceives advantages it cannot exploit in an economy where full employment restricts the supply of labour to manufacturing, where it is difficult to reward skill levels and productivity gains because of a combination of low differentials and high direct taxes. The homogeneity of labour representation is now fragmenting and cannot be based on a deal between the manual workers' federation, the LO, and the employers' SAF. By the end of the century the white collar union federation TCO will rival the LO in membership and will have different priorities. J.K. Galbraith's 'culture of contentment' seems to have spread to Sweden. Many Swedes are now tax-resistant and willing to support economic liberal policies.

In Germany, too, the structures of corporatism are weakening. National industry unions are less representative of their members than they were in a less differentiated industrial structure based on heavy industry. Germany has many medium-sized firms in new and more diversified industries that do not fit into the old classifications, nor do many flexible broadly-skilled workers who bridge the manual–managerial divide. Union density is falling and many ambitious younger workers are reluctant to involve themselves in union affairs. A substantial gap has opened between the rank-and-file and the union leaderships in Western Germany over such questions as asylum seekers and paying for the costs of integrating the East. Unions are refusing to accept that workers should carrry the main tax burden *and* practise wage restraint. Their uncharacteristic militancy is due to the fact that they are driven by anger from below.

Neither of these examples show that all structures of corporatist bargaining are doomed. What they do indicate is that highly-centralized bargaining between big unions and big employers is less and less representative of economic agents and of society as a whole. Therefore, such bargains when they are struck command less legitimacy. The forms of representation of interests need to become more socially inclusive in a new way: more flexible in accommodating a wider range of interests, such as small- and medium-sized enterprises and new types of workers. New corporate bodies need to have more bottom-up legitimacy, arising from regional and firm level cooperation between employers and employees. In an associationalist system this gap would be bridged by new forms of enterprise. More broadly-skilled and well-educated workers, the sort of people needed for the competitive industries of the future (whether in manufacturing or services), increasingly will not identify with the old centralized structures that could speak for a more homogeneous manual working class. Solidarity cannot be taken as a given, it has to be built-up from active cooperation in more complexly-divided and more individuated populations.

The combination of increasingly socially fragmented but geographically localized labour and internationally footloose capital does not bode well for national level corporatist economic governance. One cannot comfortably rely, as in Scharpf's strategy, on exploiting existing legacies of solidarity and social democratic representation to offer employers a responsible workforce, a bargain they cannot refuse. The way has to be found to a new system of national interest representation, one that is differentiated enough to be inclusive of the more diverse economic interests in modern society and yet that is cohesive enough to promote cooperation rather than self-seeking conflict and lobbying. A new kind of corporatist concertation might be based, first, on processes of cooperation at regional level and, second, on the bargaining of regional and industry representatives at national level. This would be different from the present system where these industries and regions are not represented separately, but through the interests of the participants in them as either employer or worker. Associative structures thus offer a way forward in coordination through corporate social governance. The spread of cooperative and mutual ownership would tend to reduce the current gap between the wage worker, who sees the firm as a mere means to earn a living, and the manager, who acts as a steward of external providers of capital. Both would have distinct positions but common interests in an ongoing, self-governing association. Such forms of ownership would also help to facilitate the regional collaboration of firms and public–private partnerships.

Labour would thus be united with the enterprise and capital would be rooted in the locality, rather than vanishing into the international market. New forms of capital made possible through cooperative and mutual ownership of enterprises and new types of financial institutions, such as regional industrial savings banks or industrial credit unions, would mean the capital funds would tend to be recycled regionally and invested in local work and wealth. Mutual financial institutions would be non-profitmaking and would provide investors only with a guaranteed rate of interest for their deposits. Most equities and the vast bulk of capital are the savings and financial assets of workers. These assets are controlled by large financial institutions like banks, insurance companies and pension funds. If there were alternative, secure and attractive forms of investment, then people could invest in the future of their own area – securing work and revenue for their own neighbours and children. Centralized financial institutions redirect these funds, as do large national and international manufacturing companies, often rendering their own investors or workers unemployed by investing not in local industry, but in resort hotels halfway across the globe or by relocating output to another country. The funds that could benefit localities are regularly generated by their citizens and get siphoned-off elsewhere. An economy in which mutual institutions predominated would tend to localize basic capital and, hence, require less regional redistribution in the long run, because output and employment would be more evenly distributed between regions.

If regional networks and the collaboration of mutual enterprises uniting capital and labour are the forms of economic co-operation of the future, national corporatist structures remain the best remedies against economic turbulence available in the short-term, and where they exist they should be maintained or revitalized if possible. It is no part of an associative democratic argument to undermine resources of economic governance that exist now, by claiming superior capacities for governance in the future. But such structures are clearly trading on political legacies and industrial structures that are more or less rapidly being under-mined. The national representation of economic interests is essential, because even in a strongly-regionalized economy there will be major inter-regional issues that require resolution and co-ordination, and that are either too numerous or too specific to be handled at the level of the trade bloc.

In moving toward new structures, the first move is to persuade the major interest federations to begin to take account of the diversification in firm structures and the change in the composition of skill. The CBI, for example, cannot speak for all industry in Britain. It is really the voice of the largest firms. Associationalism in promoting new and varied forms of ownership would help to do this. The new firms and public–private regional partnerships might seek representation on their own account, parallel to existing national organizations like the CBI. In promoting a new model of a relationship between work, management and capital, associationalism would show that there is a 'third way' between the internationally-oriented managers of big business and the defensive organizations of localized labour. For just as we cannot rely on the continuing vitality of the legacies of social democracy, so we cannot rely on the ongoing commitments of business to a national framework. An increasingly internationalized economy would gradually demolish the existing loyalties of managers and major firms to nations and their institutions. Were that to occur, social governance of the economy would become ever more difficult in the face of footloose capital, a power that could demand facilities from the public agencies in any given locality and yet refuse inconvenient regulation. Hitherto, German and Japanese managers have remained strongly nationalistic and this has been part of their countries' success. But in an internationalizing economy these are given cultural and institutional inheritances that it will be increasingly difficult to sustain in their sites of origin, and virtually impossible to transfer from one national context to another.

If this analysis is correct, then the political consequences are disturbing if there is no new attempt to promote solidarity and cooperation. Conventional social democratic strategies are undermined in those states whose corporatist structures are weakening. They will face a new politics of social conflict and self-interested lobbying to which they are unaccustomed. But the main losers are those societies that have *chosen* to embrace these consequences, that have abandoned social coordination in favour of the market principle. Here, lack of cooperation between the major organized interests, the turbulence that follows from poor economic coordination, and the effects of the orientation of the major firms toward short-term market success, will act as a disincentive to long-term investment in new capacity and the continuing development of quality production. This will lead to poor economic performance relative to those competitors who can maintain such sources of solidarity and concern for the long run. Poor economic performance in a market-dominated society leads to intensified competition between social actors. The result is social fragmentation and the collapse of the remaining bases for solidarity as the successful firms and localities pull away from national commitments, and are unwilling to damage their own competitiveness by contributing to general programmes of economic revitalization or specific initiatives to reverse industrial decline in less favoured industries and localities. Such firms and localities will subscribe to exclusive interest organizations that lobby to direct public policy to their own advantage. They will gain in influence since they have the resources to campaign and the state fears to compromise the remaining islands of success or to drive them abroad. Economic failure leads to social fragmentation, and that leads to political blockage. Consensus policies become impossible as winners and losers diverge more dramatically and become mutually antagonistic. The result is that the social sources of competitive failure become self-reinforcing and so infect the political system so that it is incapable of taking effective political action.

If this sounds alarmist then one should take pause, for it is all too close to the situation in the UK today and this process of self-interested and exclusive bodies lobbying for advantage came to dominate politics under Reagan and Bush. If corporatism of the centralized kind, heavily dependent on the continued allegiance of national capital and organized labour is becoming less effective, then in societies like the UK and the USA, where market-based policies have predominated, it becomes essential to find and stimulate new sources of social solidarity starting from the bottom-up, thereby creating new forms of coordinative interest group representation. Associative democracy is the most obvious and most promising route to that end.

Learning from manufacturing success

Earlier on in this section we saw how flexibly specialized production, new firm structures and new forms of regional economic governance were effective responses at the sub-national level of the firm and the region to the turbulence of the 1970s. Why then, it might be asked, is there a problem? Why have not all firms and societies adopted these practices and thereby restored their economic competitiveness? The answers to these questions are numerous, but in the main they stem from certain regions and nations having the cultural and institutional conditions to respond in this way without an explicit 'theory' of how and why to do so. Flexible specialization and regional collaborative governance have not yet developed into a highly-generalized and widely-diffused ideal-typical model of industrial efficiency in the same way as standardized mass production and large-scale corporate organization did. The grip of economic liberalism and free-market solutions as a response to the crisis of the 1970s has also prevented the reception of such practices taking place in other countries and regions. The UK, for example, given its centralization in the 1980s could hardly have responded to economic decline by a sophisticated strategy of industrial regeneration implimented by local government.

In the 1980s certain countries, (West) Germany, Japan, but also Northern and Central Italy, succeeded in weathering the crisis of the early 1970s and creating, once again, the conditions for manufacturing growth. Japan is the most obvious success story, and the management shelves of British and American bookstores groan with volumes whose message is 'learning from Japan'.

But *what* are we to learn? The answer depends in part where one looks for the key to Japan's success. If one looks at the level of state–economy relations then the obvious fact is the close association between state and business elites. This stems from the forty-year rule of the Liberal-Democratic Party, from Japan's bureaucrat-dominated system of government, and from the common educational background and close mutual links between officials, politicians and managers. This has been called 'corporatism without labour' and the key institution of that corporatist intervention is MITI (the Ministry of International Trade and Industry). Even if one accepts this analysis, ably developed by Chalmers Johnson in *MITI and the Japanese Miracle* (1982) and rejects other accounts that emphasize market-based reasons for success, there is a problem. MITI can only work in a state that strongly diverges from the liberal model of a neutral public power that does not actively discriminate between one economic actor and another. Its system of 'administrative guidance' only makes sense if firms are disciplined enough to accept it in the majority of cases and yet possess the profitability and competitiveness, occasionally, to reject what they consider ill-founded directives, as the motor industry did in response to ill-considered merger proposals in 1975.

If one looks at the level of the firm, then the best-run and most successful major Japanese companies have managed to create a business-oriented simulation of the cooperative enterprise advocated by associationalists. Typically, Japanese firms have had low income differentials, a common employee status for core workers – including manual workers – and the creation of a conception of the firm as an ongoing collective enterprise to which all members contribute and with which all identify as part of an ongoing career within that particular enterprise (Dore, 1986; 1987). Japanese managers have not ceded authority to labour in certain vital dimensions of policy, but they do rely upon workers individually and collectively acting with autonomy and responsibility both to resolve problems and to improve performance.

While Japanese firms have been growing rapidly, have ploughed back retained profits in new investment, and their managers have remained committed to sharing common hours and conditions with labour, they have been able to avoid wider questions of authority. Workers have had a unique experience of security and prosperity compared to Japan's recent past. But, while many individual components of the Japanese system, from a common employee status to quality circles, are relatively easy to copy, the pace of work and the commitment to enterprise over and above home and leisure are not. Western employees will not accept them and the Japanese do not try to impose them in their full rigour in Western subsidiary plants of their own firms. Western employees *do* like the lack of rigid status distinctions that Japanese management introduces in transplants to the West. It remains true, however, that Western workers will not make the same commitment as wage employees, without a share of ownership or authority. Moreover, the intensity of Japanese work practices is now being questioned in Japan, and many younger Japanese are reluctant to live exclusively for the firm.

The alternative accounts of Japanese success, like David Friedman's *The Misunderstood Miracle* (1988), stress the importance of flexibly-specialized small- and medium-sized firms and industrial districts as a corrective to the big firms and national government story. The conception of Japanese corporatist co-ordination as exclusively an affair of the government and the major firms, and that labour unions are merely 'yellow' company organizations is clearly very one-sided. Japan does have responsible, but effective, national unions in both the public and private sectors, and these bargain in a synchronised way during the annual wage-fixing round or *shunto* (Dore et al., 1991).

In the case of Germany, the institutions of national and regional coordination are clear, but their role is far from easy to copy. The Bundesbank is a federally representative institution, and (in most circumstances) independent of central government (Kennedy, 1991). It has consistently followed an anti-inflationary monetary policy, but it has only been able to do so because of the strong international competitiveness of manufacturing industry and the fairly consistent moderation of the union movement in making wage claims. Even so Germany has traded growth and employment for a strong currency and low inflation. Equally central to

Germany's success has been the dominance of the financial system by the big industrial banks and the ongoing relationship between the big banks and the major manufacturing firms symbolised by inter-locking directorships. The German financial system is closely regulated, the stock market has nothing like the influence it has in the UK, and the financial system is relatively insulated from international pressures. Neither the Bundesbank nor the German system of industrial finance can be maintained indefinitely if the EC develops a common monetary system and a more deregulatory and competition-oriented policy to give effect to the Single Market. A European central bank will not be the consensus-oriented and representative federally-structured institution that the Bundesbank is, and will lack political legitimacy because of this.

At the level of the region, some of Germany's Länder, like Baden-Württenburg, have developed successful supply-side policies to aid their industrial districts. At the enterprise level German workers have enjoyed in major manufacturing industry a system of co-determination with representation on a works council and on the supervisory board of the firm. Similarly, industry, labour and the state cooperate to sustain an elaborate system of industrial training and apprenticeship.

In Italy's case, weak central government has enabled regions and municipalities to take an active part in economic governance, if they had the political energy and cohesiveness to do so. Italy did not fall prey to monetarist fashions in the 1980s and its governments have, through a mixture of default and design, followed an expansionary course, trading inflation for growth. The adjustment to ERM entry after 1979 was made possible by the social interests collaborating with the state to sustain a limited form of incomes policy. Italy is now a strongly-divided society, with fundamental conflicts between the successful regions in the North and Centre and the failing ones of the South. These divisions have been savagely reinforced by the austerity measures introduced in the wake of the electoral crisis of 1992 and the currency crisis that followed it in the autumn. Italy's large firms have suffered severely in the recession of the early 1990s, and it is also questionable how well the small- and medium-sized sectors will fare without rapid growth in the domestic enonomy.

None of these models of success is thus easy either to copy or to sustain entirely on its own terms. In all three countries industrial districts, small- and medium-sized firms, and cooperative and co-ordinative national institutions have provided at least some of the keys to success. Each country has, in its way, bridged the gap between state and civil society, allowing a closer and more effective form of governance of the economy. Each has also developed institutions that mirror or simulate those of an associative economy. This shows that there is every reason to believe an associative economy would be more successful than economic liberalism and that associationalism is easier to introduce by institutional reform than by the Western states seeking to copy, say, the ensemble of Japanese practices or, even more difficult, the spirit that informs them. We shall now develop the model of the associative economy drawing on what we know from the experiences of successful economies, but carrying them further. In doing so, we shall also pay attention to the strong anti-collectivist and individualist values, and the activist civil society based on voluntary associations, that are characteristic of 'liberal' societies like the UK and the USA. It is no accident that they embraced economic liberalism most strongly. An associative reform would seek to preserve political liberalism, whilst promoting the cooperation and coordination in economic relationships that economic liberalism denegrates and destroys.

Associative reforms

The aim of an associative reform process would be to move toward an economy in which small- and medium-sized enterprises are more salient than at present, where ownership is firmly rooted within a locality, where capital is predominantly raised within the region, and where collective services and economic regulation are provided by public–private partnerships between trade associations and the regional government. Smaller enterprises are more easily subjected to democratic governance by their own members and community representatives. The argument here is not against large-scale *per se*, neither claiming that 'small is beautiful', nor holding that local relations are inherently less alienating than long-distance or international ones. Small enterprises can be viciously exploitative and authoritarian, as sweatshops demonstrate. The local can be the merely provincial. Often, moreover, the large-scale *is* necessary.

The reason for decentralization in both state economic management and the structures of firms is that this makes for both more informed and more accountable decision-making. If the future belongs to quality, in both the products and in the lives skilled and individuated economic agents demand, then it can only be had by intimate knowledge of the processes whereby products are made and the people who produce them. Partnership between public agencies and firms, between managers and workers, between capital providers and firms, will only work if there is close knowledge and the expectations that lead to trust. All the databanks, EPOS systems, satellite links, etc., will not provide the knowledge of persons necessary to trust. Indeed, remote information systems and hierarchical authority tend to demand 'transparency', the creation of relationships based on formalized tasks and statistical reporting. Management that demands total visibility from the top-down and reserves to itself all information and powers of decision, that abandons workers and customers to a miasma of PR and advertising hype, remains all too common. It tends to vanish where quality is demanded and where ongoing interactive relationships are essential to quality. Management that lives by accounting data and the short-term is less and less effective in the competitive business of selling goods. It remains rife in sectors where service ought to be the primary goal – in public health, education and welfare agencies.

The concern for quality is in essence the belief that firms will only prosper by offering a genuine service through the goods they sell. Japanese management in the most successful companies does believe in offering service, and it has managed to get large enterprises to behave like small ones. In part this is because these enterprises do depend on small ones. Major Japanese companies have been able to reduce inventories through just-in-time sourcing of components and have been able to enter into partnerships with allied firms to develop a continuous upgrading of components. This has been achieved by developing an ongoing social relationship with suppliers through relational sub-contracting, in which a supplier by offering service to the bigger firm is rewarded by an ongoing relationship based on trust, where the supplier will receive information, advice and even capital investment to meet the demands of quality. That relationship is complex, open-ended and not 'transparent', rather it is based on the exchange of knowledge through trust.

National economic decline and local economic revival

Advanced information systems can greatly aid such relationships but they are no substitute for them. Much of the reason why Northern England has deindustrialized, and Northern Italy hasn't, is because in the former local firms were often the subsidiaries of larger holding companies that saw them as mere accounting units, whereas in the latter, enterprises were tied into the fabric of the locality and its network of supporting relationships providing capital, sharing work and giving owners and managers the commitment to keep going. British firms are shut for many extraneous reasons: for not making 'enough' profit to satisfy dividend-hungry investors – although they are trading well; to concentrate production elsewhere; to sell the land on which the factory stood; or simply because nobody has the knowledge or energy to turn the enterprise around.

An associative economy embedded in strong local institutions is likely to prove both innovative and tenacious. It will, moreover, permit a more even regional distribution of economic activity, by stemming the tide of deindustrialization and by permitting locally-directed processes of reversing industrial decline. If associative democratic reforms are to become practical politics it will be as a means of reversing decline in failing economies, like the UK, and also of systematizing and conserving existing *ad hoc* routes to micro success against macro-economic turbulence, as in Italy.

In a country like the UK, confronted with serious deindustrialization, the need for a new industrial policy is evident.. Yet Britain's central state has had an abysmal record since 1945 as a means of reversing Britain's industrial decline. It should be evident that the vast majority of Britain's major firms cannot be expected to lead an economic recovery: they are overwhelmingly enmeshed in holding company structures that allow their subsidiaries too little autonomy; they have generally failed to adopt the new production methods; all too typically they practice extremely hierarchical forms of management; they are often heavily involved in sectors like defence or aerospace that are in serious decline; and they are dependent on dividend-hungry arms' length financial institutions and a stock market that all too easily facilitates external and hostile take-over bids if the share price slips. Even successful and innovative large companies like ICI found it difficult to survive in this business environment. ICI responded by attempting to split into two distinct companies. Large firms have typically, moreover, withdrawn from the regions where deindustrialization is most developed.

This is not to deny, of course, that in a country like the UK, whose institutions of economic regulation are so fundamentally defective, that major conventional national legislation aimed at the major companies and organized markets is not necessary. In Britain, the whole system of financial dealing, industrial finance, corporate governance and competition policy needs a thorough overhaul. This may or may not happen with a future reforming government. The problem is if it is imposed on failing institutions and enterprises from the outside, when their managers are fundamentally ignorant in many cases of the degree of their failure or the route forward. One could not expect much enthusiasm for reform in Britain's boardrooms. Whereas, in the construction of alternative financial institutions, in the building of new local networks, and in the creation and revitalization of smaller firms in neglected and declining areas, a vast amount of effort will be liberated because hope will have been restored. Britain's major firms will clutch at any financial help that is offered them, but they will change their structures and practices with the greatest reluctance.

The most obvious kind of regeneration *not* to proceed within this context is a *dirigiste* central government industrial policy to be able to pick winners with the aid of Britain's big firms. Rather, central government ought to facilitate *local* economic action by appropriate permissive laws and by assistance of an appropriate kind. This might include:

- building-up a network of mutual capital providers through appropriate tax incentives – such bodies would be non-profitmaking industrail investment banks for a region or industry. If building societies can succeed in attracting citizens' savings to finance housing through suitable tax concessions to investors, then the same can be done for industrial credit banks and with far more urgent need;

- encouraging public–private partnerships in the major regions (in advance of formal structures of regional government) in order to promote training, technology transfer, collective services, etc.;
- giving priority in the structure of tax allowances to companies for investment in manufacturing, with special incentives for companies with less than 1000 employees in particular;
- the giving of incentives by government to cooperatives, labour–capital partnerships and other forms of employee involvement in firms' ownership and governance, such as Employee Share Ownership Plans (ESOPS).
- that government promote competition, discourage mergers and encourage firms to decentralize and to contract-out as many operations as possible to associative tenderers (we will consider this in more detail below).

Such policies will take time to act, but a failing country's industries can only be effectively rebuilt relatively slowly by effort and enterprise, not by ministarial fiat or 'national plans'. Given the right incentives, even in a far from propitious macro-economic climate, the associative and small-to-medium-sized sector would begin to expand and to do so in places hitherto without hope of seeing firms opening again in manufacturing, except through regional subsidies. Britain is a spectacular example of economic decline, but its difficulties show that associative economic reforms could make short-term political sense, and, therefore, how they might get started. It also emphasises *why* local control and a regional basis to the economy is essential, neither to withdraw from the international market nor to accept low-tech, low-quality local products, but to have the capacity to compete and in order to distribute work relatively evenly between regions.

The associative conception of the economy need not be parochial, nor need it reject innovation and investment in new technologies. The Japanese township of Sakaki examined by Friedman (1988) is an excellent example of a small industrial district that combines intensely local economic loyalties with production of goods like medical testing equipment for international markets. At the same time, an associative system would allow those who believe for Green and/or religious reasons that such international trade is wasteful and destructive to build their own highly-localized and self-sufficient communities and benefit from the public policy toward the promotion of associative enterprise to do so. The great advantage of associative ideas in this respect is that they can accommodate a wide variety of types and objectives of economic institution: it is not tied to a single model of enterprise like the large hierarchically-managed mass production firm.

An associative dimension to the economy is not being proposed here entirely for extra-economic reasons, such that full democratic accountability requires the diffusion of ownership and an end to hierarchical authority in civil society. These are far from intrinsically bad reasons for seeking associative reform, but such changes will not be accepted if they are held to involve less economic efficiency and produce less wealth. The argument here is that associative structures are in line with major changes in economic organization, which favour quality products and skilled workers with some autonomy. Such changes mean that associationalism is a social route to economic efficiency, just as flexible specialization is an organizational route to industrial efficiency.

The dangers of an internationalizing economy

At the same time, the danger of an international economy increasingly dominated by major hierarchically-governed transnational corporations is not inconsiderable; were such an economy to develop, then effective regulation and governance of markets by regions or nations would become impossible. Such global companies would try to square their top-down authority with involvement and identification for their members, particularly as not all operations could be run from a global head office. Firms would try to compensate for the effects of markets within their own structures, but would leave all without to the mercy of largely unregulated market competition. Governments would become mere municipalities providing local services. This vision is presented in more positive terms with much rhetoric about quality, service and the wisdom of the market in Kenichi Ohmae's *The Borderless World* (1990).

Associationalism offers a coherent answer to such thinking and explains how we can compensate for the relative decline of the capacities of national economic management, and at the same time preserve the community relationships that most people continue unreservedly to desire. Security in social relationships enables people to have the courage to take risks and to be socially and technologically innovative. As we shall see below, associationalist welfare would reinforce such security, giving every adult a Guaranteed Minimum Income (GMI). This would give a cushion against risk and allow people to construct new and, often to begin with, marginal enterprises. Security thus encourages risk-taking. An associative economy would encourage people to set up in business for themselves, as self-employed artisans or traders, or in small firms. It would make capital easier to obtain for the small firm or partnership, provided employees were encouraged to join in through co-ownership schemes and participatory management. Such a society would be attractive to those who do not like to be regimented, but it would not exclude schemes of participation and formal representation in large enterprises too.

It is likely in such an associative economy that participation in paid employment or self-employment would be almost universal, even if only part-time or intermittently over an individual's life. Associationalist reforms and a GMI scheme would go a long way to abolish both dependence on big organizations to provide waged work and the current division between the employed and unemployed. An associative society and economy, because it would be diverse and open to enterprise, would not be egalitarian, there would be differences of wealth and success, but it would less readily condemn people to the powerlessness of unemployment or leave them utterly destitute. The successful would have to pay relatively high taxes for the security that all enjoy, but they would consequently have no reason to feel threatened either personally or politically by the propertyless. Such an economy would retain a considerable measure of flexibility precisely because wages and incomes would *not* be equal. Hence successful firms that wished to expand could offer training and higher wages and attract the lower paid or partially employed. The problem with a state-engineered full employment economy, like Sweden's, is that it is inflexible. High taxes mean that it is difficult to offer significant differentials, and employees have little incentive to shift from public sector jobs to manufacturing, even in attractive work environments like Volvo's new plant at Uddevalla, Gothenburg.

An economy in which associative forms of organization came to predominate would systematize those processes of public–private cooperation and coordination that already exist in the best-organized industrial districts and also generalize them across the society. The wider economy would gain all the benefits of regulatory decentralization and the trust-based relationships characteristic of such well-governed districts. But the associative democratic basis of such economic institutions would add something else, the means to reduce conflict and to make cooperation easier. Self-governing enterprises that were more accountable to their members would tend to reduce the conflicts that have their locus in authoritarian structures and status differences within firms, conflicts that are the basis for the institutionalized divisions between workers and managers in political organizations. Also, as associational forms permit pluralism, there would be ample scope for different types of firms and different types of local public–private relations. The result would be to diffuse and decentralize the interests that lead to conflict. Civil society would be more open-textured and less dominated than it is now by big companies, big unions, and their respective political organizations. The result of such diffusion would be to make collaboration between enterprises and the public power less problematic, and, therefore, to ensure an ongoing dialogue between them.

Market socialism and its limits

An associational economy would create that effective communication between the public power and civil society that Durkheim understood to be essential for economic and social stability. It incorporates the lessons of both Solidarism and Guild Socialism, without being tied to either political formula. It is open to a wide variety of doctrines, including genuine market-oriented libertarians. It also gets over a fundamental defect of most versions of a 'third way', in that it permits the combination of extensive social governance and markets. This is what the classic market socialist revisionist arguments have been unable to do. Too often these are an uneasy synthesis of socialism in the enterprise and neo-classical market theory outside. The economy is composed in market socialist theories typically of workers' cooperatives, and they are linked one with another and the consumer through market exchange.

The problem with such market socialist theories is that they tend to treat the economy as if it were reducible to its component parts, to enterprises and households, and see markets as a neutral means of linking the two. If inequality is abolished within the enterprise, then the basic source of intractable social problems is removed. Get ownership and control within the enterprise into the right balance, add to it an effective competition and anti-monopoly policy to prevent firms getting too big, and then markets will be able to opperate as efficient allocative mechanisms: the consumer will be protected by competition and the producer rewarded relative both to the success of the enterprise and her or his stake in it. This is to assume that firms should be related only by markets and that their main relation is competition, any 'distortions' of the market have to be justified by exceptional arguments that greater inefficiency would result otherwise. The problem here is that the exceptions are too numerous and too important for such a principle of public intervention to work.

Most market socialists' arguments are imprisoned in the triadic structure of independent company, market and state intervention. Yet markets will tend to direct investment and economic activity toward areas where short-term returns are best and current market information appears to be sufficient for decision-making, such as securities, commodities and real estate. But industrial investment tends to be long term and to demand more information, especially qualitative information, than current market signals can provide. Market socialism assumes that the major social problems are related to inequalities of power and wealth located within the enterprise. Associationalism raises authority within the enterprise as one important issue, but the decentralized and co-operative governance of the economy as another. Associative governance supplements the market and does not supplant it, but it does not merely intervene to regulate behaviour and correct market failures as state intervention does, it also provides an alternative and supplemental system of qualitative information to that of the market. Combined with markets, associative governance could improve decision-making and, therefore, economic efficiency.

However, such qualitative information can only be had through cooperation in a locality. Surely then, there is no more than local economic governance based on such cooperation and the exchange of quality information through networks based on trust? The market socialist might reply that markets are neutral and impersonal, they can operate on any scale, and where necessary they can be corrected by state intervention, again on a large scale. Are not associative relationships intimate and their trust contextual, fragile and difficult to replicate? Associationalism may be a good idea but it fails in the face of complexity and the large-scale.

The answer to this is twofold:

- first, that local relationships can be institutionalized and still retain their intimacy and their capacity to transmit quality information. *Ad hoc* and spontaneous arrangements in industrial districts need to be systematized into an 'industrial public sphere'.
- second, that associationalism provides the route to combining 'intimate knowledge' and a capacity to govern on a large-scale. It does so because as given units are self-governing entities, whether companies or regions, they can be left within a general legislative framework to regulate those activities that are their exclusive concern. It also does so because it incorporates the pluralist premise that different levels of authority can be restricted to their specific functions and be accountable for them alone. Higher level bodies need not be omnicompetent agencies like sovereign states. In performing a function they can gather the specific information necessary to perform it by collaborating with a definite range of other bodies that are relevant to that function alone.

Industrial districts and economic governance

There is no one best model of how to govern an industrial district, but there are some lessons that can be learned from existing districts. The aim of an industrial public sphere must be to consolidate that 'industrial atmosphere' that Alfred Marshall found to be the moving force of industrial districts like S.E. Lancashire in his *Industry and Trade* (1919). An industrial public sphere is an open-textured set of interconnecting networks and institutions to which all economic actors concerned are free to contribute. It is more general than specific contractural or cooperative relationships between firms, that may be closed to others for mutual advantage, or the provision of services by a public authority, which may involve some element of administrative discretion. It provides the context for more specific coordinative governance through the provision of collective services, local sources of investment finance, activities organized by trade associations and labour unions, and ongoing partnerships between firms. It requires either a sponsor or an obvious point of constellation between networks and activities. At the most formal that might be a corporatist forum, a regional economic chamber, underwritten by the regional government, and into which more local or industry-specific bodies channel their own networks and forms (Sabel, 1993).

A region linked in this way has a centre in which the shape of the local economy and its problems can be discussed. Discussion can lead to local legislation, to public provision and coordinated action. An industrial public sphere turns a district from a series of co-present firms and networks into a body capable of prevision and remedial action. It can mobilize support for the public financing of industry intelligence, market research and collective R&D. This is essential if coordination is to be flexible and capable of initiating change, of solving the problems Cole's national guilds could not. Many industrial districts do tend to stagnate either because their patterns of coordination are too informal or are tied to very specific mechanisms that inhibit product and technical change. An industrial public sphere is Durkheim's 'social brain' on a regional scale. It would make the economies of regions resilient and tenacious, organized bodies capable of responding to new competitive pressures and preventing decline through remedial action. A public sphere is not an administrative machine, nor is it a state agency, it is neither public nor private. Above all it is a means for circulating information and a forum for discussion.

But surely this is an over-political fantasy? Hard-headed business people will not waste valuable time and energy on such arrangements, nor surely can they benefit from information and services which are public, common to all relevant firms, and give them no special competitive edge? This is to suppose that the firms in a given industry are most successful when they concentrate their energies on competing one with another, and seeking exclusive advantages. There is a good deal of evidence that the reverse is true, that if the balance between cooperation and competition tilts too much toward the latter, then the whole population of firms may lose out (Best, 1989). Firms, like individuals, benefit from environments where prosperity and success are widespread, and for them to succeed it is not necessary that others should fail. It is a great deal easier to rise to success as a fashion designer in Milan than in Wigan, or to sell hams if they come from Parma. This is also to see the determinants of a firm's success as predominantly set by what goes on *inside* it. However, listening to others in a trade association or a regional economic chamber may save hours of labour and a great deal of money, it may help to cement networks in which contacts are made. Few business people now despise networking, and the formal arrangements of an industrial public sphere are like networking for the region as a whole.

The EC as a federal economic regulator

Regional economic governance will work for certain dimensions of policy but not for all. Hence the need for a distribution of governance functions between different levels of authority, and the means to keep each level exclusively to its particular functions and to make it accountable to those below it. This is the essence of the principle of federation and the logic of subsidiarity. In economic governance a complex division of labour is necessary, and must be adjusted over time to meet changing circumstances. Associationalism, because it is committed both to the federal principle and to the self-government of the units of any federated authority, can adapt to the new internationalized economic environment more easily than the traditional doctrines of state-centred economic governance.

If we accept that the governance capacities of the national state are now and for the foreseeable future limited in an internationalizing economy, then we should also conclude that a trade bloc like the European Community is one effective way of managing the most internationalized of the dimensions of economic policy, such as trade and monetary policy. At the very least, such blocs make the negotiation of international compromises possible by reducing the number of parties to the bargain. A body like the EC is not, however, a super-state. It is not a scaled-up version of the nation state. It can do things nation states cannot do and yet it cannot do other things that remain the province of the nation states and the regions within them. If, for example, the EC is capable of sustaining an expansionary policy unlike France, it cannot create either the legitimacy for the specific policies of public spending or credit creation necessary to sustain such a policy or the forms of co-operation of the social interests necessary to implement it (Hirst, 1993).

The EC is not a state, but a confederal public power. It enjoys the powers it has by treaties entered into by the member states. Thus the EC is a clear example of a public power limited to certain functions only, and answerable to its member bodies for the performance of these functions. If the Maastricht Treaty is signed, the Union will become a fully political body and the EC's populations common citizens of the Union. All citizens have rights against their governments at national level through the European Convention on Human Rights. All national states must accept and incorporate into their law common EC legislative directives. EC policy is currently made by agreement by the states and the Commission. Europe thus has a complex of inter-locking political entities, each with specific powers and capacities, none of which is in the strict sense 'sovereign'. Unless Europe fragments, the principle of federation will become ever more relevant in understanding and shaping its structure.

The EC should gradually come to handle those dimensions of economic policy common to Europe as a whole:

- monetary policy – ultimately through a common currency;
- the common framework of general regulatory rules;
- competition policy for corporations that operate on a European scale;
- policy for technologies and skills that can only be handled at the European level, and require coordination at that level;
- inter-regional redistribution to meet common social and infrastructure standards;
- provision of infrastructure common to the whole continent, e.g. air traffic control.

Other levels of economic governance will be handled by nation states and regions. We have seen the crucial political role of nation states in economic management through the creation of consensus. We have seen the role of regional economic governance in supporting industrial districts. The principles of subsidiarity and self-regulation allow the lesser agencies to perform certain functions exclusively and without being subordinate to a higher authority in doing so. Within a common framework of economic regulation and citizens' rights, nations and regions are free to determine policy and to raise revenue to support it. These activities are answerable to democratic mechanisms of accountability for such policy at national and regional level.

If nations and regions diverge in pursuing specific economic and industrial policies, so be it. They perform specific functions and have autonomy within the sphere of competence of those functions. The same principle applies to firms with democratic mechanisms of accountability in respect of national and regional legislation. *How* they meet framework standards and how they resolve disputes is their own business. Regulation can be devolved because those concerned can be trusted to make it for themselves and all relevant interests have an effective say. The result is that regulation can be simplified by being specified, the higher regulatory agencies need not legislate for each and every contingency. Hence one of the central economic liberal objections to regulation, its tendency to proliferate and generate complexity, can be answered through the political mechanisms of federation and institutional self-government.

Democracy and trust may come far cheaper than the institutionalized suspicion that arises from leaving affairs solely to be coordinated by contract and market exchange. It is impossible for contracts or the laws regulating them to eliminate all contingencies or provide remedies for all risks. The increasing recourse to litigation and the use of insurance mechanisms is a way of compensating for trust and for ongoing social relationships that attempt to avoid or repair damage. A society that flees from the obligations of other institutions into the one 'neutral' institution of the market generates such costs, and it also has to cope with greater uncertainty.

It is only by building trust and cooperation at the basic level of the economy – in its firms and localities – that higher-level institutions can function in this way. It is futile to expect the politics of an exclusively competitive market society to be more than the struggle of exclusive and self-interested groups for particular advantage. Cooperation can be built out of cooperation, trust out of trust. Units divided by suspicion and conflict will find it difficult to cooperate one with another, except to further conflict. Bosses uniting for the sole purpose of resisting workers and *vice versa*. Coordination through cooperation of the representatives of economic agents, in a word, corporatism, will only work if those agents are themselves experienced in cooperation. Hence the need to rebuild economic democracy from the base of the democratization of the enterprise.

The new firms

If there is no best model of how to govern an industrial district, the same is even more true of how to govern the firm. We now have the good fortune to approach the governance of firms in a period when this complexity is beginning to be recognized. On the one hand, the demand for economic democracy has been prised loose from the exclusive grip of advocates of 'workers' control'. It is now clear that there are more stakeholders in industry than just the immediate producers, and that corporate governance must reflect this. Corporate governance is no longer an exclusively socialist issue, rather it concerns the relationship of the firm to the wider society. On the other hand, the diversity of firm structures is beginning to be recognized as both economically inevitable and desirable, there is now no good reason to argue that industrial efficiency has to be sought exclusively through economies of scale and, therefore, through large enterprises. There is no general case for the concentration of ownership and the building-up of larger firms, and because of that it is easier to argue for more democratic and accountable, less hierarchical and autocratic, management structures.

It should be evident that changes in industrial structure have breathed life into the idea of a democratic economy based on a plurality of sizes of firms and styles of governance. Small-and medium-sized firms have grown in relative importance and also in their autonomy from large ones. Larger firms have decentralized and loosened their structures, and some have aimed at a flexible and recombinable 'moebius strip' character, capable of perpetual reorganization. Large firms do remain, however, and they are particularly important in international trade in manufactured goods between the industrial countries. Even if many of these firms have introduced flexible and decentralized structures, this is within the limits of ultimate control through ownership or part-ownership by the head office. Partnerships between firms and joint ventures complicate this picture for the managements of the participating firms, but they also make the self-government of the units in question more difficult.

The logic of *industrial* concentration based on economies of scale in production has weakened, but the relevance of other logics favouring concentration have not declined in the same way. There are many firms far larger than the maximum that plant size would justify. Production may not require large firms, but major fixed R&D costs, extensive investment in marketing and sales networks etc. may do so. This is particularly true if the firm is selling in a wide range of international markets.

There are other pressures to concentration of ownership that have little to do with industrial necessity, the *financial* pressures toward concentration of ownership have accelerated, even as those stemming from production have declined. The divorce of financial operations from the direct investment in new plant and processes, conjured up in the phrase 'casino capitalism', has fostered the concentration of ownership of industry based on stock market opportunities and lending by the banks or bond issues to finance acquisitions. This is most marked in countries like the UK and USA with very active stock markets and with relatively few institutional limits on corporate acquisitions. This process in the mid-1980s was driven by stock market conditions and surplus capital. It led to processes of hostile acquisition of firms or mergers that were often devoid of either manufacturing or marketing logic. In the USA, otherwise viable firms have been bled dry to service high interest rates on the bonds issued to facilitate acquisition. In this context top management becomes ever more powerful, decentralization and participation go by the board, and in consequence the operations of subsidiary firms will tend to suffer from such remote control. Such a financially-driven form of control cuts against the logic of product up-grading and the continuous improvement of quality, since what is required is the highest possible percentage return on the costs of acquisition.

Financially-based conglomerate holding companies all too often lack a *raison d'être* in operational necessity. They are, moreover, black holes for the existing structures of corporate governance: they are beyond the control of the formal machinery of shareholder representation, and they are also unaccountable to their employees. This industrial concentration without economic rationality for consumers, workers, communities or many of the shareholders turns large-scale firms into a pure form of ownership divorced from managerial necessity. Head office control here is a weakening rather than a strengthening factor for the subsidiaries, and such ownership patterns have helped to promote deindustrialization.

How then to deal with such corporate structures? The reason for intervention is ultimately economic efficiency and the social benefits that stem from it, and not democratization *per se*. Traditional socialist remedies like nationalization can hardly make any sense here. One of the main reasons for nationalizations was to rationalize industries through concentration. However, in this case the component parts of such conglomerate firms often make little industrial or administrative sense when gathered together. External regulation will hardly have much effect either. The answer is a general policy of promoting economic decentralization and the self-government of the units thus made autonomous. Decentralization is different from conventional competition policy in that it does not prevent mergers or break-up trusts because of the threat of monopoly; it goes further and seeks to encourage firms to reduce to the smallest size consistent with their core operations. Such a policy is general. It is not just targetted at the more irrationally-structured conglomerates. Firms that need large-scale networks can be accomodated, and by other ways of achieving these at lower capital cost than exclusive ownership. We shall return to our model of decentralization.

Corporate power and corporate property

Before we do, it is necessary to reconsider the corporate form, because any challenge to existing patterns of corporate governance will be violently resisted by those managerial interests affected as a fundamental assault on 'private property'. Robert Dahl's *A Preface to Economic Democracy* shows that to link corporate property with property *per se* is a gross *non sequitur*.

The corporate economy is relatively recent. In Britain and the USA, the corporate form of organization became widely established only in the third quarter of the nineteenth century. In Britain, for example, the 1862 Companies Act made corporate status readily available for the first time. It protected the ordinary investor through the dual devices of limited liability and the system of governance that envisaged the firm as a republic of shareholders, each with certain basic common rights. That structure is now taken for granted. Whilst it remains substantially intact despite later legislation, the majority of companies are not effectively accountable to their shareholders. Most shares are held by financial institutions, who in normal times support management as a self-perpetuating oligarchy. The real check on management is the share price and dividend levels. If these fall unacceptably then the institutions will frequently favour either a boardroom coup or acquisition by an external bidder. The private shareholder's role in the governance of the company extends little further than being sent proxy forms for the Board's nominees, or, exceptionally, attending a routine annual shareholders' meeting. Employees and the communities in which firms operate have no specific rights in company law, and it places directors under no specific obligation to pay attention to their interests.

Corporate property enjoys very real privileges granted by the public power through company legislation. These privileges are available to any citizen who wishes to form a limited company, but they confer on private entities immense power. Without those privileges corporate power could not survive. First of these is limited liability, without which the World's stock markets would be empty. Second, is the grant of legal personality and the right of the company to hold property and act as a legal agent in its own right (distinct from its shareholders and servants). Third, as a consequence of corporate personality, is that managers enjoy certain legal immunities when acting as servants of the company.

Companies cannot be viewed as private bodies, as mere associations of citizens who have chosen to pool their property. Corporate property is a creature of particular laws and cannot be identified with property as such, as if any alteration of the terms of the former were an attack on the latter. The bulk of corporate wealth is made up of the holdings of financial institutions – the source of which is the financial assets of ordinary citizens. These assets are neither controlled nor owned as equities by most ordinary citizens: they are in the hands of pension fund trustees, or insurance company and unit trust fund managers. In many cases, as with pensions, these savings are a necessity and citizens take them for granted. They forget the immense power that their assets give to financial institutions and to other company managements nominally acting on behalf of shareholders. As Berle and Means (1932) recognized, responding to the way in which the defects of corporate regulation and corporate governance had contributed to the 1929 Crash in the USA, the divorce of ownership and control conferred on corporate managements powers that are better compared to those of feudal barons than of merely private associations of citizens. The divorce of ownership and control might be better described as the effective possession of the company's assets by the management. Citizens as holders of financial assets, as employees, as customers or as members of communities, have little or no right to intervene in corporate governance. In that sense corporations remain autocracies, and some can be tyrannies for their employees, regulating every aspect of their lives.

Corporations are too powerful to be regarded as private associations, but rather than be nationalized or subjected to worker control, they need to be made into bodies that are 'public' to those involved in them, to be governed by the participation of their stakeholders. Companies need to be encouraged by public policy to evolve into self-governing associations that are sufficiently representative of their stakeholders to continue to enjoy the privileges of corporate status. But how can corporate power be subjected to citizen control? Are not many companies too huge to be effectively governed by particular constituencies of workers or by local communities? Are not some companies, including many of the most important, multi-national and beyond the regulation of any particular state? Will it ever be politically possible to re-regulate such companies and democratize their governance? Surely, this would inspire fear of a socialist takeover?

New structures of corporate governance

For the moment we shall lay the issue of political possibility of such change on one side and consider the questions of how corporations might be governed, might be restructured so as to be made governable, or might be sidestepped altogether.

What is clear is that associationalism requires a more complex and long-lasting process of reform of corporate governance than that envisaged only a few years ago when the central issue for those advocating change was the representation of the workers' interests. For those purposes a single industrial democracy statute might suffice, such as that envisaged in the British Labour government's Bullock Report of 1977. In that document union representatives were to be elected to company management boards in equal numbers with shareholders' appointees, and were to be balanced by a number of community representatives agreed by the two sides. One could not avoid drawing the conclusion that the latter were there simply to avoid a stalemate, and not primarily to represent a significant stakeholder interest in its own right. Similarly, representation was based upon the unions rather than democratic elections by the whole workforce, solely in order to appease the union interest rather than to further the democratic governance of companies. In what follows we assume two processes of change, an incremental growth of alternative structures, and a more focused programme of legislative action.

To begin with the former, there are a wide range of possible routes to incremental company democratization. These include the use of alternative financial institutions like regional investment banks, mutual manufacturing investment funds (non-profitmaking agencies that would be like building societies for manufacturing and attract ordinary citizens' deposits), and industrial credit unions (where non-profitmaking firms would bank their short-term trading surpluses and their funds not required for immediate investment). A population of cooperative firms would be built up by giving preference to new ventures that fitted a range of models of governance and by requiring existing firms to move in this direction if they wanted the benefit of mutual funds. Thus the building of mutual and alternative financial institutions would be crucial for the construction of an alternative cooperative manufacturing sector.

These funds would be greatly favoured by national legislation giving a privileged tax position for investors and for the institutions, provided the latter remained non-profitmaking. Given permissive legislation and perhaps some 'start-up' grants, existing institutions like building societies might set up branches in this area and other associations like churches might do so too. This would mean that rebuilding the institutions of economic ownership could proceed at a natural pace dictated by the level of energy and enthusiasm in civil society. It might well be, given the religious interest in ethical investment and the environmentalist interest in promoting the use of renewable resources and earth-conserving technologies, that this pace could be quite rapid and that success would be rapidly copied.

Legislation might also require firms that wished to take advantage of general tax advantages for manufacturing investment would have to comply with a number of democratizing conditions; as a bare minimum, to recognize trade unions and to give unions access to solicit members, to establish a codetermination machinery and a works council, and to establish an Employee Share Ownership Scheme (ESOP).

Transnational companies (TNCs) would have to be tackled rather differently in an incremental scheme, and one envisages that they would be put under pressure by public opinion in the advanced countries that are their major markets. It is probable that this pressure would be focused by concerned international associations that combine to campaign against such TNCs utilizing their global position to exploit low-wage workforces in less developed countries or permit serious environmental damage. We can already see from existing campaigns of this type that such firms will in the main be very vulnerable to bad publicity and will fear such boycotts.

One target of such international campaigning might be to get the most publicly-aware TNCs to accept the idea of an international corporate senate. A corporate senate is an advisory body composed of persons of unimpeachable integrity to whom management would bring major new plans for social vetting and to which the unions or campaigners in particular countries could appeal to air and to investigate their grievances. A corporate senate with no more than moral authority, and that dependent on corporate goodwill, may seem feeble, but in future such transnational corporations will need the goodwill of international public opinion and this device should not be spurned as mere window dressing.

Let us accept that this strategy of gradual mutualization can only work within nation states if a careful balancing act is practised, that enough power and fiscal autonomy is devolved to regional governments and other quasi-public agencies to support the growing cooperative and small-firm sector, whilst at the same time the national state retains enough power to regulate the activities of the biggest corporations. Big corporate power has required big government, in part to check it and in part to provide it with assistance, against international competitors in particular. If the Jeffersonian and Distributivist aim of diffusing the ownership of productive property remains valid, then it can only be accomplished by a state powerful enough to protect small property and to prevent big corporate power from enjoying monopoly privileges over it. Many associationalists were naive in believing that they could ignore the state. Many Labour Movement radicals were equally naive in believing that they could utilize nationalization and regulation by the central state as the main means to protect workers and their families. A pluralist state need not be a weak form of government, nor need the functionally-specific powers of a national level of government amount to omnicompetence and sovereignty. Pluralism thus allows for central regulatory powers, whilst also creating decentralized forms of governance. Associative democracy allows for government that is extensive in the scale of its operations but functionally limited in the scope of its powers. Within that limited scope it can have capacities as great and more effectively legitimated than the conventional nation states of today. Thus the existence of big corporations need not act as an insuperable block on strategies of the decentralization and federalization of power.

How might the public power charged with the task of regulating big corporations act to promote associational objectives within them? First, to outline some principles, such a government cannot dogmatically seek to convert all big companies into small mutual associations. Some economic activities *do* need to be carried out on a large scale. Second, a government committed to associative reform should encourage companies to follow their own strategies, to identify with the objectives of the reforms, and to see the benefits of doing so. Government needs to operate as far as possible with measures that are general to all corporations and as neutral as possible between them, rather than highly-targetted and discriminatory practices of regulation that will be as unpopular as, and as strongly resisted as, nationalization.

Thus anti-concentration legislation would be reinforced to prevent further mergers or take-overs, unless a convincing case could be made that they were in the public interest. Existing firms would be provided with incentives to deconcentrate wherever possible. Large firms – especially public utilities – would be required to introduce economic democracy measures either by legislation or to qualify for tax concessions and other benefits. Let us consider each of the possible institutional arrangements for these strategies in turn.

Many firms need to operate on a large-scale, but the larger and more complex the firm, the more difficult it is to envisage effective democratic input by interests other than senior management on the policy of the firm as a whole. However, firms often do not need to be as large as they happen to be for any given scale of operations. They are often carrying processes and activities that could be hived-off, and that as smaller units, could be more democratically governed.

The first aim of reforming governments committed to economic success and therefore open to associationalism should thus be to diffuse ideas about the institutional logic of pursuing 'quality' and the competitive advantage of doing so. Free consultancy services should be provided that stress the virtues of the more democratic and mutualist structures but which remain pragmatic about meeting business objectives.

Governments committed to reform should encourage and provide incentives for large companies to slim-down by deconcentrating, and should require all companies above a certain size (say 1000 employees) to carry out a decentralization audit (with appropriate external assessors) and to offer 'non-core' activities either to management–worker buy-outs or as contracted-out services. The aim would be to reduce firms to a core of absolutely necessary activities that must be under direct control (strategic management, R&D and crucial manufacturing operations), and to get to this level firms would follow a strategy either putting services out to external tender, with the requirement that they give preference to associatively-structured firms such as cooperatives, or offering peripheral activities up for management–worker buy-outs, or take-over by smaller mutual companies.

Another strategy would be to encourage firms to constellate their group structures, to adopt partnerships with other firms, to explore ongoing practices of cooperation with other firms, and to subscribe to or to co-finance specific-function services (such as an international dealership network or generic R&D). In this way firms could enjoy the advantages of the large-scale without incorporating them in a single management hierarchy.

If the democratization of companies were to become a fully legitimate objective with voting publics, and accepted widely in a number of advanced countries, then all large companies might be required to conform to new legal requirements for corporate governance. In particular, all firms that had failed to democratize and to actively restructure on their own behalf, and that were above a certain size (say 500 employees or $100 million capital) would be subject to legislation that aimed to change the way that they are run in a more associative direction.

In order to achieve this companies would be required to meet the following conditions:

- that they establish a two-tier board, including a Supervisory Board representing shareholders (one third shareholder representatives, one third employee representatives elected by secret ballot of individual employees, and one third community representatives – chosen from a list provided by regional or national bodies representative of consumers and other associations, and approved by a majority of the representatives of the first two groups), and that board would appoint the Management Board charged with the operational running of the company but answerable to the Supervisory Board;
- to place upon the members of both boards the legal duty to consider and to give due regard to the interests of shareholders, employees, consumers, the community and the environment when making decisions;
- that the Board institute a Works Council charged with the co-determination of company policy and below it a comprehensive system of participation involving all employees;
- that the company give a Japanese-style lifetime employment contract to all full-time employees with more than two years' service, and that it establish a single employee status with the same holidays, pension rights, terms of service and social facilities;
- that part-time employees be granted similar rights if they have worked for more than sixteen hours per week for two years and that the Management Board undertakes to ensure that employment practices are not devised to evade the legislation, directors being personally liable;

- that new share issues and mergers require a 60% majority of the Supervisory Board;
- that the company institute an ESOP.

In some countries these requirements would involve very little extension to company law. In other countries these requirements may appear draconian to managers who are used to exercising their prerogatives with little or no check. These requirements are little more than an amalgam of Japanese and German best practice and would not in themselves render firms uncompetitive. On the contrary, employment security would compel firms to be competitive, because it would reduce the easy option of laying-off workers. Workers would have security only while the firm was trading viably, and so they would have no reason to be complacent. Management would lose certain privileges, they would have to consult and their own activities would become more transparent. That would be a huge shock to many of Britain's managements, for example, who have enjoyed all the perogatives of control and also high salaries, whilst failing to deliver an internationally-competitive performance. Where the companies in question are privatised public utilities, with a new monopoly position with regard to the consumer, the perogatives of top management as they stand now in the UK are quite indefensible. In that case the interests of internal democratization and external regulation probably mesh together moderately well, as broadly representative Supervisory Boards are less likely to seek to profit at the consumers' expense.

Nevertheless, all of these reforms could easily be presented as an assault upon business. Supporters of economic liberalism are basically corporate apologists and believers in the principle that the managers of corporate hierarchies, with all the powers of central planners in their private empires, really do know best. We may be at a point when legitimacy of the defence of management privilege as if it were identical with the rights of private property is about to take a tumble. Authoritarian managers may be one of the main victims of the end of the Cold War. There is some prospect that issues of productive property and corporate governance may be depoliticized, in that they will in Carl Schmitts' terms cease to be the source of fundamental socio-political antagonisms. We are emerging from a century-long 'social war' as bitter as the religious wars of the sixteenth and seventeenth centuries.

Until recently to tamper with the structures of corporate power was to threaten private property, even though those structures were relatively recent products of legislation and the basic forms of private property long pre-dated them. The problem was that state socialism and specifically Soviet-style socialism compounded all forms of property. Socialism as 'class struggle' threatened to eliminate large and small propertyholders as an economic group, and socialism as 'revolution' threatened the abrogation of individual political rights. Those threats were cemented into the global conflict of the Eastern and Western blocs. The fear of a superpower committed to objectives wholly contrary to those of Western citizens united all social groups, from the most powerful manager to the average householder with some savings. Property and democracy were both threatened, and so to alter the former in any significant way was to weaken the latter. Anyone who was not a 'proletarian', i.e. almost anyone, could fear for both their property and their liberty under socialism. Hence the greatest concentrations of unaccountable economic power (both personal and corporate) could enjoy mass support through the defence of existing property rights.

If citizens can be convinced that corporate wealth is in the main *their* wealth in another guise, that it is too little accountable to them and managed by people who seldom take their interests as workers, pensioners or small savers into account, and that some other equally partisan interest will not rise to power in consequence of changes in corporate governance, then the prospects for the reform of corporations are better than they have been since they were created by legislation. Corporations are not like voluntary self-governing associations, since most of those directly involved in them or indirectly subject to their decisions have no say. Corporate structures can only enjoy the autonomy of 'civil society' if they in fact belong to it, if they cease to be autocratic and unaccountable to the majority of those who are members in fact, but at present have no rights to participate in their governance. The problem for top managers in a post-state socialist era is that they are few in number, and that even a great many executives in subsidiary companies might welcome a reform that enhanced autonomy.

In the UK, at least, survey data show that the public has low expectations of the behaviour of company managements and that their actions have little legitimacy. The Fifth Report of the *British*

Social Attitudes survey (1988) shows the public to be distinctly sceptical. When asked to 'suppose a large company *had* to choose between: doing something that improves pay and conditions for its staff; *or* doing something that increases profits', respondents showed a low opinion of managers – 80 per cent thought the firm would act to increase profits, while 69 per cent would personally choose to improve pay and conditions for staff. When questioned further, 52 per cent of respondents thought profits should go to new investment in the firm, but only 41 per cent expected managements to do this; only 3 per cent favoured extra benefits to shareholders and managers, against 34 per cent who expected firms to increase dividends, and a further 21 per cent who expected a bonus to top management.

The Ninth Report of the *British Social Attitudes* survey (1992) confirms that these attitudes have remained relatively stable. When asked where 'a large profit in a particular year' *would* go, 54 per cent replied that firms would distribute them as dividends or as bonuses for senior management whereas only 3 per cent thought profit *should* go to that source. Similarly only 28 per cent thought profits *would* go on investment, and 42 per cent thought that they should. When asked who benefits and who *should* benefit from the profits made by British firms, the response was: 90 per cent thought shareholders and managers do benefit, whilst only 18 per cent thought shareholders should benefit, and only 3 per cent directors, whilst 44 per cent thought employees should benefit, and 32 per cent the public generally (1992: 135–6).

One must always be highly suspicious about the political payoff of attitude data, this comes from a country where dividend levels are exceptionally high and where directors' salaries and bonuses have received considerable publicity. However, the underlining attitudes of the public hardly seem hostile or contrary to associationalist values. The British public, at least, seems to see companies as national institutions performing a service to society, and, therefore, fulfilling public obligations. Firms are expected to provide work and to sustain national prosperity, not just make a profit for their shareholders (whoever they happen to be). This is after more than a decade of the Government's extremely active advocacy of management's perogatives and an enterprise culture.

The public will probably begin to support even radical reforms that diffuse power, and will oppose changes that concentrate it or give too much influence to one interest. In that sense associationalism is very much in tune with the new democratic spirit abroad in the world. For if publics throughout the world are gloomy about the economy, and see few economic alternatives, they remain strongly in favour of democracy and enhanced autonomy for the individual citizen. The reform of corporate structures through associational democracy makes sense in that context since it is against top-down authority, against concentrated power without the defence of strict economic necessity, and in favour of participation by all shareholders. It is thus quite unlike the 'workers' control' that has raised fears of unchecked producer power and has consistently failed to win widespread public support.

The unions as associations

But what about the trade unions? Surely, they as large organizations have much to fear from the growth of self-governing associations in the world of work? Would it not render their defence of workers' rights and the negotiation of wages and conditions obsolete? Might not a system in which ownership and wage labour gradually began to fuse, in which many workers draw a significant portion of their income through their assets as shareholders, make unions a thing of the past, since they are a consequence of the wages system? The answer is that unions would still have a role to play. For the long foreseeable future the great majority of workers would still receive the main part of their income as wages. Even in a system in which workers had strong incentives to remain with the firm, few workers would wish to be inescapably bound to it and without the security and the bargaining power that a labour market organized and regulated by both law and union activity allows.

Wage determination would remain important. It would need to be institutionalized to correspond to a change to associational economic governance. Wage determination could well take place at three levels in an associative economy:

1   national bargaining between the major interests – the state, conventional employer's representatives, federations of associations and

the unions – leading to a fixed-term accord for overall pay norms;

2 regional councils in which public bodies, associations and unions operate arbitration machinery to settle disputes about the application of norms to groups of workers – at this level unions would also cooperate to ensure the provision of collective services such as training for firms and workers in the region;

3 unions would ensure the firm's compliance with laws governing labour contracts and ensure that internal representative arrangements were democratically arrived at.

There would be a legal right to strike, but the combination of internal self-government in firms and the unions' participation in collaborative institutions of supra-firm wage determination would be designed to make strikes measures of last resort. The system of self-government in firms would be based on free votes of individual employees rather than through the union branches, thus maintaining the unions' independence and also preventing them from taking control of firms' internal decision-making procedures. Unions would therefore remain voluntary bodies to which individual workers could choose to subscribe. Like every other association they would be required to meet minimum legal standards of democratic self-governance. They would strive to enforce fair contracts for employees so that firms could not create 'labour rackets' under the cover of self-government.

In the associational welfare system we will consider in Chapter 7, the unions could greatly extend their role as providers of welfare and other services compared with their position today. Unions would be eligible to get funds under the 'write-in' provisions the individual's taxes, to receive funds proportional to membership and to bid for projects from the reserves. Unions would potentially control very large funds to use for the benefit of their members. They could also contribute to training policy through co-determination machinery, and perhaps control training funds and offer training themselves. The benefits of belonging to a union would be very real for members. Unions would provide benefits as associations in civil society and directly organize welfare. The unions would directly carry out policy instead of campaigning for it to be done by the state, and they would be directly responsible to their own membership for the success of that policy. They would have to compete with non-socialist associations like churches in providing welfare.

Unions would not, however, directly organize or own production (such activities would be *ultra vires* under associational law). Thus associationalism would be quite unlike syndicalism. Workers would be free to not join unions, and the various self-government procedures of firms would be independent of the unions. Workers, therefore, would not be compelled to be part of a rigid top-down corporatist structure, and unions would have to win and keep members to ensure influence. Workers would have their union to protect them if for some reason a firm became riven by factional strife or dominated by a management clique. They would also have unions to ensure that their job rates, skill classifications and training were protected. Unions would have an interest in and would help to maintain labour mobility and, therefore, the liberty of the worker.

This account has tried to claim a good deal for the capacity of associative reforms to regenerate economic activity, that by enhancing the structure of social governance of the economy it would promote those forms of non-market coordination and cooperation that are essential to sustain market performance. At the same time one need not claim too much for associationalism. Associationalism is part supplement and part substitute, how much it is of either depends on political feasibility and on the extent to which such reforms are required. Associationalism seeks to create a 'civil society' worthy of the name, in which the division between the public and the private spheres is transformed, in which governance extends beyond the state into the wider society, and in which the centralization and hierarchical direction of the state are reduced to the bare minimum. In such a 'civil society' individual rights and the principle of choice are protected, the blurring of the public–private division does not lead to greater state compulsion or intrusion into the private realm. At the same time the capacity of society to govern itself, through cooperation and through participation in voluntary associations, is enhanced. Greater economic governance is possible without an extension of the powers of the 'sovereign state' and its bureaucratic agencies.

6

Thick Welfare, Thin Collectivism

Narratives of collectivist welfare

For the better part of a century, the growing and changing bundle of public services denoted by the term 'welfare' has been identified with state provision by supporters and critics alike. This identification is built in to the conventional narratives of the rise of the welfare state.[1] The dominant account that prevailed into the 1970s was strongly pro-welfare and could be seen as a social democratic variant of the Whig interpretation of history. This chronicles the magnificent journey whereby, as reform succeeded reform, we arrived at that largely satisfactory state which is the present. The narrative begins with the replacement of the old social order by the era of *laissez faire*. The market becomes the dominant form of social organization and is protected by the nightwatchman state. Liberalism allows all competent citizens to fend for themselves by their own efforts and enterprise. Public provision is made to paupers only, and on terms of dire necessity and at a standard sufficient only to sustain life. However, neither the liberal state nor the market could cope with the social consequences of rapid industrialization, urbanization and the breakdown of traditional communities and statuses. Hence the inevitability of collectivism, that is, the development of public services provided as of right to citizens and organized by the state; these services being

1 A broad definition of the 'welfare state' is used here, including a wide range of publicly-provided services such as education and health as well as transfer payments and income support.

funded either through taxation or compulsory social insurance schemes.

There were always counter views that saw the rise of comprehensive state welfare less as a magnificent journey, than as the steady imposition of a collectivist yoke. Hilaire Belloc's *The Servile State* (1913) saw in the British Liberal Government's social insurance legislation of 1911 a fundamental threat to liberty. In a society based predominantly on wage labour, the working class became the new helotry; as workers lacking independent means, they are defined as of a particular status and regulated through the mechanism of social insurance legislation. Belloc feared that the New Liberalism had become illiberal and would ensure the welfare of the state's subjects at the price of their freedom, forcing them to submit to compulsory regulation in wider and wider areas of life. Belloc's answer was Distributivism, to ensure through the widest possible distribution of productive property, the means of providing one's 'welfare' whilst earning one's livelihood. Friedrich Hayek's *The Road to Serfdom* (1944) is not specifically an anti-welfare tract, but is an argument against planning. It saw in Western liberal societies the seeds of a drift toward collectivism that posed a threat to the allocative efficiency of the market and to the liberal state. Hayek accepted the need for social insurance and limited institutions for the relief of poverty. But he feared the assumption of state omnicompetence and the provision for every social need by state action. A comprehensive welfare and public service state cannot but interfere with the market and civil society. Its officials are ineluctably driven to promote the expansion of such a state at the expense of private freedom. Comprehensive welfare and measures to ensure economic security at the expense of markets are thus but a way-station to a full command economy and the death of the liberal order. Belloc and Hayek were both eloquent and influential writers but there is about their works the air of a desperate last-minute protest against the inevitable. Both see collectivism as a growing menace, but also as the dominant political trend. Utilitarian bureaucrats are taking freedom from the people in the name of administered welfare, and the people are too doped by the drug of a secure life for them to protest. Welfare collectivism was not in fact the road to serfdom, nor did it contribute to the growing power of Communism, quite the reverse.

As historiography, neither the pro- nor the anti-welfare state narratives will hold water. The point worth retaining from this story of the rise of welfare collectivism is that the most diverse political forces could attach themselves to, promote and utilize the ideas and institutions of comprehensive state welfare. Hence the tone of despair of the opponents of statism and collectivism. They felt embattled against an idea supported across the political spectrum from extreme conservatives to radical socialists. Moreover, this constellation of diverse ideologies and parties around the institutions of the welfare state meant that the institutions could grow steadily and persist through changing political conjunctures and despite the victory or defeat of one political party or another. Thus the institutions grew through, and often despite, the diverse rationales offered for them and the different strategies they were supposed to embody, and they developed in ways that, therefore, escaped those rationales and strategies.

Collectivist welfare grew steadily because, far from being an orphan, it was claimed as the child of many political parents. Conservatives were early, if pragmatic, exploiters of social legislation, state unemployment and sickness insurance provision, and state public services. They saw the need for the preservation of the social order *against* the market. Regulation of the market posed few problems for aristocratic and authoritarian conservatives, who saw the state in a more exalted role than as the minimalist guardian of a market society. Ruling elites could also easily find non-egalitarian rationales for collectivistic welfare and redistribution. They shared with other political groupings the rhetoric of 'national efficiency'. A large, healthy and competent populace was a precondition for survival in the competition between nations, in commerce and in war. Whether at the front or in the factory, the ordinary citizen would in fact serve the state better if he or she were healthy, adequately fed, properly housed and literate. Such social engineering, conceding a place 'albeit a subordinate one' in society to the worker, might well be sufficient to contain the challenge of revolution and socialistic collectivism.

Social liberals provided a more coherent rationale for collectivism and welfare, and, in general, did so earlier and more comprehensively than most European socialists. Most of the latter remained at least notionally committed to the solution of the problems of poverty, unemployment, poor housing, etc., through the reconstruction of society on the basis of comprehensive public ownership well into the twentieth century. The English New Liberals developed early on an elaborate rationale for intervention in markets, one that was seen as a means of maintenance of the market system itself. Unregulated markets could not of themselves deliver enough of goods like education or health to enough of the people to ensure a sustainable economic and social order. Market failure in the 'social' field threatened the efficiency and the very survival of the market system itself. Moreover, there were utilitarian advantages in collectivism – collective provision through the state would be both economical and uniform in its delivery, ensuring common standards of service at low cost. A measure of equality promoted social efficiency as well as social justice, enabling individuals to be more productive than if they were unaided by public support. Furthermore, all this could be accomplished without too much redistribution; state organized and underwritten insurance schemes would enable the mass of the employed population to protect themselves against a wide range of contingencies without an excessively heavy burden on general taxation.

As the twentieth century wore on Social democrats and non-revolutionary socialists increasingly appropriated and expanded this social liberal strategy. Increasingly, they came to see the welfare state as the core and most comprehensive feature of their socialism, far more important than the partial nationalization of industry. The combination of comprehensive and universal welfare provision with redistributive direct taxation came to be seen as the means to ensure social equality. The strategy of promoting equality through welfare became the ideological core of democratic socialism in the West, once it became clear that the socialization of the means of production as a whole was an impossibility within the constraints imposed by liberal-democratic parliamentary government. Indeed, the provision of welfare was seen as redefining that state, the role of welfare was to be as the capstone of the new mass democracy. To legal and political equality that gave the same rights of formal citizenship to all were to be added state-secured entitlements to the means to a decent life that made each person an independent social citizen. In the concept of 'citizenship' of T.H. Marshall (1949), the welfare state came to embody both a political ideal and a strategy of social provision. Democratic socialists were convinced that only comprehensive *state* welfare could ensure universal and uniform provision. Thus the growth of state provision was identified with the pursuit of an egalitarian strategy. It was not just a means to relieve poverty or to tackle social problems, it became the core of the political project to even out power and influence in society through the equalization of the conditions of living. The paradigmatic text of the new revisionism, C.A.R. Crosland's *The Future of Socialism* (1956), made the pursuit of equality the defining feature of modern socialism, and the provision of welfare services and redistribution were the means whereby equality was to be attained.

Welfare states developed and functioned in ways that seldom corresponded to the political rationales, or realized the strategic objectives of these diverse political forces or ideologues who claimed them for their own. Thus, on the conservative side, Bismarck's promotion of social insurance schemes in late nineteenth-century Germany can hardly be said to have been more effective in containing the growth of the SPD than were his anti-socialist laws. On the socialist side, the post-1945 British welfare state could hardly be said to embody Marshall's or Crosland's vision. It neither promoted a major redistribution of income and wealth, nor did the pattern of its welfare services show much evidence that a 'strategy' of equality had informed the shaping of their provision (Le Grand, 1982).

Be that as it may, by the post-1945 period most modern Western states had collectivist systems of welfare provision, some far more comprehensive and universalist than others. These systems and public spending generally expanded during the long post-war boom and then began to experience severe difficulties as unemployment and inflation both rose substantially. Soon after this the political 'consensus' over mass state welfare was shattered. However, it was always less a true consensus about objectives and values than a common acceptance of the same institutions for divergent political purposes.

The intellectual challenge to comprehensive and universal welfare provision came from a new and revitalized economic liberalism. If growth could not be programmed, if it was uncertain and volatile, then every effort had to be made to protect the non-state, supply-side, sources of growth, and, in particular, to minimize the burden of direct taxation on private sector incomes. Welfare expenditure by the state was simply a drag on the wealth-creating power of the economy. If possible, general public expenditure was to be cut as a percentage of GDP. Many economic liberals argued that welfare merely converted its recipients into clients and prevented them becoming active, wealth-creating, economic agents.

Economic liberalism and the 'culture of contentment'

The seventies ended throughout the 'Anglo-Saxon' world in particular, with a determined intellectual and political assault on the welfare state. In the UK, USA, Australia and New Zealand more or less sustained efforts were made by both labour and conservative governments to curb the growth in public spending on welfare and to rationalize provision on economic liberal lines. By now it is clear that such economic liberal solutions to welfare problems are in ruins: they have not improved service delivery or quality, they have not tackled the perceived problem of an 'underclass' trapped in a 'dependency culture', and they have not contributed to increasing the rate of economic growth by reducing the overall tax burden on the mass of income earners.

The economic liberal agenda has lost some of its intellectual legitimacy in the face of these failures, but the mass attitudes that have provided political legitimacy for free market quick-fix solutions still remain. The economic rationalizers were the members or the servants of democratically elected governments. The rich can hardly vote their own party into office, rather it is a significant number of middle and lower income earners, the supposed beneficiaries of welfare state provision who vote for parties that promise lower taxes and that try to contain public spending on welfare.

J.K. Galbraith's *The Culture of Contentment* (1992) has provided a straightforward and widely accepted explanation for the failure of redistributionist and welfare politics. The post-war mixture of sustained economic growth and welfare spending provided the means for the majority to escape into relatively comfortable and 'middle class' conditions, where in consequence collectivist solutions seem to them less necessary. The new mass middle class are reluctant to make major sacrifices for that socially containable and politically ineffectual minority who have not benefitted in the same way. Welfare states are thus the victims of their own past successes. There is an element of truth in this thesis, but it neglects the extent to which people are not just tax resistant, and underplays the fact that they also have other good reasons not to support simply spending more on existing forms of bureaucratic state welfare. The real problem is that supporters of the extension of state welfare services have been unable to come up with a clear new strategy that encompasses reforms to both funding and service delivery. Rather they have sought to break down public resistance to 'more of the same' by moralizing and the patronage of possessing superior principles. Resistance will only be overcome by new ideas that inspire people, and not by schoolteacherly social democratic exhortation to be altruistic and pay-up.

If we look at the main problems that limit public willingness to be taxed for welfare provision they are threefold:

1   throughout the Anglo-Saxon world we find the deadly combination of uncertain growth and high expectations of private consumption on the part of the mass of the employed – the result is resistance to taxation, although survey evidence in the UK also shows that a substantial majority would prefer high standards of welfare services and health to be publicly provided at low direct cost to the consumer;
2   that people are widely resistant to the bureaucratic deformations of mass welfare services (administrative discretion, low public accountability and the absence of a 'consumer' culture in the provision of services) – people do not want to be supplicants, to have to wait and to be treated rudely in squalid circumstances;
3   that the alleged benefits of national public services – fairness and equal treatment – are by no means apparent to consumers or available in fact, there is considerable variability in the way services are delivered between regions and households in most countries, thus 'national' services are by no means uniform (for example, there were marked disparities in provision between regions in the pre-1979 NHS in the UK) nor are 'universal' benefits equally distributed, or specific services and benefits effectively targeted at those most in need.

The problem that most supporters of a social democratic mass welfare ethic fail to accept is that state bureaucracies do not empower citizens. The vast majority of citizens expect to be treated as articulate, sensible individuals in charge of their own affairs and not as objects of tutelage. Yet state welfare bureaucracies habitually patronize and at worse demean a high proportion of recipients of their services. In the UK, for example, post-1945 local authority housing involved many absurd and humiliating restrictions on tenants, one could not even paint one's front door the colour one pleased.

Is the problem welfare or the state?

The position is, therefore, one of stalemate. Social democrats have no new ideas and the public will not trust them simply to spend public money on more of the old services. Economic liberals have failed to revitalize or transform stagnant welfare states that survive – underfunded and ineffective – in the absence of anything better. How can the deadlock be broken?

Before we can answer that question, we must tackle another one which is presupposed by it. Should we be concerned with revitalizing state welfare? If welfare states have grown up piece-meal and to a large extent independently of the rationales of their diverse political sponsors, then surely we should treat them merely as a social fact and not seek to add new rationales and strategies to existing ones? This response surely will not do. Welfare states have come to encompass a large part of that which the vast majority of human beings value – the education of their children, the preservation and restoration of their health, the maintenance of the aged and the sustenance of the poor. Societies did these things to the best of their ability before there was a generalized market society or there were modern welfare states and we could hardly cease to do them to the best of our ability and resources without sinking into barbarism.

Yet here is the central problem of modern welfare states, that they appropriate to officials and bureaucracies things that the common people have in the past done for themselves. The people gave to charity to relieve the poor, they ran local schools from parish fees, they cared for elderly relatives. Now they pay taxes or receive state benefits, and bureaucratically administered institutions provide the services. This is not to say that all bureaucracy is inherently alienating or that all welfare personnel must be cynical and uncaring, quite the contrary. Many welfare state institutions were established with high ideals of disinterested and benevolent service, and many doctors and teachers or attendants in old people's homes do act out of an ethic of service and give a high quality of attention of their clients. The NHS in Britain still has a very high reputation with the vast majority of the population for this very reason, and because most people value the principle of free access on the basis of need. The issue is one of citizens' involvement with and responsibility for these services.

In fact, however good or bad the service delivery personnel are, citizens have little access to these institutions other than in the capacity of clients, as objects of administration. They have no control over the content or the delivery of welfare services. The result is that they relate to them as passive consumers when they receive a service, and not at all when it is provided to others outside their own immediate family circle. Because they have no say in the service they do not see themselves as helping to provide welfare for others, as they did when they gave or now give charity directly to the poor. Bureaucracy takes away citizens' responsibility and numbs their response to the need of others.

The purpose of the foregoing is not as the preamble to a plea to recreate the pre-modern pre-industrial face-to-face community in which social life was simple and spontaneous. That is both crassly unimaginative and impossible. It is, however, essential to create circumstances in which the consumers of welfare have far more capacity to determine and shape what is provided. Only in that case will they identify fully with the services in question. Is it possible to have collective consumption of welfare services without the collectivism that accompanies state provision? Collective consumption and provision on the basis of need are both economical and fair. Markets as the sole basis for provision of health, education, care of the elderly, etc., will leave large numbers in dire need, and the majority uncertain of their long-term prospects even if they stay in well-paid work. The problem is to devise a form of collective consumption that does not alienate control and responsibility from the individual.

Thus we do need to approach the problem of the welfare state afresh and to consider whether the primary problem lies with welfare or the state? Welfare is necessary once we remember what it is – our children educated, the sick cared for – and do not look at it merely as a share of GDP or as a slice of our tax demand.

Bureaucratized and centralized welfare encourages us to do the latter. That is because the modern state is too large, too centralized and too remote. We need to go back and question the link that began to be established a century ago between welfare and the state. We need to question whether some fusion is not possible between the voluntary and decentralized approach, which lost out to state welfare, and the conception of comprehensive well-funded public services, which the national state appeared to provide and localism and mutual aid could not? The economic liberals have questioned the link between welfare and the state, but only to question welfare and to deny it any role other than that of a minimum safety-net for the very poor. The time has come to question the state, the better to promote welfare.

An associationalist welfare system

The answer as to how the deadlock can be broken is deceptively simple and can be summed-up in two sentences:

1 to devolve the provision of public welfare and other services to voluntary self-governing associations;
2 to enable such associations to obtain public funds to provide such services for their members.

It will be obvious that this is to transfer the associationalist principle to the field of welfare. This is not done out of an urge to consistency or dogmatism, but because associationalism has a vital role to play in resolving the specific dilemmas of welfare state provision. If that were not the case, it would be perfectly possible to rely on associative governance in certain other social fields and leave core welfare activities as bureaucratic services managed or overseen by the central state. Associationalism does not operate on the principle of take-it-all or leave-it-entirely.

Associationalism is a scheme of social governance. Its fundamental objective is to renew and democratize modern societies by transforming the division of the public and private spheres. It publicizes civil society and pluralizes the state. Governance of activities is devolved to associations, this makes the 'private' a sphere of social cooperation and collective governance through voluntary bodies. At the same time the 'public' sphere becomes the association of associations, that is, the mechanism for providing both the rules and the funds that enable the various self-governing private institutions to work.

I have argued that associationalism can deliver all the libertarian political benefits economic liberals claim to seek from the market without the same scale of economic costs and injustices that unregulated markets impose. It also offers the benefits of voluntarism and mutualism without the problems of funding and the extreme variability of service delivery that localized self-help and charity was held to involve by the advocates of centralized collectivist welfare earlier this century. Associationalism is an idea that simultaneously proposes solutions to the problems of funding, service delivery and citizens' involvement that is attractive to those citizens seeking greater autonomy, that is easy to understand in principle, and which neatly explodes the terms of the conflict between economic liberalism and welfare collectivism.

Associationalism offers first of all extended governance *without* big government. Economic liberalism fostered the delusion that the answer to over-extended and unaccountable government was deregulation, the result has been the unwanted and unintended consequences of 'free' markets in welfare. Governance is essential: modern industrial societies need extensive policing to ensure that acceptable standards are set and complied with. This is true even in straightforward commercial transactions where consumers have to be able to trust the honesty of the vendor and know that they can obtain relief through public agencies if that trust proves to be unfounded. The problem is govern*ment* not gover*nance*. Government becomes too big, too multi-form and too bureaucratic in struggling to cope with all of those diverse tasks that complex modern societies of necessity impose.

The advantages of self-governing voluntary agencies rather than state bureaucracies in welfare are threefold: first, personnel will be more committed to an agency with whose principles they are in agreement and which is chosen by them as a place of work for that reason; second, self-governing voluntary associations will be internally accountable to their members, this ensures a first-line form of policing of service delivery by members and reduces the load of inspection and rule-setting on the state; third, the delivery of welfare services through voluntary agencies effects a separation between the service provider and the state as the 'governor of governors', whereas at present the state is in the contradictory position of providing services through its bureaucratic agencies and also acting as the guarantor of the standard of those services.

In the second place, associationalism offers *thick* welfare, *thin* collectivism. Bureaucratic collectivist delivery of welfare typically entails high administrative discretion on the part of providers and low consumer choice. For that reason it is less and less attractive to the even moderately successful. Market-based insurance schemes can hardly serve as the general answer to this problem. They can assure a high and uniform level of welfare provision only in a society of mass affluence, that does not have a substantial pool of long-term unemployed and that lacks a significant underclass. Even then, market-based systems entail serious distortions in provision due to strong financial incentives for suppliers to over-deliver services.

Associationalism, by contrast, both promotes consumer choice and, because of the joint producer-consumer self-governance of associations, also provides a mutual check on the tendencies to over-consume and to over-produce that are inherent in any form of decentralized welfare provision. In such a system individuals can craft the package of services that they need. This is because of the high level of choice in the type and mode of services on offer, due to the fact that service providers are voluntary organizations in competition and that their provision is mainly demand led. Consumers have a large element of choice in the services they receive, but also considerable discretion in determining the overall level of funding for them. Thus when it comes to paying for services, individuals will tend to behave differently from how they do now. Employed consumers with a substantial disposable income will have high discretion in controlling what public welfare services they get, and, therefore, will be willing to accept higher taxation if services meet their perceived needs and offer good value compared to private provision. The poor will get common minimum entitlements, but still will be able to choose which agencies should fulfil them. The system is not egalitarian, but it would tend to promote higher overall welfare spending and would incline most individuals toward meeting their needs through collective consumption. Welfare expenditures would tend to rise to the extent that consumers see *they* can control services and that they benefit from consuming collectively. Associationalist structures thus have the potential to unblock the tax constraint on welfare spending, since they take the responsibility for making service provision decisions from the state and place it in the hands of the consumers.

Associationalism is a well-established idea and its principles are easy to understand. Why then has it not already gained widespread acceptance as the new basis for welfare systems? The answer is because it is not a technical quick-fix solution. It requires fundamental changes in the forms of authority predominant in both state and civil society.

Social democrats tend to be hostile to associationalism because it lessens the power of the state. They remain committed to their perception that only the state can offer true welfare, because it is supposed to be able to deliver universal and uniform benefits. This is an illusion, no system of welfare can ensure, over the long run, equality and uniformity between localities and types of household.

An associationalist welfare system involves a quite different political principle. It offers greater empowerment, rather than the illusory hope of equality of outcomes, as the means to the goal of social justice. It recognizes that such empowerment cannot come from state centralism and the inevitable bureaucracy that accompanies it, but only from decentralization and a degree of popular control. An associationalist welfare state would be decentralized and pluralistic, it would be divided into self-governing regions, into distinct and competing voluntary associations, and into different functionally-distinct service sectors. No single agency would have omnicompetent control over all the others, rather at best a limited and functionally-specific power of inspection, rule-setting or funding. This political model looks messy to statists because of the inherent weakness of top-down control in such a federative system.

However, as we noted earlier, not only are the advantages of centralized sovereign state power more apparent than real, but the pressures sustaining state centralism have lessened and the forces inclining toward more federative and plural organization have strengthened. The problem for social democrats is that the nation state has lost a good deal of its centrality as the main economic and social regulator – and yet it is essential to their project of a uniform and comprehensive national welfare state.

We have also seen that the pressures toward regional economic regulation and the regionalization of economic activity have grown apace. The divisions of the levels of prosperity *within* nations are as substantial as those between them. If nation states are loosing salience upwards to economic blocs like the European Community, and downwards to regionalist practices of economic regulation and regional sources of citizen identity, then the project of a 'uniform' national welfare state is undermined – in Europe at least. Italy offers the clearest example of the regionalist rejection of national redistribution. The regional autonomist Northern Leagues protest that the south of Italy produces 25 per cent of GDP and consumes 49 per cent of it.

The only possible long-run answer to this crisis of national states in Europe is a federalist solution, in which EC, national and regional governments accept specific and partial functions in welfare. The EC would set minimum framework standards for social welfare. It would then effect the supra-national redistribution between richer and poorer regions to meet them. Regions would then be free to determine welfare policies consistent with their explicit political objectives and their underlying economic performance. At present this is unlikely since national governments are unwilling to concede such redistributive powers to Brussels, and such common welfare standards that do exist are well below the standards of the richer nations.

The real problem for economic liberals in accepting associationalism is not their addiction to the free market, rather it is their commitment to a strong central state that protects market freedoms (and in particular ensures that there is no political or social obstruction of the market from local government or voluntary associations like labour unions) and their commitment to the corporate dominance of economic and social provision. The two go together, centralized state power and top-down corporate management. Decentralization and the principle of self-governing voluntary associations are threats to economic liberals (with a few honourable and genuinely libertarian exceptions), because the freedoms they really value are those for corporations to act in weakly-regulated markets. Modern economic liberalism is passionately addicted to management, and convinced that top-down authority and hierarchy are the only routes to social efficiency.

Economic liberals are also centralists and anti-federalists because they seek tightly centralized monetary and fiscal control.

A genuinely federal system would leave regions considerable autonomy in their tax levels, their levels of public borrowing, and the extent of their public service provision. It might be thought that the best solution for economic liberals would be to endorse a form of negative federalism, in which richer regions had no responsibility to contribute funds to poorer ones. The problem is that such cynical federalism would quickly fail if the poorer regions had genuine autonomy and political voice. The advantage of centralized states for economic liberals is that tight budgetary control can limit the extent of inter-regional redistribution, and yet concentrated power prevents the poorer regions doing much about it.

Associationalism would be a radical change because it would empower citizens and it would break-up the current ossified private hierarchies that ensure that most of civil society is a domain of authority and not of freedom. The citizen, at work and in purchasing private welfare (insurance), is at the mercy of largely unaccountable corporations. Associationalism, by beginning to restore citizen power to civil society, would threaten corporate dominance. Associationalism has not been seized upon as a solution to contemporary welfare problems because it is radical: too decentralist for social democratic conservatives wedded to the nation state, and too democratic for corporate apologists in the guise of economic liberals. It might, therefore, appear to be marginal, except for the facts that existing doctrines of social organization are bankrupt, that the problems of providing and paying for welfare are very real, and that it is implausible that sophisticated and individuated publics in industrialized societies will continue to accept passively the existing patterns of authority forever.

Associationalism has the advantage that it can be added slowly and experimentally to existing welfare states as a limited principle of renewal and reform. It is not just another slick idea for funding, since it offers both recipients and providers of welfare a say in its governance and delivery. It is also compatible with a variety of methods of funding and can co-exist with those elements of collectivism and bureaucracy that are inevitable and inescapable. However, the basic principles of mainstream associationalist welfare provision must be laid down. Associationalism will always be attacked as impractical and utopian if, that is, one does not show that it could form a complete and satisfactorily functioning welfare system in and of itself. In the absence of such a demonstration it can hardly be effective as a principle of reform, since people will have little idea of what they may be moving towards as they use this principle more and more. Only the practical can be truly inspirational.

In what follows it will be assumed that we are describing the welfare state of a fully-developed associationalist society, where governance is federal and by region, and functional and by association. In the course of presenting the welfare state we shall, in fact, describe the institutions of the associationalist commonwealth and its taxation and legal systems. It must be emphasized that there is an element of arbitrariness in this. The same principles could be developed with other institutions. Associationalist institutions could be developed with less emphasis on the principles of equality of service and access on the basis of need. The model I have created grafts federalist and associationalist institutions onto principles that are closer to those of social democratic supporters of welfare than they might at first suppose. Whilst a national uniform welfare state is no longer the goal, provision is not primarily dictated by ability to pay and access to key services, like health, is on the basis of need.

The trouble with conservative decentralization

This is important to emphasize because it is necessary to differentiate associationalist conceptions of welfare very strongly from, for example, the various initiatives of Britain's Conservative Government to decentralize certain services such as education and health. The problem with these initiatives is the partiality of the decentralization and the lack of democratic accountability in the component units. The result is a decline in social governance that is seldom matched by gains in economic efficiency on the social scale.

The British government pursued two main programmes in the early 1990s. In education the main initiative is Local Management of Schools (LMS). This enables schools to become formula-funded self-governing entities largely independent of Local Education Authorities (LEAs). In health, the creation of an 'internal market' in the NHS aims to create a separation between agencies purchasing public health care in bulk, the Health Authorities (HAs), and the hospitals providing it. Trust Hospitals are encouraged to opt out of Health Authority control and become self-governing corporate entities. Schools and hospitals are locally managed, but this gives them at best limited autonomy as the central government reserves its powers both to control the funding framework and also every detail of their operations. The British government continues to run a centralized command economy in welfare, whilst talking the rhetoric of local control, consumer choice and the market.

Control has been appropriated almost exclusively to top-down management. Teachers and health workers have no say as of right in how their affairs are conducted. They are to be the objects of hierarchical administration, not partners in an association. The governing bodies of these organizations, to which management is nominally responsible, do not adequately represent either service providers or consumers.

Such organizations amount to privatization within the welfare state. They are removed from LEA or HA control, but are subject to no public control other than that of central government. Had the Conservatives had as their main aim the discrediting of the idea of decentralization, they could hardly have made a better job of it. They have hijacked the rhetoric of local control and consumer choice, whilst wrecking it in practice. However, the Conservatives may not have set back the associationalist agenda in welfare as much as appears, at least among providers.

If, in an associationalist reform, welfare sector workers are offered some genuine say in policy, some check on top-down management, and if the organizational and cultural concomitants of an ethic of service are restored – then we can expect a degree of support from such workers, both at professional and manual levels. Similarly, parents and patients may soon discover how thin is the rhetoric of 'choice' when they are compelled to attend a hospital 80 km away because it is cheaper for the bulk-purchasing Health Authority, or when they find that their locally-managed school practises selection and their own children are excluded. It should not, therefore, prove difficult to keep associationalism free of the taint of the Conservatives' reforms, and even present it as a panacea for some of their consequences. Associationalism is neither right-wing nor left-wing in principle. However, it is different from the sort of institutions we have been describing, which are in essence managerialist.

One should also remember in this context one essential advantage of associative democracy: that democratic local control simplifies regulation. Higher federal bodies confine, in the main, themselves to creating framework legislation, outlining in broad terms the regulatory ends to be achieved and then local bodies or associations decide through consultation how it shall apply to them. Thus, for example, in the case of safety legislation – all sides within a plant have a say and agree on the detail. In consequence the legislation can be looser than if the aim were to restrain the actions of one party with a high degree of discretion; management. If management had the discretion to implement loose framework legislation, it would do so in its own interests. Hence in a society of undemocratic organizations, the rules governing them from outside must be complex in order to cover as many contingencies as possible. Conversely, whilst legislation can be looser because lesser bodies can be trusted to implement it more fairly if they are democratically accountable, the *administrative* discretion of higher bodies can be more circumscribed in a self-administering and federal system.

If common standards are applied, then they need to be agreed federally and by consultation. This may appear cumbersome, it always does to those who believe in snap management decisions and top-down authority. It has the *advantage* of being cumbersome, of having to accommodate the various interests and taking time. Any agreement thus reached will not be lightly undone. This is in complete contrast to the style of modern British government: ceaseless centralized legislative and administrative interference in the welfare sector and society at large is the norm, but inconsistency is also the rule, and policy contradicts policy as the centralized system seeks to cure the errors of one hasty and arbitrary decision by another. Properly presented, a confederal and associationalist system might begin to look attractive to harassed teachers so buried under mountains of paper about curriculum change that they can barely teach, or to doctors struggling to implement endless shifting guidelines.

7

An Associational and Confederal Welfare State

The associationalist welfare system – principles and funding procedures

We turn from the polemics of the present to the serene stability of our model confederal and associational welfare state. The easiest way to present such a welfare state is to state some basic principles:

- that provision is by voluntary self-governing organizations that are partnerships between the recipients and the providers of the service. Such associations will be at least formally democratic and recipients will have an annual right of exit;
- that such organizations are funded predominantly from public sources (possible methods are outlined below) and are subject to public inspection and standard-setting;
- that any voluntary organization – church, trade union, charitable trust – may establish as wide or narrow a range of welfare services as its members choose (e.g. a Muslim charitable foundation may wish to establish schools, hospitals, old people's homes, and so on). It is assumed, therefore, that (at least in urban areas) there will be a range of competing services with which citizens may choose to register;
- that all such organizations must meet conditions of registration to receive public funds, among these would be compliance with public standards, acceptance of exit rights and recipient choice (e.g. to register with a Catholic school but with a 'neutral' Trust hospital), and participation in the public/associational governance of the whole system. It is assumed here that standard-setting, allocation of funding and inspection would be 'consociational'.

Such a fully developed associationalist welfare state would be federal in that the core organization of provision would be the region, at which level public funds (including inter-regional transfers) would be collected and distributed. Associations would cooperate with one another in the public governance of the distinct services and of the whole system, sending representatives to public bodies that perform the central regulative and distributory functions. Voluntary associations would thus enter into public governance in a decentralized state. Thus the associationalist principle would not only renew welfare provision, but also the state and government itself. The associations would be democratically self-governing internally, and would also contribute to a system of federated indirect democracy in the governance of the regional welfare state. Representative democratic bodies would remain at central and regional level, and would be standard-setters of last resort. Citizens would have several 'votes' and, moreover, the most important power of exit from direct service providers. The state would retain major reserve powers, to curb excessive growth in aggregate spending and to challenge standards of provision, but it would not have the unilateral powers available to politicians and officials in bureaucratic collectivist systems. Welfare professionals would be subject to strong public pressure and yet have far more say in how their own unit and the service as a whole is run.

Having set out the principles of the system in synoptic form, it is now necessary to describe it serially and in far greater detail. First, we shall examine how associations would be funded and how individuals' entitlements would be determined and related to organizations. Second, we shall examine the overall architecture of the system, how taxes are set and funds distributed between the major entities in an associationalist confederal commonwealth. Then we shall examine how any activity, like education or health, is organized on associational lines. Finally, we shall consider the problems such a federal and associational welfare system might give rise to and how they might be dealt with.

To begin with we will make a simplistic distinction that is necessary to our exposition, that between basic and specific welfare needs. In the case of the former we shall assume that in a civilized society everyone who is a member has by right an entitlement to certain fundamental necessities: food, shelter and clothing, and that these are available to all irrespective of age or status. In the case of specific welfare needs those may be determined by a general status (sick person, school-age child, pregnant mother, etc.) or depend upon more specific and complex circumstances (such as mental incapacity, disability, and so on). Entitlements to welfare in the case of general statuses would be automatic and based on a funding formula deemed appropriate for that status. More specific cases would involve discretionary assessment by some agency to ensure that the person in question received the bundle of services appropriate to their condition.

Basic welfare needs might be met with or without reference to associations. A person receiving such funds might buy food in a commercial shop or might pay-in a portion of their income to a cooperative rooming house for single people run by a charity. The point is that such funds are not distributed through associations but to individuals. In the case of status-dependent formula funding, the individual registers with the association as a provider and the association then receives the appropriate share of the formula-funded resources for the relevant statuses. In the final case, individuals could either present themselves to associations who would assess and 'sponsor' them for specific programmes and funding – making a claim for discretionary funds to the relevant public bodies – or they would come under the few remaining elements of compulsory state supervision in the system – for example, a child-battering family might be assigned for supervision and family therapy to a cooperative of social workers who have contracted with a municipal council to perform certain duties for a per case fee or an overall fixed cost. Individuals would have complete discretion over certain resources, the choice of an association to meet their needs in certain other circumstances, and in some cases would be subject to compulsion. Associations would be funded in a variety of ways depending on how they associated with the public. Thus a home for elderly disabled people might receive a portion of the residents' basic income in cash as a charitable body (and claim tax immunity for it, whereas a commercial lodging house could not), receive part of their disability pension money under formula funding, and also receive case-by-case or block-grant funds from the relevant public body charged with discretionary funding for the disabled. It is evident that this system is sufficiently complex to combine the elements of choice and compulsion, universalism and specific benefits adjusted to need.

How might this combination of basic and specific needs be funded? The answer is that it could use for different purposes, and in different combinations, any or all of the existing methods of funding welfare: general taxation, public or private insurance, markets and private purchases, charitable donations, etc. Here we will merely sketch out a possible model of funding based upon the schema of basic and specific welfare needs outlined above.

Guaranteed minimum income

First, let us assume that the simplest way to meet basic welfare needs is a system of universal entitlements, and that this is funded from general taxation. The most effective way is through a Guaranteed Minimum Income scheme (GMI): in which every individual adult receives as a transfer payment or tax credit a (low) basic income assured by the federal commonwealth. Such a system would be economically sustainable at present if the level of basic income were pitched low enough.

How low is a matter of much dispute. For example, the figures proposed for the UK by Hermione Parker in 1985 involve supplementary payments for such categories as the elderly, lone parents and the disabled to make them viable (Walter, 1989:41). For a GMI scheme to provide a truly liveable basic income at current prices it could not be less than US $500 per adult per month, plus child allowances. At this level, even with the rationalization of existing welfare programmes, taxes would have to be substantially increased in both the UK and the USA. However, a GMI scheme is economically feasible should we be willing to pay for it. Western societies are wealthy enough to assure economic security and dignity for all their citizens as of right if they wished to do so.

A GMI scheme would not even be necessarily unattractive to the mass of employed tax-payers since it would put a fairly high floor on their taxable incomes. In could also be used to simplify the tax system and would make it fairer, if the GMI tax credit became the only major tax allowance available. Assuming therefore, that tax revenues fell somewhat as a result of this floor on taxable incomes, GMI would have to prove itself fiscally efficient in other ways. It would help to simplify the administration of welfare since many distinct programmes providing what is in effect basic welfare could be rolled-up in it: unemployment benefits, other income support, basic state pensions, child allowances, etc. This would both reduce administrative overheads by cutting the number of programmes, but also by cutting out the elements of discretion in these programmes and the personnel involved.

The principle of GMI or Basic Income has strong advocates across the political spectrum, even if we exclude Milton Friedman's Negative Income Tax (which is not truly universal). It has left-wing advocates like Andre Gorz and Philippe Van Parijs. It is supported by futurologists like Alvin Toffler. It has found favour with the Greens, particularly in Germany. Claimants' advocates like Bill Jordan support it, as do some conservatively-inclined enthusiasts like Sir Brandon Rhys Williams and Hermione Parker. Because the principle of GMI makes sense and can appeal across conventional political divisions, whereas conventional welfare state issues tend rigidly to reinforce them, then it has some hope of being successful. The GMI principle has the same capacity to be claimed by a 'plurality of parents' that social welfare and social insurance had in the late nineteenth and early twentieth centuries. That is a sign that it may answer very basic needs of social organization. It is the one reform that would make extensive associational experiments possible, since it provides a basic plank of universal income support on the basis of which large-scale experiments that led to diversity and heterogeneity in provision might be acceptable. Associationalism can renew welfare institutions like hospitals or old people's homes on an extensive scale *within* existing funding structures. For the basic funding framework to move in the direction of associationalism and federalism, then the security of a GMI scheme would be an essential pre-condition. GMI is thus the key reform if an associationalist welfare state were to be built, rather than that existing welfare states merely be reinvigorated by associationalism.

We assume that, as things are at present, a feasible GMI would provide just sufficient to live on. It is, therefore, unlikely to promote idleness and take away the incentive to work. These fears are ludicrous in a society with high unemployment (ten per cent and above) where there are large numbers of people desperate for work and who cannot find it. They will hardly be deterred from taking non-existent jobs by a GMI scheme any more than they would be by the dole. Unemployment benefits and other welfare payments actually deter the unemployed from supplementing their income. They offer the options of enforced idleness or illegal work. A GMI scheme, on the contrary, provides its recipients with a positive incentive to work. As it is given to all adults, neither pensioners nor those who have lost a full-time job are debarred from working. GMI need not create a 'poverty trap' that threatens the poor with loss of income if they take paid work. Wage income, while taxed, would always be positive. A GMI scheme would greatly expand the potential labour force and would undercut one of the main motivations for the 'black economy'.

Left-wing proponents of conventional welfare object to a (low) GMI scheme on precisely these grounds, that it is a form of new Speenhamland system, and subsidizes low-wage employers out of general taxation. It is true that employers would take into account GMI when assessing what taxable income to pay. This is inevitable, but the question of low wages is essentially a separate one and is best addressed by minimum wage legislation.

Many economic liberals would view the combination of GMI and minimum wage rates with horror. Together they would prevent poverty wages, by setting a guaranteed social subsistence level and a guaranteed minimum hourly wage over and above that for those in paid employment. The result would certainly be to make many low wage jobs currently in existence both illegal and unattractive. That is why these measures are resisted by those who believe that poverty wages are essential if labour markets are to work efficiently, that is, that at some structure of prices demand equals supply. This is pure dogma and serious economists like Solow (1990) argue that labour markets do not and cannot behave like perfectly competitive markets. This is because the unemployed cannot and do not 'bid' for the jobs of the employed, and because people in and out of work have social standards about the sort of wages consistent with different types of work. There is no reason to seek to preserve low-wage, low-productivity, low-skill jobs as such; unless, that is, one is addicted to a theory about the labour market that values its formal efficiency over the substantive creation of wealth. Also, as far as those theoretical dogmas are concerned, a GMI scheme is an interference with the market and a labour de-motivator, but then so are unemployment benefits and other welfare measures currently in existence. Any form of income support above starvation level will interfere with the labour market as conceived in economic liberal dogma.

The sort of GMI scheme that might be feasible at present may appear to put public income support in a provocative form, since it is a universal cradle to grave economic entitlement. As a universal benefit however, it is less of a problem to justify than a mass of specific programmes targetted at particular groups such as the sick or the unemployed. Moreover, as a universal benefit, dependent on nothing more than social membership, it makes the point that wealth is, in large measure, social. The efforts and talents of individuals do indeed contribute to the total wealth of society, and they are rewarded more or less proportionately. It would be foolish either to deny that some individuals are more industrious, skilful and successful than others or to seek to inhibit effort and enterprise. However, skills, knowledge, access to institutions, even the level of demand for goods are social phenomena. Individuals contribute to producing these phenomena, but they cannot – as individuals – create all the conditions of their own livelihood or personal success. Individuals' locations (both geographical and social) and their temporal placement (in boom or slump) contribute to their success or failure – 'luck' is in large measure a social good. Thus those who were born in a prosperous locality, with ample work, and who enter employment during a long boom have no right to assume and to judge that those in a poorer locality seeking work at a time of slump are responsible for their own fate.

The crasser pedlars of free-market apologetics will say that markets are always open to talent, skill and effort (the more intelligent economic liberals will not; they will present it as the best allocative mechanism in an imperfect world). That is to make the exception, the rags to riches entrepreneurial story, the moral basis for the rule. But societies cannot live on fantasies in modern times, nor can their less successful members be expected to defer to such myths. The poor are not a credulous peasantry, starved of information and dulled by starvation. The modern poor may not pass exams, but they are sophisticated individuals, open to the prospects available to others. They know that opportunities are not, and probably will never, be equally distributed. If wealth is, in a large measure, social, then poverty cannot be made an entirely individual stigma. To plead against the claims of social justice, as

the Hayekians do, that the market cannot be 'fair', that it dis-
tributes success and failure by blind formal processes that are
ignorant of all considerations of social justice, is to state an obvious truth. That the market is not fair is exactly so, and for that
reason markets alone cannot be permitted to distribute the wealth
of society.

A GMI scheme has other reasons for being a core principle in
an associationalist welfare state than that it can cope with large-
scale unemployment or offer simplified and fiscally efficient welfare. The former rationales may be necessary to get it introduced.
As a scheme of income maintenance it has more to offer than just
being a way of providing for those without work, or for those too
old to work who have no private pension. If we assume an economically successful society with a low level of unemployment
(below five per cent) – then a GMI scheme ought to be sustainable
at a much higher level than basic subsistence. In that case, given
that the conditions of a dignified life are provided as of right by the
Commonwealth, then people could really choose when or whether
to work. That people might enjoy lifetime economic security and
be freed of the goad of poverty to drive them to work is absurd
to an economic liberal. That it is so considered by them is to
accept a diminished account of all human purposes including a
diminished account of why we work.

It is also to ignore the fact that we may never be able to pay for
all the work that needs to be done. In such a successful economy
we assume most people do work (whether full- or part-time) for a
substantial part of their lives, and are at least adequately paid.
However, each citizen would have sufficient income to pursue
activities that the market does not value but which may be either
personally valuable or socially useful. They may do this for part of
their lives. In particular they may choose to undertake voluntary
service. A GMI scheme would thus increase the potential personnel of the welfare state in areas not covered by paid labour and
formula funding. People may choose to drop out of work or take
part-time work to care for their children (and not be poor as a
result). People may choose to care for very elderly relatives or
friends. A well-funded GMI scheme could give families and
households the option of providing for their welfare at home. In
an ageing society this may well be more economically rational
than collectivist institutional welfare. The same may be true of

moving from a society of tired two-income families and emotion-
ally neglected latch-key kids. A GMI scheme would also allow
organizations to offer labour-intensive services that formulas did
not cover, relying on volunteers sustained by a GMI scheme and
moved to cooperate from conviction in the worth of the enterprise. GMI would also help to end the rigid division between
(paid) work and (idle) retirement. In an associationalist society,
the active old would be a vital resource for welfare organizations;
engaged in voluntary service in substantial numbers they would
provide a good deal of the personnel for many associations. They
would, in particular, provide a means to carry on charitable work
additional to or which did not qualify for public funding.

Choosing welfare

We have argued that citizens will use their federal GMI and other
incomes to meet certain basic welfare needs without further reference to the Commonwealth. They may purchase these things from
associations or on the commercial market. More specific entitlements would be met at the regional level from general taxation
and the complex a particular citizen received would depend on her
or his age and various statuses. We assume here that entitlements
would be defined for each specific provision area like education or
health. The formula for funding these specific entitlements would
be determined at the Consociational Funding Council of the regional government. Each individual's choice of an association as
provider would thus carry a specific level of formula funding with
it, determined to be sufficient to meet the normal contingencies
of such needs. Each citizen would have to register annually in
advance with a service provider for each relevant service. An
entitlement to a definite quality and quantity of service would
be specified in a 'contract' between citizen and association. We
assume that the majority of citizens would re-register regularly
with the same provider of each service and that the annual social
costs of citizens switching from one provider to another would be
small. The citizen would, however, have an unquestioned right of
exit, and organizations providing a service would have to accept
registrations for that service alone and could not bar a registree
because they had not signed on for a 'package' of services offered
by the different organizations of an association.

Funding to the service-providing organizations created by associations would thus follow from citizens' elections to use a particular service. The formula would give the means to carry on the service assuming a certain scale of operation ($f \times n$), where f is the funding formula and n is the minimum feasible number of registrants. Voluntary associations would receive funds proportionate to membership in effect, and in practice the bigger and more popular ones would be able to offer better services, given economies of scale. People could choose large or small depending on their preferences, and local information centres would provide materials on the previous year's membership and the terms offered by each service provider. In urban areas at least, citizens would have a wide choice of providers of services offering different philosophies and styles of provision. Even if people chose a very small association – a village school cooperative, for example – they will do so *because* of its smallness and locality, and despite the fact that it could offer 'less' than a large school gathering in children from a wide area. Thus the formula component should work for services like primary education and primary healthcare, allowing n to be a relatively small number. The system would thus be driven by citizens' choice in the type of providers and by the consociational machinery in setting formulas, in which associations (governed as partnerships of producers and providers) would predominate. Thus *citizens*, not bureaucrats, would choose the type of welfare services they liked. The pressures toward centralization and rationalization would undoubtedly be checked – few people would choose a basic care hospital 50km away before a local one.

Associations would be under strong pressure to provide services their members wanted and to heed their opinions, otherwise they could suffer rapid and potentially extremely damaging losses from the 'exit' choices of their dissatisfied ex-members. They would also have strong incentives to expand their memberships and compete with one another. Citizens' elections would thus work like a market, but one driven by consumers' choice of the provider. This would contain purely producer preferences and also eliminate the bureaucratic distortion of 'pseudo-markets', where officials pick the lowest administratively-determined price on offer in a bulk-purchase of a service for their clients who have no say in the matter. The combination of GMI and formula funding by citizen's elections to use a particular association would give the federal and regional governments relatively low control of the pattern of services – it allows an extensive welfare state without centralized bureaucratic control. At the same time because it is funded from general taxation, and federal and regional governments have the ultimate fiscal powers, the overall level of expenditure on welfare can be controlled and subjected to representative bodies elected by the whole people. The danger of a decentralized choice-driven welfare state eating up larger and larger proportions of GDP by the unintended consequences of individual discrete decisions is, therefore, remote.

We assume that the combination of GMI and formula funding will consume the great bulk of welfare funds (about 75 per cent). This still leaves the question of more specialized discretionary welfare services and how they might be funded. It also raises the question of how to maintain some elements of flexibility, since together GMI and formula funding are *intended* to be inflexible, that is, to give citizens high choice and officials low discretion. Nevertheless, the system as described would leave little room for changes that are not driven by citizens' elections and consequent changes in service providers' membership.

As far as specific welfare needs involving assessment and discretionary allocation are concerned, these can be met in a number of ways: by a residual bureaucratic collectivist system funded out of taxation and 'top sliced' when the formula-based allocations are made at regional level; by allocating funds for such services as above, but inviting service providers to bid for contracts to meet them (private psychiatric practices, social workers' cooperatives, etc., would thus take over these functions, subject to inspection and contract compliance); by building a component for such services into the formulas on which citizens' elections are based, citizens' either choosing a contingency provider for general welfare services, or one of the major provision areas (e.g. health) taking over problems like disability, compulsory psychiatric care, etc. and this provision being specified to citizens when they choose.

As for flexibility, two mechanisms are possible, one in the hands of citizen consumers of welfare, and one in the hands of professional providers. Citizens need a mechanism that will enable them to respond to areas of perceived need, either in cases where there is little or inadequate provision, or where formulas fail to give the

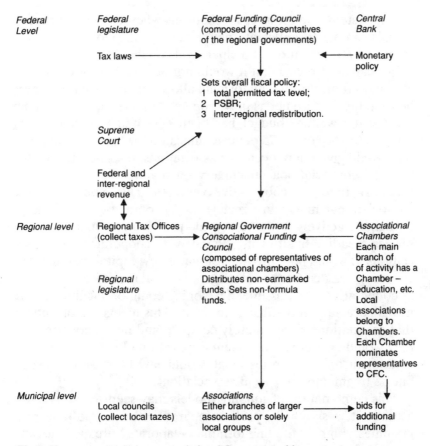

Fig 1 How taxes are set in an associational Commonwealth.

level of service that certain groups of citizens deem necessary. The simplest way to cope with this is to institutionalize citizens' voluntary initiative by ring-fencing a portion of a citizen's tax payments (say five per cent) and enabling citizens to annually assign that revenue to up to five organizations of their own choice in proportions they deemed fit (for example, the whole five per cent might go on a charity researching a particular disease, or it might go one per cent to each of five service-providing organizations the citizen registers with, to top up each of their formula funds). Such allocations could be purely altruistic or used to benefit a service of direct relevance to the citizen – thus a group of citizens could band together to improve the services at a small rural hospital where formula funds did not provide certain desired facilities.

The system also requires mechanisms whereby welfare professionals can act to anticipate major needs, can pool resources to create on a regional or municipal level collaborative ventures for major capital projects that it would not be possible for each association to fund through its formula allocation, and simply to plug holes in the welfare net as they crop up. Assume that some 15 per cent of the welfare budget has been allocated to discretionary services (on top of the 75 per cent allocated to GMI and formulas) that would give ten per cent for associations to spend through the regional consociational machinery on major new projects, bids for extra funds or cooperative ventures. This would give the consociational machinery real teeth, encourage associations to participate actively in it and provide professionals in a particular service area like health with the means to cooperate across associations. It would both provide for major new capital spending and encourage associations to manage a particular service in a region as cooperatively as possible, developing common facilities where it was necessary and efficient to do so. This meets the objections that associations would merely compete and not cooperate, that they would encourage inefficient duplication of expensive capital equipment, and that professionals would have little *esprit de crops*, but be fragmented in specific associations.

This combination of funding models may seem very complex, actually it is simplicity itself compared with the multiple programmes, complex funding formulas, elaborate bureaucracies and so on of the current British welfare state. In so far as it is complex, the funding system derives from a desire that there be a 'separation of powers' in welfare funding, so that different functions, interests and objectives are accommodated. Within the system different agencies have different powers:

1 thus federal and regional governments set overall levels of tax, determine the broad budget headings, and allocate welfare funding between different methods (e.g. tax, insurance, tax concessions, etc.) – we have assumed here a system wholly funded from direct taxation for purposes of simplicity;
2 a high proportion of expenditure on welfare is in either a form where it is exclusively controlled by citizens (GMI), or where citizens choose the provider of the service who administers the formula funds;
3 discretionary welfare is provided on several different principles;

4   there are elements of citizens' and producers' initiative to make the system capable of change and responsive to need;

5   in the last instance, compulsory collectivist welfare interventions are retained, for that residual component that cannot be accommodated to citizens' choice and these are overseen by democratically account-able bodies.

The system accommodates choice, it also allows for profes-sional efficiency, but it does both in a system where power is distributed federally and associationally, in which there is no single centre. The welfare system is confederal in its political principles and primarily based on associations for its services. It is a dispersed decentralized democracy.

The architecture of an associationalist common-wealth

Devising the institutions of an imaginary state has a monomania-cal ring to it. The purpose here is not to devise a perfect commu-nity, but simply to show how the complex funding procedures outlined above fit in with a possible constitutional architecture that does not violate common sense. The scheme is outlined in figure 1. We assume that the system is confederal and that regions delegate powers and resources up to the federal government. The federal government is solely concerned with inter-regional issues. Thus its legislature sets a common framework of laws nec-essary to ensure that citizens enjoy the same basic rights between regions. The Supreme Court adjudicates on constitutional dis-putes between regions, and protects the rights of citizens against the regional governments. The Federal Funding Council is com-posed of representatives of the regional governments, it deter-mines overall fiscal policy and the level of inter-regional transfer of revenues to redistribute income between the richer and poorer regions. The principle operative in such inter-regional transfers is neither that a central government separate from and above the regions imposes redistribution on them, nor that individual regions always act like sovereign entities at an international gathering, and bargain how little they can get away with in external calls upon their resources. The federal level must be cooperative if it is to be confederal: that is, the regions meet collectively and reach an agreement through debate, if they cannot the matter is put to federal arbiters elected by the regional governments. Regional governments in this scheme will not be centralized mini-statelets, but themselves will disperse power to different agencies and to associations. The Federal Funding Council would receive from the legislature the common framework legislation of the federation, it would receive through the various deliberative bodies representing associations considered views on common minimum standards in welfare, and it would receive the draft budgets of the regional governments. From this it would evolve annually a set of minimum service standards appropriate for all federal citizens and the fiscal implications thereof. It would then establish the level of inter-regional redistribution consistent with meeting those standards across the federation. It would operate on the principle that all competent entities must be able to meet those standards and that wealthier regions may only provide welfare *above* those standards after they have subsidized the poorer ones in meeting them. This principle allows richer regions to keep down their total tax levels only if they can persuade poorer ones to accept lower framework standards, and if we assume both sides have the power of vetoing a proposed deal and placing it in the hands of federal assessors (whereupon last year's formulas are adopted), then this creates a balance of forces between the regions that at the price of procrastination prevents a *dictat* on either side.

Regional governments collect the taxes and pass on the share needed to pay for federal institutions and inter-regional redistribution. It is at the regional level that welfare associations operate as far as funding is concerned. The GMI system operates across the whole federation and is the core of the common framework standard-setting for welfare between regions. Assuming regions provide federal taxes, pay GMI at the agreed level, and abide by federal laws regarding the rights of individual citizens and of other regional governments, then the principle of federation means that they can organize internally as their citizens please. However, to avoid stretching the imagination or the reader's patience too far we shall suppose that there is a 'typical' region whose welfare and funding institutions we may describe.

Associations providing welfare will provide most services at the municipal level, and they will be either purely local groupings (e.g. a parent–teacher cooperative school association in a small town) or local branches of larger associations (the regional Catholic old people's welfare society, for example). Each association at local level will be governed by a joint board representing producers and consumers, weighted according to a formula registered and accepted at regional level with the Consociational Funding Council (CFC). Each association will be engaged in a distinct branch of activity through its organizations (as we shall see below). For each main branch of activity, local associations meeting together nominate representatives to a regional level Associational Chamber. Each branch of activity, health, education, etc., has a chamber. Each chamber serves as the professional, regulatory, standard-setting and deliberative body for that activity in the first instance – providing the primary level of supra-organizational regulation. Each chamber sends representatives to the regional Consociational Funding Council. This body sets standards of service and monitors them by inspection; it receives and audits the registered memberships of associations arising from citizens' elections, and it decides on bids for discretionary funding from associations and chambers. It thus creates the regional welfare budget which it passes to the regional legislature (composed of elected representatives) for approval and it also serves as the highest level of supra-organizational regulation (other than actions through the courts and appeals to the Supreme Court).

Associations are democratically governed by providers and consumers separately electing representatives to a council of management. Chambers and the Consociational Council are structures of indirect and corporatist democracy, staffed by professionals and active volunteers. The existence of an elected regional legislature, and of a structure of federal law and courts protecting citizens' rights, ensures that any tendencies toward the corporatist system acting against the wishes of individual citizens above associational level can be checked. Associations and the consociational machinery both provide levels of governance and regulations as well as provision within the system. Regulation is impossible if it does not go along *pari passu* with the delivery of the service, but service providers cannot be the sole regulators as is the case with bureaucratic collectivism. In the associationalist system voluntary agencies are given broad scope to govern themselves, but ultimately in an associationalist Commonwealth representative assemblies and the courts are governors of last resort. However much associations and the regional consociational machinery are left to interpret 'framework' legislation by means of their own cooperative, consultative and democratic procedures, the legal state retains the power to assess and adjudicate whether the law has been complied with in those sections where it strictly delimits the rights of individuals and the obligations of associations. In the same way, the state will not refuse existing means of ensuring that agencies steward public funds and conform to common publicly agreed purposes: thus regional tax officers, auditors for the Consociational Funding Council, and more specific task delivery inspectorates would be available to ensure that taxes were spent legally, that associational membership rolls were accurate, and that professional standards of service were complied with. Because the state does not directly organize services, because they are in the hands of voluntary associations, does not mean that the state has fewer powers of inspection than existing welfare states, merely that its task is less impossible. As we have argued, as the state does not directly perform the task of provision of welfare, so it has the capacity *vis-à-vis* associations to act as the guardian of the public in matters touching on financial competence and probity, and on service quality.

Associations in a Commonwealth of the type we have been considering are voluntary bodies, freely formed by citizens. There is in this argument no requirement that *all* associations conform to public standards, other than of the most minimal kind (the Society for the Propagation of Racial Abuse would be outlawed, associations would be compelled to distribute audited accounts to their members, and to count one person as one vote). That is, unless they sought to receive public funds for public welfare or other purposes, in other words, to participate in the system of public governance through organized civil society. Organizations that wished to practise purely private charity, to eschew the public realm, and to keep to themselves, avoiding all formal consociational machinery, would be free to do so. An associational Commonwealth should not be more restrictive than existing liberal societies, without compelling reason and wide democratic support. Such free-standing associations could fund themselves by charitable donations and even, perhaps, from the five per cent tax write-in provisions.

Any association accepting public functions must participate in the structure of consociational and state governance of associations as a condition of tax-based financial support. It must accept being part of a collaborative and consultative system of coordination of an association's activities and cooperation in social governance. Associationalism is a form of social governance in which associations are to perform public functions, and not merely a scheme to direct public revenues to private purposes. The purpose of the corporatist and indirect democracy of the Chambers and the CFC is not merely to ensure that public funds are well spent, it is to provide a coordinative and collaborative structure whereby associations can cooperate. With such a structure, as we have noted above, associations can achieve the advantages of economies of scale that large public and corporate bureaucracies claim as a major advantage without the associated problems of 'bigness', but without loosing their distinctive style. They could pool funds to create capital-intensive facilities for common use, they could create services, like in-service training, that smaller associations could not afford and to which they could subscribe. This coordinative machinery is rather like the 'industrial public sphere' envisaged for an associative economy, and likewise enables smaller and more intimate associations to function as well as or better than large ones.

The coordinative machinery also enables common standards to be developed, problems considered by deliberation on the part of a wide range of experienced professionals and volunteers, research to be funded, and a means of communication established between organizations. This is vital as we saw when we discussed the process of 'Ottomanization'. An associationalist society without a thick 'public sphere' would not promote the liberty of the citizen as well as one in which citizens could choose associations without committing their whole life to them, and yet in the knowledge that those bodies were outward-looking enough to learn from others and be able to change. No sensible person wants the variety of styles of provision and social values that is the great advantage of an associational system to be produced at the price of parochialism and conservativism on a social scale, each inward-looking community going along in its own rut. In a technological and knowledge-based society this would be fatal, and without the coordinative machinery of the Chambers and the CFC it would be difficult to develop and to diffuse knowledge in areas like medicine.

Associations would be funded regionally, but they may choose to organize federally, regionally or muncipally depending on their aims and objectives. A religious group (Catholics, Muslims, etc.) may have members spread throughout the country, and wish to provide a wide range of welfare services for them. A group may have a strong regional concentration on ethnic, linguistic or cultural lines and may wish to organize on a regional basis (but perhaps with local chapters in other regions organized municipally, thus, for example, there used to be strong London Scottish and Irish associations that did perform some welfare functions). Again, a group of parents and teachers may simply wish to provide local non-denominational education through a cooperative primary school association. The level at which an association organizes is a matter of choice for its own members – although, of course, that choice would be policed by associational law, which would set the conditions in which associations could refuse membership, the minimum procedures for ensuring democracy in self-governance, and the justice of their disciplinary procedures. The aim of such rules would be to facilitate the democratic choice of associations, and not to specify what they should do otherwise.

However, the limits of accountability for public funds would impose some limits, and, therefore, some *ultra vires* actions in fiscal matters. First, funds distributed within a region to associations could only be spent within the region – the process of inter-regional transfers will be fraught enough, without certain agencies practising their own inter-regional redistribution on top of it. Similarly, formula funding per citizen choice will be for certain purposes, health, education, etc., and the formula per service weighted accordingly. Therefore, funds received by consequence of membership elections cannot be vired from one purpose to another; education to health, or public funds for welfare to religious purposes. Hence associations would be required to create distinct organizations for each publicly-funded purpose they engage in and spend, and account for those funds within that organization. The association may pursue as many purposes as it likes, but only if it creates distinct branches of organization corresponding to public funding for each one that it engages in. The administration of the non-welfare activities of the association, for example, paying the priests and maintaining the buildings of the Catholic Church would have to be paid out of private charity. The bodies involved would be legally distinct, and have different membership and decision procedures. Thus a Catholic Hospital Association would include all who have elected to be members for health purposes and would be distinct from Church leaders as such or the clergy, it might thus decide to offer services contrary to orthodox church doctrine. As each organization is distinct, so its membership is free to decide to leave as it pleases and cannot be compelled to join or leave other organizations of the association.

These conditions may appear to go against the principles of organizational autonomy, but they are essential if an associative democracy is to preserve accountability for public money and if citizens are to have choice in welfare. No association is bound to accept these conditions, it can remain a private entity. The conditions imposed on an association's behaviour by the standards evolved by legislation and by the coordinative machinery would also be restrictive. Let us assume that hospitals would be required to accept emergency cases brought in by ambulance if they were nearest, regardless of the membership or views of the patient. Hospitals that could not accept this would not be funded for casualty services – a Muslim hospital that insisted on treating only Muslims would find it could not offer the kind of cover its members would desire. One can imagine a gradually thickening series of these rules growing as inter-associational problems arose. In certain areas it may even be the case that the associational system would be as complex as a state collectivist one. However, the volume of rules and directives constantly issued to ensure uniformity in a highly-centralized bureaucratic system lead one to suppose that an associationalist society would be at worst no different in this respect, and have a lot of other advantages besides.

The problems of an associational system

No system of social organization can be without problems. The issue at stake here is whether any of the problems likely to be foreseeable in an associationalist welfare system are so serious as to render the enterprise void and self-defeating.

The first problem is one raised by those who see in collectivist welfare the major advantage that it can act paternalistically on behalf of the poor and uneducated to offer them services they could not otherwise obtain on terms equal to the more fortunate in society. This paternalism is not necessarily just a cloak for a bureaucratic collectivst will-to-power, it may be sincerely felt and has often contributed to underpinning the ethic of service. One thinks of Titmuss' high-minded advocacy of universalism and disinterested benevolence in such works as *The Gift Relationship* (1970).

Associationalism need not oppose disinterested service, but it is quite against bureaucratic paternalism, and it does favour active citizens concerned for their own affairs. It might appear, therefore, that associationalist welfare will favour the well-educated middle classes with a 'consumer' mentality and the skill to work the self-governing components of the system. The system would exclude the poor and unskilled by the complexity of choices required. Actually, by giving the power of exit, the system would empower the poor to a considerable degree, and one that did not require them to participate extensively in the democratic machinery of an association. They could walk away from bad schools, for example, something that is difficult to do in a collectivist-bureaucratic system. Likewise, because the system could easily be made open to campaigning associations as much as to others, it would enable those groups actively concerned to improve the position of the poor in partnership with them to obtain public funds by persuading poor people to make membership elections on their behalf. It would also enable alternative groups and non-establishment groups to set their own welfare agendas in ways that current bureaucratic welfare states do not permit (for example, providing proper medical services for 'travellers'). For these reasons, associationalism has a strong potential to attract radicals, who favour alternative and democratic organization, as well as those who favour the principle of consumer choice.

The next major problem often foreseen by critics is that the system only really allows for a wide range of choice in densely-settled urban areas. There is would be possible, for example, for

Catholic, Jewish and 'neutral' hospital associations to compete for members. But what about rural areas, where there may be only enough formula-funded members for one small unit? Will not services be worse and choice restricted?

The first point to be made in response to this objection is that this affects centralized collectivistic systems too, and rural residents may have *no* local services at all – their children being bussed 20 km away, or the nearest major hospital being 50 km away. Associationalism would, at least, enable rural residents to choose to create a simple community school or community hospital. It might not allow the same choice as in the city, but it would be *local*. The second point in response is that small local units need not be ineffective if they can subscribe to, or cooperatively pool, wider services, e.g. the schools in a rural area may collectively contract with a service provider of, say, specialist training, personnel management, skilled music teaching, etc. Small school boards of less than 20,000 children could be viable on this basis and not offer significantly worse services at no greater cost up to the age of sixteen. The small school (25–100 pupils) could survive semi-autonomously within such a collaborative school board structure. The third point to make in response is that it would be possible to provide some choice in rural areas if associations, each with quite small memberships in a given locality, were to pool resources to share common facilities, for example, Catholic and Muslim school associations co-locating and sharing access to a science laboratory for their small schools.

Critics raise the problem of how a choice-based system of provision copes with contingencies people think they will never need, or will never have imposed upon them, such as long-term compulsory psychiatric care or statutory social work supervision? We have dealt with this issue in the course of this chapter, however it is worth summing-up the answers here. First, associationalism can easily accept residual elements of state bureaucratic provision in areas like the police, social work, etc. Second, there is nothing to prevent one of the core formula-funded services being miscellaneous 'welfare provision', and citizens signing on with a publicly-approved provider of supervisory services of their choice. This would not apply to monopoly services like the police, but, for example, parents with dependant children might be required to register with a health visitor or child welfare agency. Third, there is no reason why the major services like health should not include a broad range of services, including compulsory psychiatric hospitalization, within their formula-funded activities. Associationalism is not like anarchism: it does not proport to abolish the state, nor does it imagine that associations are not engaged in the task of government, and that, however much choice individuals may have in the agencies that perform that task, and however large a democratic say they may have in how it is carried-out, voluntary agencies will constrain their members in certain ways and, in some cases, exercise elements of compulsion on behalf of the public power in specified circumstances on members. Associationalism cannot create a society without constraint for the simple reason that the latter term is an essential part (if part only) of the former.

Another problem we have alluded to throughout is the issue of the potential for heterogeneity in associationalist welfare provision, and of gaps in the net of services. In one sense, an associationalist welfare system is *designed* to be heterogeneous, to offer people the choice of options in style of welfare. Centralized bureaucratic welfare states do not achieve homogeneity in provision, nor do they offer much choice to compensate. The answer to undesirable heterogeneity and incompetence of services is, however, simple: the system is designed to be more democratic and responsive than a state-centralist system, so citizens have numerous mechanisms at their direct control to address perceived problems; the state in both its representative-legislative role, and in its corporatist associational role, is a standard-setter and inspector, and can comment upon and act to check deficiencies in provision; the system has the mechanism of a ten per cent discretionary element in the budget allocated through the consociational machinery that can plug gaps; finally, citizens have the cushion of a GMI scheme, so that they cannot fall through the welfare net altogether into basic poverty, something that most current welfare states do not guarantee.

In discussing the political aspect of associationalism we considered an objection that is often made by defenders of state-centralized and bureaucratic welfare provision against any system that relies on strong elements of voluntarism, as the associational system outlined here does, and that is, how can one ensure that enough people give enough of their time to sustain the activity? If the objection is that most people will wish to play little active part in the self-governance of their associations, and will give little attention to choosing carefully, then the answer is that the associationalist system does not intrinsically require a high level of involvement, and that if people are satisfied with what they get from minimum commitment so be it. The associational welfare services will, in the main, be delivered by paid professionals, and they will have some substantial democratic input into the system. One might claim, as a result, that they will be *too* influential and will introduce a producer-based set of interests into the system. They may do so, if they are wholly and negatively self-interested, and if the citizens make no effort to stop them or find no dissatisfaction with the result. Either case is unlikely, and the citizens have a formidable battery of means available to make their dissatisfactions felt, if they choose to do so. As for the cadre of energetic volunteers who participate actively in the governance and operation of associations, will there be enough of them, and will they be too different from Joe and Josephine Public to really reflect their interests? The answer to the first question is itself a question, how much is enough? At present there seems to be no problem in finding enough people to undertake the work of voluntary governance of associations, *if* they identify with their purposes. Difficulties tend to occur when governments try to create structures that require volunteers, but without creating the conditions of excitement and commitment in the 'public'. The Conservative Government's attempt to get British industry voluntarily to sponsor and to govern the new City Technology Colleges (selective 'magnet' schools) has been an ignominious failure, as has the attempt to find large numbers of school governors from business for the new Locally Managed Schools.

British managers are not, probably, less public spirited than other managers or less public spirited even then the citizenry at large. The reason they have not come forward is that the government tried to draft them as its voluntary vanguard and for its own purposes. It is difficult to draft people into voluntarism. Britain, as we have seen, has had one of the most lively associational cultures in the Western world and a strong voluntary charitable sector in welfare. Bodies like Oxfam and the Royal National Lifeboat Institution show that the voluntary principle can create and sustain large-scale organizations that are efficient providers of vital services. They must, however, grow up by voluntary effort. This shows us an important lesson. An associationalist welfare state cannot be created by government fiat, it can only grow slowly by a variety of processes as people, politicians and officials come to see the value of associationalism and voluntarism as means of reforming welfare states.

Thus one assumes that the welfare system we have been describing as an accomplished fact will grow gradually and piecemeal, at a pace that the voluntary principle can sustain. We have explored the imaginary complete system simply to show it is possible, that piecemeal change could evolve toward this system without entertaining disaster. Gradual but steady 'parachuting out' of services from the centralized welfare state might occur as groups of professionals take the chance of democratic privatization, and seek volunteers and consumers of the services to go with them. Similarly, decentralizing reforms can occur that do not require a complete associationalist system to be in place, but rather tend to promote it. A GMI scheme could be introduced as a modification of centralized welfare, in itself it would simplify and improve the system even without extensive associational provision. The introduction of the five per cent voluntary tax donation to up to five associations would help to fund the voluntary sector and without the risk of bureaucratic intervention that current state support for charities' activities entails.

The question of how far the voluntary governors of an extensive associationalist welfare system would be like the average consumer of the services, and how far their interests might coincide, is almost impossible to answer. If we assume a passive, uninterested and ignorant populace then, presumably, the voluntary governors will be as remote from, and patronizing to them as bureaucrats are at worst today in a collectivist system. However, given what we have seen about how the system as a whole can only come into being gradually, and by voluntary effort, this seems unlikely. To develop fully such a welfare state, the associations composing it would have required large-scale citizen support and positive public choice. It would be odd then to imagine that citizens would become suddenly passive, indiffferent to the choices available to them, when the system reached full development. Associationalism is not like building a command economy or turning one with 'big bang' rapidity into a free market. It is more like liberal or social democratic reform; it will grow steadily and be fuelled by the past success of reform, or not at all.

A last problem remains to be considered: it is the most difficult of all and we have already discussed it in general terms when considering the issue of 'Ottomanization and also of the normative basis for the associational system in Chapter three. Associationalism does raise some acute dilemmas in that the desire to allow the maximum democratic self-governance to associations, and the desire to preserve the rights of individuals, will often come into conflict. We have tried to argue that this is not qualitatively different from the dilemmas faced by liberalism in general when confronted by divergent standards within the community. The issue here centres on education, and the passionate commitment by liberals, democratic republicans and socialists that there be a common educational system in which, as far as possible, all citizens participate, that it should be secular and that it should promote common citizenship. These are worthy aims and it would be wholly wrong to brush them aside. An associationalist system *must* be more culturally and socially pluralistic than this republican model would desire; it will allow explicitly religious and other value-centred forms of education to receive public money. It creates fundamental problems about the curriculum. Can Torah schools be permitted, where children receive only a traditional Jewish education? Should Christian fundamentalist sects be allowed to teach 'creation science' with public money?

These are not easy questions, nor are they confined to an associationalist Commonwealth. They would occur where there is a measure of decentralization and local democracy and a high concentration of believers in a particular value system, as we see in the constant pressure for creationist teaching in the South of the USA. Associationalism would sharpen them acutely, however, since it seeks democratization through social self-governance. The central ethical principle that provides a way out of this morass is that associations are voluntary, as we have repeated several times; they must be communities of *choice*, not of fate. Citizens must be at least in principle able to informed enough to choose for themselves between different options and individuated enough to be able to choose. Education in blind conformity to given community standards thus violates the first principle of an associationalist society, that its communities must be voluntary. They will have different values; they will make demands on the loyalty of their members, but ultimately they must let them go if their members choose. The associations of a pluralistic society that can survive under modern conditions cannot be like 'existential' communities, wholly absorbing the life and loyalty of their members except at the price of the decomposition of the Commonwealth, and the loss of variety and choice for the citizen, avenues of potential change and renewal.

The fundamental principle to which associationalists and liberals together must adhere is that adult citizens do not own their children, they do not own their future lives as social beings. The public power has no interest, either in preventing the formation of identity or in peddling a multicultural pluralist mush as a substitute for religion and culture, but it does have an interest in ensuring individuation. That means the public power has the right to determine elements of the core curriculum in schools, to insist that schools in receipt of public funds conform to certain standards, and, in the last instance, to remove children from their parents. An associationalist system will reserve this latter right, *in extremis*. Satanic abuse is largely a myth fabricated by over-imaginative fundamentalist Christians and by credulous social workers, but, if it were true that there were widespread associations of devil worshippers, one could hardly let them be in the dogmatic belief in unlimited cultural pluralism and an absolute right to democratic community self-determination, come what may. This is, of course, a *reductio ad absurdum*, but it makes the point well enough that, however they may be drawn, the public power has the right to set limits to the conduct of associations and that the foundation of that right is the liberty of citizens and of future citizens.

The civic culture of an associationalist society will have a different logic from that of democratic republicanism, one closer to liberalism in its giving primacy to the individual's right and capacity to choose. An associationalist welfare state would set common standards, it would enforce a thin but strong morality based on an ethics of freedom. Republicanism claims the larger part of the citizen and demands identification with the state as a community, not just as an association with important but limited functions. Associationalism allows the citizen to choose the communities he or she will create with others, and demands in return the duties of respect for others' rights to choose.

Suggestions for Further Reading

This book was originally conceived as a modern version of G.D.H. Cole's *Guild Socialism Re-stated* (1920a). It has changed radically from the idea of updating an associational socialist classic for three reasons. First, because social relations have changed considerably since Cole wrote his book. Second, because there are certain fundamental weaknesses in the basic associationalist concepts that Cole was using (as we have seen in Chapter 3). Third, because this book is written to offer radical ideas of social reconstruction to diverse audiences, many of which are in no way part of the associational socialist tradition. It is designed to appeal to socialists and non-socialists alike. It does retain two elements of Cole's project. One is that it does include a practical and reasonably detailed account of institutions, it is not just a statement of values or principles. The other is that it is intended to be reasonably accessible to a non-specialist audience. For that reason I have not included conventional footnotes, in order to make the book read more easily and to keep it to an acceptable length. Suggestions for further reading are given here, with full bibliographical data. A list of works referred to in the text is given separately, and works cited here and also cited in the text are given here in the short form, e.g. Cole (1920a).

Modern associationalist arguments and critiques of representative democracy

The most thorough modern statement of an associative democratic case is John Matthews' *The Age of Democracy* (Oxford

University Press, Melbourne (1989)). Other examples are: Martell, Luke (1992) New ideas of socialism. *Economy and Society*, 21 (2), 152–72; Schmitter (1988); Schmitter and Streeck (1985); Yeo, Stephen Three socialisms: statism, collectivism, associa-tionalism. In W. Outhwaite and M. Mulkay (eds), *Social Theory and Social Criticism: essays for Tom Bottomore*, Basil Blackwell, Oxford (1987) – republished by Gregg Revivals, Aldershot (1992). See also the special issue of *Politics and Society*: Secondary associations and democracy, 20 (4), (1992), especially the main paper by Joshua Cohen and Joel Rogers – they and John Matthews use the term 'associative democracy' and I have adopted it rather than my earlier usage of associational democracy for convenience and commonality.

Boris Frankel (*The Post-Industrial Utopians*, Polity Press, Cambridge (1987)) discusses a number of Green and post-industrial thinkers, notably André Gorz, who share elements of the associationalist agenda. John Burnheim (*Is Democracy Possible?* Polity Press, Cambridge (1985)) mounts a powerful critique of representative democracy and bureaucracy, but argues for 'demarchy' rather than associationalism, that is, the direct participation, Athenian-style, of citizens in government. I have criticized this (1986) in *Sociological Review*, 34 (3), 669–73.

For critiques of representative democracy that do not simply reject it, David Held's *Models of Democracy* (Polity Press, Cambridge (1987)) is a balanced discussion of the different varieties of democratic theory. David Beetham's Key principles and indices of democracy (*The Democratic Audit of the United Kingdom*, Charter 88 Trust, London (1993)) is the best short statement of what modern democratic principles entail; see also Hirst (1990); Cohen, Joshua and Rogers, Joel (1983) *On Democracy*, Penguin, New York; Bowles, S. and Gintis, H. (1986) *Democracy and Capitalism*, Routledge, London; McLennan, Gregor (1989) *Marxism, Pluralism and Beyond*, Polity Press, Cambridge. The special issue of *Economy and Society*: State, democracy, socialism, 20 (2), (1991) contains important papers on the redefinition of democracy: David Held's Democracy, the nation state and the global system, 138–72, which poses the need to take into account the internationalization of social relations and the consequent inadequacy of national-level political processes, and Barry Hindess' Imaginary presuppositions of democracy, 173–95, that frontally attacks the idea of a 'self-governing community'. For intelligent neo-republican attempts to renew democracy using the concept of 'citizenship' see Chantal Mouffe's The civics lesson (*New Statesman and Society*, 7 October 1988) and Michael Walzer's The good life (*New Statesman and Society*, 6 October 1989) and his *Spheres of Justice* (Martin Robertson, Oxford (1983)). For the approach to democratic renewal using an Eastern European concept of 'civil society' see John Keane's *Democracy and Civil Society* (Verso, London (1988)). These ideas are criticized in the first chapter of Hirst (1990).

Classic associationalist arguments

There is no satisfactory single book on the history of associationalism, mainly because it was such a diverse movement. On the English political pluralists the best source remains David Nicholls' *The Pluralist State* (Macmillan, London (1978)); see also Hirst (1989). Other discussions include: Eliott, W.Y. (1928) *The Pragmatic Revolt in Politics*, Macmillan, New York which also discusses syndicalism, fascism and corporatism; Follet, M.P. (1918) *The New State*, Longmans Green & Co, London; Hsiao, K.C. (1927) *Political Pluralism*, Kegan Paul, Trench, Tubner & Co; Magid, H.M. (1941) *English Political Pluralism*, Columbia UP, New York. On the defects of functional democratic arguments see Kelvin Knight's The myth of functional democracy (PhD Thesis, University of London (1990)). For Cole see Wright, A.W. (1979) *G.D.H. Cole and Socialist Democracy*, Clarendon Press, Oxford and for Laski see Zylstra, B. (1970) *From Pluralism to Collectivism: the development of Harold Laski's Political Thought*, Van Gorcum, Assen. Guild Socialism is considered by Glass, S.T. (1966) *The Responsible Society: the ideas of the Guild Socialists*, Longmans Green & Co, London and Carpenter, N. (1922) *Guild Socialism: an historical and critical analysis*, D. Appleton & Co, New York. Matthews, Frank (1979) The ladder of becoming. In D.E. Martin and David Rubenstein (eds), *Ideology and the Labour Movement*, Croom Helm, London is especially valuable.

For Otto von Gierke see his *Community in Historical Perspective* (Anthony Black (ed), Cambridge UP, Cambridge (1990)), especially the editor's introduction, and his *Political Theories of the Middle Age* (Cambridge UP, Cambridge (1900) – reprinted 1988), especially the introduction by F.W. Maitland which is a major interpretative essay; see also Lewis, J.D. (1935) *The Genossenschaft Theory of Otto von Gierke*, University of Wisconsin Press, Madison WI. On Robert Owen see Taylor, K. (1982) *The Political Ideas of the Utopian Socialists*, Frank Cass, London; Harrison, J.F.C. (1973) *The Quest for a New Moral World: Robert Owen and the Owenites in England and America*, Macmillan, London. For G.J. Holyoake see Gurney, P. (1988) George Jacob Holyoake: socialism, association and cooperation in nineteenth-century England. In S. Yeo (ed.), *New Views of Cooperation*, Routledge, London.

On Proudhon see: Vincent, Steven, K. (1984) *Pierre-Joseph Proudhon and the Rise of French Republican Socialism*, Oxford University Press, New York; Ritter, A. (1969) *The Political Thought of Pierre-Joseph Proudhon*, Princeton UP, Princeton NJ; Vernon, R. (1863) The introduction to Pierre-Joseph Proudhon's *The Principle of Federation*, pp. xi–xlvii.

On corporatism see Cawson, Alan (1986) *Corporatism and Political Theory*, Basil Blackwell, Oxford; Black, Anthony (1984) *Guilds and Civil Society*, Methuen, London, especially Chapters 17 on Hegel, 18 on Gierke & Tönnies and 19 on Durkheim; Bowen, R. (1953) *German Theories of the Corporative State 1870–1919*, McGraw-Hill, New York; Elbow, M. (1953) *French Corporative Theory, 1789–1948*, New York. Boswell, Jonathan (1990) *Community and the Economy: the theory of public cooperation*, Routledge, London is a powerful re-statement of neo-Durkheimian and Christian communitarian ideas for economic governance.

Doctrines of economic governance

On Soviet-style state socialism it hardly seems necessary to offer much critical literature; Alec Nove's *The Economics of Feasible Socialism* (Allen & Unwin, London (1983)) offers the most stinging critique in the course of an attempt to construct a feasible and non-dictatorial socialist system. For other attempts to restate socialism, along 'democratic planning' lines, see Devine, Pat (1988) *Democracy and Economic Planning*, Polity Press, Cambridge, or through 'market socialism' see Le Grand, J. and Estrin, S. (eds) (1989), *Market Socialism*, Clarendon Press, Oxford and Miller, D. (1989) *Market, State and Community: theoretical foundations of market socialism*, Oxford University Press, Oxford. It will be evident from the text that I do not think either democratic socialism or market socialism a viable alternative, modern societies are at once too politically and culturally pluralistic to accept such projects, and in the market socialist scheme the 'socialism' in question allows too little of the coordination above enterprise level that modern economies need for their governance.

On Keynesianism Hall, Peter A. (ed.) (1989), *The Political Power of Economic Ideas: Keynesianism across nations*, Princeton UP, Princeton NJ offers the best survey of the different national receptions and of German and Japanese coolness to demand management; Weir, M. and Skocpol, T. (1985) State structures and the possibilities for 'Keynesian' responses to the Great Depression in Sweden, Britain and the United State. In P.B. Evans, D. Rueschemeyer and T. Skocpol (eds), *Bringing the State Back In*, Cambridge UP, Cambridge reinforces the point of the variability of national strategies and their determination by state capacities and political conditions. Cutler, T., Williams, K. and Williams, J. (1986) *Keynes, Beveridge and Beyond*, Routledge & Kegan Paul, London offers a brilliant exposition of Keynesianism as 'liberal collectivism'; Smith, K. (1984) *The British Economic Crisis*, Penguin, Harmondsworth offers a good account of the collapse of post-war British economic policy and also a lucid exposition of Keynesian economic theory. Tomlinson, Jim (1990) *Public Policy and the Economy since 1900*, Clarendon Press, Oxford is a sustained account of the reception, application and eventual failure of 'Keynesian' macro-economic management in the UK.

On economic liberalism: Smith (*The British Economic Crisis*) offers an accessible critique of both 'free market' and monetarist economic theory; see also Smith, D. (1987) *The Rise and Fall of Monetarism*, Penguin, Harmondsworth; Thompson, G. (1986) *The Conservative's Economic Policy*, Croom Helm, London; Thompson, G. (1990) *The Political Economy of the New Right*, Pinter, London; Tomlinson, Jim (1986) *Monetarism: is there an alternative?* Basil Blackwell, Oxford. For economic liberal policies in Britain see: Gamble, A. (1988) *The Free Economy and the Strong State*, Macmillan, London; Hirst, P. (1989) *After Thatcher*,

Collins, London; Keegan, W. (1984) *Mrs Thatcher's Economic Experiment*, Penguin, Harmondsworth; Smith, P. (1992) *From Boom to Bust: trial and error in British economic policy*, Penguin, Harmondsworth. On the American economy's structural problems and economic liberalism and its failure in the USA see: Bluestone, B. and Harrison, B. (1982) *The De-Industrialisation of America*, Basic Books, New York; Kuttner, R. (1991) *The End of Laissez Faire*; Magaziner, Ira and Reich R.B. (1983) *Minding America's Business*, Vintage, New York; Reich, R.B. (1983) *The Next American Frontier*, Penguin, New York; Thurow, L. (1980) *The Zero-Sum Society*, Basic Books, New York; Thurow, L. (1987) *The Zero-Sum Solution*, Penguin, Harmondsworth. A stinging reposte to the belief that Britain's manufacturing failure can be found in anti-industrial attitudes is David Edgerton's *England and the Aeroplane* (Macmillan, London (1991)) and on the anti-manufacturing bias of economic liberalism see Chapter 5 of Hirst (1989).

Current realities

For an assessment of the impact of the internationalization of economic relations on the possibilities of natural economic management, the role of trading blocs, and the likely prospects for the European Community as a form of federal economic governance see: Hirst, P. and Thompson, G. (1992) The problem of 'globalization': international economic relations, national economic management and the formation of trading blocs. *Economy and Society*, 21 (4), 357–96. On the changing strategies of manufacturing production and flexible specialization see: Piore and Sabel (1984); Hirst, P. and Zeitlin, J. (1991) Flexible specialisation vs post Fordism: theory, evidence and policy implications. *Economy and Society*, 20 (1), 1–56; Badham, R. and Matthews, J. (1989) The new production systems debate. *Labour and Industry*, 2 (2), 194–246; Sabel, C. and Zeitlin, J. (1985) Historical alternatives to mass production: politics, markets and technology in nineteenth-century industrialisation. *Past and Present*, no. 18, 133–76; Streeck, W. (1991) On the institutional conditions of diversified quality production. In E. Matzner and Wolfgang Streek (eds), *Beyond Keynesianism: the socio-economics of production and employment*, Edward Elgar, London.

On the importance of regional economies and industrial districts generally see: Sabel, C. (1989) Flexible specialisation and the re-emergence of regional economies. In P. Hirst and J. Zeitlin (eds), *Reversing Industrial Decline*, pp. 17–71, Berg, Oxford; Zeitlin, J. (1992) Industrial districts and local economic regeneration. Overview and comment in F. Pyke and W. Sengenberger (eds), *Industrial Districts and Local Economic Regeneration*, pp. 279–91, IILS, Geneva; Zeitlin, J. (ed.) (1989) Local industrial strategies, special issue of *Economy and Society* (vol. 18, no. 4).

On 'intimate knowledge' and the 'industrial atmosphere' of industrial districts see Marshall (1919); Beccattini, G. (1990) The Marshallian district as a socio-economic notion, and Brusco, S. (1990) The idea of an industrial district: its genesis, both in F. Pyke, G. Beccattini and W. Sengenberger (eds), *Industrial Districts and Inter-firm Cooperation in Italy* ILO, Geneva. For the concept of an 'industrial public sphere' see Hirst, P. and Zeitlin, J. (1989) Flexible specialisation and the competitive failure of UK manufacturing. *The Political Quarterly*, 60 (2), 164–78; for the benefits of collective services see Brusco, S. (1992) Small firms and the provision of real services in *Industrial Districts and Local Economic Regeneration*, pp. 177–96. On the role of trust and the balancing of cooperation and competition see Lorenz, E.H. (1992) Trust, community and cooperation: toward a theory of industrial districts. In M. Storper and Allen J. Scott (eds), *Pathways to Industrialisation and Regional Development*, Routledge, London, and on the pernicious effects of competition on a small population of firms see Best (1989).

For studies of two modern industrial districts, both of which have proved strongly competitive in the 1980s, see: (for Baden-Württemberg) Sabel, C. et al. (1989) Regional prosperities compared: Massachusetts and Baden-Württemberg in the 1980s. *Economy and Society*, 18 (4), 374–404; Scmitz, H. (1992) Industrial districts: model and reality in Baden-Württemberg. In Pyke and Sengenberger (eds) *Industrial Districts and Local Economic Regeneration*, pp. 87–121; (for Emilia-Romagna and Italy generally) Brusco, S. (1982) The Emilian model: productive decentralisation and social integration. *Cambridge Journal of Economics*, 6 (2), 167–84; Trigilia, C. (1992) Italian industrial districts: neither myth nor interlude. In Pyke and Sengenberger (eds), *Industrial Districts and Local Economic Regeneration*, pp. 33–47.

At the more general theoretical level on patterns of governance that are neither markets or hierarchies and the emergent possibilities of trust see: Ostrom, Elinor (1990) *Governing the Commons: the evolution of institutions for collective action*, Cambridge UP, Cambridge; Sabel, C. Constitutional ordering in historical context. In F. Scharpf (ed.), *Games in Hierarchies and Networks* (forthcoming); Sabel, C. (1992) Studied trust: building new forms of cooperation in a volatile economy. In Pyke and Sengenberger, pp. 215–50.

On new constellated firm structures and the growth of inter-firm partnerships see: Moss Kanter, Rossabeth (1989) *When Giants Learn to Dance*, Simon and Schuster, London; Sabel, C. (1991) Moebius strip organisations and open labour markets: some consequences of the reintegration of conception and execution in a volatile economy. In P. Bourdieu and J.S. Coleman (eds), *Social Theory for a Changing Society*, Westview Press, Boulder CO. For the classic statement of the empirical case that corporate concentration is driven by factors other than production technology see: Prais, S.J. (1991) *The Evolution of Giant Firms in Britain*, 2nd Edition, Cambridge UP, Cambridge. On the institutional and stockmarket pressures driving concentration in the UK see Cosh, A. et al. (1990) *Takeovers and Short-termism in the UK: Industrial Policy Paper No. 3*, Institute for Public Policy Research, London; Kuttner, R. (1993) The corporation in America: is it socially redeemable? *Dissent*, Winter, 35–49 is a valuable survey of the position in the USA.

On the post-1945 success of corporatist governance and an active industrial policy, and the limitations of UK-style macro-economic management, Andrew Shonfield's *Modern Capitalism* (RIIA/OUP, London (1965)) remains unrivalled; see also Marquand, D. (1988) *The Unprincipled Society*, Cape, London; Coldthorpe, J.H. (ed.) (1984) *Order and Conflict in Contemporary Capitalism*, Clarendon Press, Oxford; Berger, Suzanne P. (ed.) (1981) *Organising Interests in Western Europe*, Cambridge UP, Cambridge; Katzenstein, P.J. (1985) *Corporatism and Change: Austria, Switzerland and the politics of industry*, Cornell UP, Ithaca NY; Katzenstein, P.J. (1985) *Small States in World Markets*, Cornell UP, Ithaca NY. The literature on the weaknesses of corporatist governance and the weakening of interest group representation by changes in industrial and occupational structure is less extensive and inevitably more recent, see: Scharpf (1991);

Kern, H. and Sabel, C. (1990) Trade Unions and decentralised production: a sketch of strategic problems in the West German labour movement, Mimeo; Sabel, C. (1987) A fighting chance: structural change and new labour strategies. *International Journal of Political Economy*, Fall, 26–56; Streeck, W. and Schmitter, P.C. (1992) From national corporatism to transnational pluralism: organised interests in the single European market. *Politics and Society*.

New structures of governance in the firm

The literature on economic democratization is vast, a good deal of it pre-dates current transformations in production methods and occupational structures, and much of it tends to rest on a 'workerist' case, rather than a stakeholder accountability and extended social governance. Therefore, only a few indicative and relatively recent references are given here. Apart from the powerful theoretical case for economic democracy made by Dahl (1985), Schuller, T. (1985) *Democracy at Work*, Oxford UP, Oxford remains the best general survey. For a valuable survey of the impact of new production methods on the democratization of the firm see: Matthews, J. (1989) *Tools of Change*, Pluto Press, Sydney. On the role of 'quality' in the transformation of management and work see: Deming, W.E. (1988) *Out of the Crisis*, Cambridge UP, Cambridge. On ESOPS see: Cornford, J. (1990) *A Stake in the Company Shareholding, Ownership and ESOPS, Economic Study No. 3*, Institute for Public Policy Research, London; Blasi, J.R. (1988) *Employee Ownership – Revolution or Ripoff?* Harper Business, New York. For stakeholder representation and the 'ownership transfer corporation' see: Turnball, S. (1991) Reinventing corporations. *Human Systems Management*, 10, 169–86. On the dominance of institutional investors in the UK stockmarket see Thompson (1990), pp. 144–6.

New strategies in welfare

It will be obvious that I am not a welfare state or social security 'expert'. In my experience such experts are immobilized in contemplating reform either by the complexity of existing systems, or by the need to defend uniform state provision and universal benefits against economic liberalism. The case that state welfare involves inevitable bureaucratic discretion and appropriates choice is a powerful implication of Jacques Donzelot's *The Policing of Families* (Hutchnsion, London (1979)) and that state and private strategies for the governance of subjects fundamentally compromise liberty and autonomy is powerfully made by Michel Foucault in *Discipline and Punish* (Allen Lane, London (1977)). The case made here for a new welfare state is not made on 'Foucauldian' lines, however. It is an attempt to combine collective consumption with consumer choice, an option not considered in Foucault's analysis. Three books on the genesis of discourses about welfare and the 'liberal' governance of subjects that are especially valuable are: Dean, Mitchell (1991) *The Constitution of Poverty: toward a genealogy of liberal governance*, Routledge, London; Minson, Geoffrey (1985) *Genealogies of Morals: Nietzsche, Foucault and the eccentricity of ethics*, Macmillan, London; Rose, Nikolas (1989) *Governing the Soul*, Routledge, London.

Barry Hindess' *Freedom, Equality and the Market: arguments for social policy* (Tavistock, London (1987)) is a powerful theoretical interrogation of both the classic liberal collectivist arguments for welfare of Crosland, T.H. Marshall and Titmuss and the economic liberal response to them. Le Grand (1982) is, despite faults, a powerful critique of the failure of post-war strategies of redistribution and universality in the UK. Raymond Plant's *Equality Markets and the State* (Fabian Tract 494, London (1984)) and Citizenship, rights and welfare (in A. Coote (ed.), *The Welfare of Citizens: developing new social rights*, IPPR: Rivers Oram, London (1992)) are attempts to restate the classic egalitarian welfarist case against economic liberalism, whilst Nick Bosanquet's *After the New Right* (Heinemann, London (1983)) outlines economic liberal social doctrines.

In proposing an associationalist system I have been greatly influenced and encouraged by two works: Charles Sabel's Equity and efficiency in the federal welfare state (paper presented to the Nordic Working Group on the New Welfare State (1989)) that argues that economic and social changes are undermining uniform national systems; and Prochaska, F. (1988) *The Voluntary*

Impulse, Faber & Faber, London which is a major reinterpretation of the role of the voluntary sector in welfare in nineteenth-century Britain, that attempts both to show that it was not predominantly 'middle-class' charity and was far from being the failure collectivists asserted. Le Grand, J. (1990) Rethinking welfare: a case for quasi-markets. In B. Pimlott et al. (eds), *The Alternative*, W.H. Allen, London makes a strong case for giving choice to working class consumers of welfare as an empowering and egalitarian device, his method, however, is vouchers rather than the system of voluntary elections where consumers choose service providers proposed here.

On Guaranteed Minimum Income see: Frankel (1987), Chapter 2 which discusses the ideas of thinkers like Gorz and Toffler on basic income; van Parijs, P. (ed.) (1992) *Arguing for Basic Income*, Verso, London which includes essays by many advocates; Jordan, Bill (1987) *Rethinking Welfare*, Basil Blackwell, Oxford; Purdy, David (1988) *Social Power and the Labour Market*, Chapters 9–11, Macmillan, London; Parker, Hermione (1989) *Instead of the Dole*, Routledge, London; Walter (1989). For Milton Friedman's ideas see: The case for the negative income tax: a view from the right (1968) in J.H. Bunzel (ed.), *Issues in American Public Policy*, Prentice-Hall, Englewood Cliffs NJ. Young, Michael and Schuller, Tom (1991) *Life after Work: the arrival of an ageless society*, HarperCollins, London do not advocate GMI as such, but show the radical transformations in social affairs that will be necessary in a society of mass longevity, to which a basic income scheme could contribute by eliminating the division between work and retirement.

References

Barker, Rodney (1978) *Political Ideas in Modern Britain*, Methuen, London.

Belloc, Hilare (1913) *The Servile State*, T.N. Foulis, London. Republished in 1977 by Liberty Classics, Indianapolis IN.

Berle, A.A. and Means, G.C. (1932) *The Modern Corporation and Private Property*, Harcourt Brace, New York. The 1968 edition is the most widely available.

Best, Mike (1989) Sector strategies and industrial policy: the furniture industry and Greater London enterprise. In P. Hirst and J.Zeitlin (eds), *Reversing Industrial Decline*, Berg, Oxford.

Beveridge, William (1948) *Voluntary Action*, Allen and Unwin, London. Excerpted in Williams, K. and Williams, J. (1987) *A Beveridge Reader*, Allen and Unwin, London.

Bobbio, Noberto (1987) *The Future of Democracy*, Polity Press, Cambridge.

British Social Attitudes Survey, 5th Report (1988), R. Jowell et al. (eds), Gower, Aldershot.

British Social Attitudes Survey, 9th Report (1992), R. Jowell et al. (eds), Dartmouth, Aldershot.

Bullock, Lord (1977) *Report of the Committee of Inquiry on Industrial Democracy (Cmmd 6706)*, HMSO, London.

Cohen, Joshua and Rogers, Joel (1992) Secondary associations and democratic governance. *Politics and Society*, 20(4), 393–472.

Cohen, Morris (1919) Communal ghosts and other perils in social philosophy. *The Journal of Philosophy*, 16, 673–90.

Cole, G.D.H. (1914–1915) Conflicting social obligations. *Proceedings of the Aristotelean Society*, NS XV, 140–9.

Cole, G.D.H. (1920a) *Guild Socialism Re-stated*, Leonard Parsons, London. Republished in 1980 with an introduction by R. Vernon by

Transaction Books, New Brunswick NJ.

Cole, G.D.H. (1920b) *The Social Theory*, Methuen, London. Excerpts in Hirst (1989).

Crawford, A. (1985) *C.R. Ashbee: architect, designer and romantic socialist*, Yale UP, New Haven CT.

Crosland, C.A.R. (1956) *The Future of Socialism*, Cape, London. Revised edition (1964).

Dahl, Robert A. (1961) *Who Governs?* Yale UP, New Haven CT.

Dahl, Robert A. (1985) *A Preface to Economic Democracy*, Polity Press, Cambridge.

Dore, Ronald (1987) *Taking Japan Seriously: a Confucian perspective on leading economic issues*, Althone Press, London.

Dore, Ronald (1986) *Flexible Rigidities: industrial policy and structural adjustment in the Japanese economy 1970–1980*, Althone Press, London.

Dore, Ronald et al. (1991) *Japan's Annual Economic Assessment*, Campaign For Work Research Report, vol. 3, no. 7, London.

Durkheim, Emile (1893) *The Division of Labour in Society*, Alcan, Paris. Republished in 1964 by The Free Press, New York.

Durkheim, Emile (1957) *Professional Ethics and Civic Morals*, Routledge and Kegan Paul, London.

Figgis, John N. (1913) *Churches in the Modern State*, Longmans Green and Co, London.

Friedman, David (1988) *The Misunderstood Miracle: industrial development and political change in Japan*, Cornell UP, Ithaca NY.

Fukuyama, Francis (1989) The end of history. *The National Interest*, Summer, 3–18.

Galbraith, John K. (1992) *The Culture of Contentment*, Houghton Mifflin, Boston MA.

Hayek, Friedrich A. (1944) *The Road to Serfdom*, Routledge and Kegan Paul, London.

Held, David (1993) Democracy: from city-states to a cosmopolitan order. In D. Held (ed.), *Prospects for Democracy*, Polity Press, Cambridge.

Hindess, Barry (1991) Imaginary presuppositions of democracy. *Economy and Society*, 20(2), 173–95.

Hirst, Paul (1989) *The Pluralist Theory of the State: selected writings of G.D.H. Cole, J.N. Figgis and H.J. Laski*, Routledge, London.

Hirst, Paul (1990) *Representative Democracy and its Limits*, Polity Press, Cambridge.

Hirst, Paul (1993) Maastricht – the missed turning point. *Renewal*, 1(1), 11–23.

Johnson, Chalmers (1982) *MITI and the Japanese Miracle: the growth of industrial policy, 1925–1975*, Stanford UP, Stanford CA.

Kennedy, Ellen (1991) *The Bundesbank*, Chatham House Papers, RIIA/ Francis Pinter, London.

Laski, Harold J. (1921) The problem of administrative areas. In *The Foundations of Sovereignty and Other Essays*, Allen and Unwin, London.

Laski, Harold J. (1925) *A Grammar of Politics*, Allen and Unwin, London.

Le Grand, Julian (1982) *The Strategy of Equality*, Allen and Unwin, London.

Marshall, Alfred (1919) *Industry and Trade*, Macmillan, London.

Marshall, T.H. (1963) Citizenship and social class. In *Sociology at the Crossroads and Other Essays*, Heinemann, London.

Ohmae, Kenichi (1990) *The Borderless World*, Collins, London.

Olson, Mancur (1971) *The Logic of Collective Action*, Harvard UP, Cambridge M.A.

Olson, Mancur (1982) *The Rise and Decline of Nations*, Yale UP, New Haven CT.

Penty, A.J. (1906) *The Restoration of the Gild System*, London.

Piore, Michael and Sabel, Charles (1984) *The Second Industrial Divide*, Basic Books, New York NY.

Proudhon, P.-J. (1863) *The Principle of Federation*, E. Denty, Paris. Translated and introduced by R. Vernon for Toronto UP, Toronto (1979).

Rendell, Ruth and Ward, Colin (1989) *Undermining the Central Line – giving government back to the people*, Chatto and Windus, London.

Russell, Bertrand (1918) *Roads to Freedom*, Allen and Unwin, London.

Sabel, Charles (1993) Constitutional ordering in historical context. In F.W. Scharpf (ed.) *Games in Hierarchies and Networks* (to be published).

Scharpf, Fritz W. (1991) *Crisis and Choice in European Social Democracy*, Cornell UP, Ithaca NY.

Schmitt, Carl (1930) Staatsethik und pluralistischer staat. *Kantstudien*, Band 35, Heft 1, 471–7. Reprinted in *Positionen und Bergriffe im Kampf mit Weimar-genf-Versailles*, Hanseatische, Verlag, Hamburg (1939).

Schmitt, Carl (1932) *The Concept of the Political*, Duncker and Humblot, Berlin. Trans lated and introduced by G. Schwab for Rutgers UP, Brunswick NJ (1976).

Schmitt, Carl (1943–1944) The plight of European jurisprudence, *Telos*, no. 83 (Spring 1990).

Schmitter, Philippe C. (1988) *Corporative Democracy: oxymoronic? just plain moronic? or a promising way out of the present impasse?*, Mimeo.

Schmitter, Philippe and Streeck, Wolfgang (1985) Community, market, state – and associations? the prospective contribution of interest governance to social order. *European Sociological Review*, 1, 119–38.

Solow, Robert (1990) *The Labour Market as a Social Institution*, Basil Blackwell, Oxford.

Titmuss, Richard (1970) *The Gift Relationship*, Allen and Unwin, London.

Walter, Tony (1989) *Basic Income*, Marion Boyars, London.

Index